D1624936

EXPERIENCING HEAVEN

EXPERIENCING HEAVEN

TRUE STORIES, PRAYERS, AND PROMISES *for* EVERY DAY *of the* YEAR

SARABETH BROWNE

New York Boston Nashville

Unless otherwise indicated, Scriptures are taken from the HOLY BIBLE, NEW INTERNATIONAL VERSION®, copyright © 1973, 1978, 1984 by International Bible Society. Used by permission of Zondervan. All rights reserved.

Other Scriptures noted are listed on the "Scriptures Noted" page at the end of the book.

FaithWords
Hachette Book Group
1290 Avenue of the Americas
New York, NY 10104

faithwords.com

Represented by Ann Spangler, www.annspangler.com.

Printed in the United States of America

RRD-C

First Edition: October 2014

10 9 8 7 6 5 4 3 2 1

FaithWords is a division of Hachette Book Group, Inc.
The FaithWords name and logo are trademarks of Hachette Book Group, Inc.

The Hachette Speakers Bureau provides a wide range of authors for speaking events. To find out more, go to www.hachettespeakersbureau.com or call (866) 376-6591.

The publisher is not responsible for websites (or their content) that are not owned by the publisher.

Library of Congress Cataloging-in-Publication Data

Browne, Sarabeth.
  Experiencing heaven : true stories, prayers, and promises for every day of the year / Sarabeth Browne. — First Edition.
    pages cm
  Includes bibliographical references.
  ISBN 978-1-4555-5507-9 (hardcover) — ISBN 978-1-4555-5508-6 (ebook)
  1. Devotional calendars. 2. Heaven—Christianity—Miscellanea. I. Title.
  BV4811.B765 2014
  242'.2—dc23

                                                            2014010838

EXPERIENCING HEAVEN

HEAVEN

It Must Have Been Angels

For to me, to live is Christ and to die is gain. Philippians 1:21

Several years ago, a philosopher and theologian by the name of Richard John Neuhaus underwent emergency surgery from which he nearly died. Neuhaus describes what happened shortly after he was released from intensive care.

"I could hear patients in adjoining rooms moaning and mumbling and occasionally calling out; the surrounding medical machines were pumping and sucking and bleeping as usual. Then, all of a sudden, I was jerked into an utterly lucid state of awareness. I was sitting up in the bed staring intently into the darkness, although in fact I knew my body was lying flat. What I was staring at was a color like blue and purple, and vaguely in the form of hanging drapery. By the drapery were two 'presences.' I saw them and yet did not see them, and I cannot explain that. But they were there, and I knew that I was not tied to the bed. I was able and prepared to get up and go somewhere. And then the presences—one or both of them, I do not know—spoke. This I heard clearly. Not in an ordinary way, for I cannot remember anything about the voice. But the message was beyond mistaking: 'Everything is ready now.'

"I pinched myself hard and ran through the multiplication tables, and recalled the birth dates of my seven brothers and sisters, and my wits were vibrantly about me."

What were those "presences" in his hospital room that night? According to Neuhaus, they were angels conveying the message that he was allowed to go somewhere with them. "Not that I must go or should go, but simply that they were ready if I was."[1]

Years later, Neuhaus died of cancer. In between his near-death experience and his final passing, friends said he seemed indifferent about when his life might end. It didn't really matter because he knew who he was and where he was going and that "everything is ready now."

Flight to Heaven

Instead, they were longing for a better country—a heavenly one.
Therefore God is not ashamed to be called their God, for he has
prepared a city for them. Hebrews 11:16

Dale Black was the sole survivor of a plane that crashed shortly after takeoff at the Hollywood-Burbank airport in Southern California in 1969. For eight months, he remembered nothing. He couldn't recall the plane crash, the ten hours of surgery, or his first three days in the hospital. Yet when Dale woke up in the ICU, he was a different person, no longer a self-centered, rebellious teenager but a young man who loved everyone, even complete strangers who walked into his room to care for him. What had happened? Dale hadn't a clue.

Eighth months later, as his memory began to return, he discovered the surprising answer. As he thought back to the day of the crash, astonishing pictures began to emerge. He remembered how he had felt when he had arrived at the hospital. There was neither pain nor fear, only a sense of curiosity as he felt himself rise up off the gurney. Suspended in midair, Dale could see his body below him, battered and covered in blood and fuel. How, he wondered, could he be in two places at once? Then suddenly his thoughts flashed back to an experience he had had several years previously.

He saw himself as a young boy who had just committed his life to Christ while attending church camp. Dale had wanted nothing more than to live completely for God. How had that boy, he wondered, turned into a person who thought only of himself? "It was all about me," he says. "*My* life. *My* career. *My* hopes. *My* dreams....I felt shame, sadness, grief."[2]

The weight of his shame began to drag him downward. Then suddenly the heaviness lifted and he began drifting up again. Noticing details in the light fixtures and in the air-conditioning ducts embedded in the ceiling, he moved out of the room and into the hallway.

"The speed of my movement increased," he says. "I couldn't stop it, couldn't steer it.

"I moved faster, faster, and faster still...

"In the darkness," he says, "millions of tiny spheres of light zoomed past as I traveled through what looked like deep space, almost as if a jet were flying through a snowstorm at night, its lights reflecting off the flakes as they blurred past...."

Traveling at enormous speed, Dale realized he wasn't alone. Two angels flanked him. "Their skin tone was light golden brown and their hair fairly short....I was fast approaching a magnificent city."

What Dale saw in that city was about to change him forever. But that's a story for another day.

The Light

"I am the light of the world. Whoever follows me will never walk in darkness, but will have the light of life." John 8:12

Dale felt himself slowing down as he approached the magnificent, golden city. Light suffused it, appearing to shine not on but through everything—trees, and flowers, and people. Brighter than anything he'd ever seen, the light appeared to emanate from a source several miles within the city walls.

"In that dazzling light," he says, "every color imaginable seemed to exist and—what's the right word?—*played*. If joy could be given colors, they would be these colors, the colors were pure and innocent, like children playing in a fountain, splashing, chasing each other, gurgling with laughter...

"Somehow I knew that light and life and love were connected and interrelated. It was as if the very heart of God lay open for everyone in heaven to bask in its glory, to warm themselves in its presence, to bathe in its almost liquid properties so they could be restored, renewed, refreshed."[3]

Remarkably, the light didn't make Dale flinch or squint. Instead of shielding his eyes, he wanted to immerse himself in it forever. This city, this realm, this heavenly place—he knew at once he was made for it and that it was made for him.

Fortunately, this place of living light, this place where God dwells—it was also made for you and me.

A Note from Jesus to You

Do not let your hearts be troubled. John 14:1

Take a moment to read these words as though Jesus is speaking them directly to you, which he is.

> *Do not let your hearts be troubled. You believe in God; believe also in me. My Father's house has many rooms; if that were not so, would I have told you that I am going there to prepare a place for you? And if I go and prepare a place for you, I will come back and take you to be with me that you also may be where I am. (John 14:1–3)*

Then close your eyes for a few minutes and imagine the kind of place Jesus is preparing right now for you in heaven. Ask the Holy Spirit to guide your thoughts. Try drawing a picture of what you've just seen or writing words that describe the scene.

We Do Not Fade Away

"I have loved you with an everlasting love." *Jeremiah* 31:3

Sometimes we speak of people living on in our memories. If we are fortunate, the memory of who we are might linger in the minds of those we have known. A few people, like Abraham Lincoln or Helen Keller or Catherine the Great or Genghis Khan, may have made enough of an impression to be remembered for centuries. But even strong memories are like mists or shadows compared to the real thing. They die away as people fade away.

But we are remembered by someone who will never fade away. Scripture calls him the everlasting God, the one who loves us with an everlasting love. But what's the point of loving finite creatures (that's us) with an everlasting love if we are merely here today and gone tomorrow?

The Bible tells us that God is like a mother who will never forget her child (Isaiah 49:15). We are always in his mind. Heaven, then, must be a place in which we exist not as shadows or mist, but as souls created out of love who've been united to God and destined to live with him forever.

Where Is Heaven?

*Then I saw "a new heaven and a new earth," for the first heaven
and the first earth had passed away.   Revelation 21:1*

Is heaven a place in the physical universe, like Trenton, New
Jersey, Mumbai, India, or even OGLE-2005-BLG-390Lb, the
ungainly name of the farthest planet from earth so far discovered? Or does it exist on an entirely different plane, removed
from space and time?

Though heaven is a place, it's not a physical place in the
universe. Rather, it's a spiritual place in which God dwells.
Though God is present on earth, heaven is uniquely his dwelling place. Even so, the Bible speaks tantalizingly of a move
God intends to make at some point in the future when Christ
will return to establish a new heaven and a new earth. Just as
the spiritual place we now call heaven is infused with the presence of God, the new earth will be completely infused with
his presence. That new earth will be our future address—a
place in which everything and everyone will exist in perfect
harmony with God and each other.

Right now, as the stories in this book will attest, when
believers die, their souls pass into the presence of God. So they
are in heaven with him. But their souls exist in an intermedi-
ate state, still waiting for the day when Christ will come to
judge the living and the dead. On that day, they will be given
resurrected bodies. Those bodies will never grow old, never
get sick, and will never die. Instead they will live forever in
their eternal home—the new earth that God will create.

New Heaven and New Earth

*But in keeping with his promise we are looking forward to a new
heaven and a new earth, where righteousness dwells. 2 Peter 3:13*

Randy Alcorn calls the heaven that people experience now the
"present Heaven." It's where the souls of the faithful go when
their bodies die.

But God's ultimate plan is not that we will live with him
forever in the present heaven but that we will live with him
forever in the new heaven and the new earth. Why is it important to know this? For one thing, the focus on the new earth
affirms the truth that we are incarnational beings, both physical and spiritual, who are meant to live in an incarnational
world. Our souls are not destined to be separated from our
bodies forever.

To miss this is to remain ignorant about God's final intentions for creation. It is like settling for meringue when God is
preparing a whole pie for you to enjoy or for five innings of
baseball when there are four more to come. Without an understanding of the new heaven and the new earth, our view of
heaven will be stunted and only partially informed.

The Way Things Are Supposed to Be

I heard a loud shout from the throne, saying, "Look, the home of God is now among his people!"   Revelation 21:3 NLT

The Bible is a big book, 923 pages of double columns in tiny type in the version lying on my desk. But only about two and a half pages of this massive book describe life as God intended it to be—Genesis 1–2 and Revelation 21–22, the first and last chapters of the Bible. If you want to get an idea of what God would like the earth to be like, read these chapters.

The rest of the Bible is all about struggle. It's about plot, character development, dialogue, and setting. Because we have always lived in the struggle portion of the story that is the Bible, it's difficult for us to envision what the world was like before things went haywire.

Because the Bible was written over many centuries, in different historical settings, by many different people, it is really a library of books. But the funny thing about this library is that all the books taken together tell one big story. It's the story of a God who so loved the world that he wouldn't let sin forever ruin it. Who so loved you that he wouldn't let sin forever ruin you.

Ever since the beginning and all the way through to the end, this God is determined to use every tragic turn and every twist of circumstance to craft the happiest ending of all. He wants to bring us home to the place we have always longed to be, living with him in his kingdom, world without end, amen.

"Your Baby Is with Me"

Your eyes saw my unformed body. All the days ordained for me were written in your book before one of them came to be. Psalm 139:16

Every day, more than 215,000 babies are born into our world, and God cares for each one. Listen to this story, told by an undercover missionary, whom I'll call Laura. In the course of her work, she encounters many pregnant women.

"The first time I examined Li Na," she says, "I had to tell her I couldn't find a heartbeat. The child she had been carrying for fourteen weeks had miscarried.

"As a nurse practitioner and a practicing Christian, I was concerned about how the news might impact her fledgling faith. Li Na had given her life to Christ weeks earlier. Employed as a makeup artist in the red-light district of a large Asian city, she had already helped five young women escape prostitution.

"Now her tears and the dark circles that quickly formed beneath her eyes bore witness to the terrible pain inside.

"So I prayed and asked friends to pray. The next time I saw Li Na, the circles beneath her eyes had vanished. She told me what had happened.

"'I didn't even know how to pray,' Li Na confided. 'I just cried out, "Jesus, where is my baby now?" Suddenly I saw a picture in my head of clouds and bright light. Everywhere was just so bright…and then I saw angels and they looked like they were dancing and rejoicing. I saw a person standing among them, but I couldn't see his face—it was so bright—the light was coming from it. But I noticed he was holding something in his arms…. It was a baby, my baby! He told me, "Don't be afraid, your baby is with me." Now I know where my baby is, and I have peace.'"

Li Na has discovered the secret of true peace. It comes, not from a lack of trouble but from knowing that we and those we love are safe in the arms of God.

What's Heaven Like?

"What no eye has seen,
what no ear has heard,
and what no human mind has conceived"—
the things God has prepared for those who love him.
1 Corinthians 2:9

It's hard to imagine heaven. Many of us think of it as a vague, ethereal place where disembodied people float around, mingling with angels and singing a lot of worship songs. No wonder heaven sounds boring. But is it?

Consider the way C. S. Lewis depicts heaven in his wonderful book *The Great Divorce,* a story about a group of accidental tourists who board a bus only to find themselves on a journey to heaven and hell. Actually, Lewis imagines only the outskirts of heaven. Even in heaven's precincts, the reality is far solider and more real than anything they've ever known on earth.

At one point, the main character gets off the bus to explore this strange new land. Spotting a daisy growing at his feet, he bends down to pick it. "The stalk," he says with surprise, "wouldn't break. I tugged till the sweat stood out on my forehead and I had lost most of the skin off my hands. The little flower was hard, not like wood or even like iron, but like diamond. There was a leaf—a young tender beach-leaf, lying in the grass beside it. I tried to pick the leaf up: my heart almost cracked with the effort, and I believe I did just raise it."[5]

In Lewis's vision, and in the Bible's vision, earth is the copy and heaven is the reality from which it has been crafted. No wonder, then, that the main character in Lewis's imaginative tale is shocked when he looks down at his feet and can see through them to the grass beneath. For the first time, he realizes that he, and not heaven, is insubstantial as a mist.

What is heaven like? Go ahead and let your imagination run wild. Just be sure that whatever you imagine is solider, more brilliant, and more real than anything you've ever seen on earth.

"I Would Be So Bored in Heaven"

The Lord your God is in your midst, a victorious warrior. He will exult over you with joy, He will be quiet in His love, He will rejoice over you with shouts of joy. Zephaniah 3:17 *NASB*

"Oh, I don't think I even want to go to heaven. Who wants to sit around on a cloud for eternity, playing a harp?"

Where did we get the idea that heaven is like that, from *New Yorker* cartoons? For that matter, why would we take it for granted that the Father is a grumpy curmudgeon with no sense of humor? In his classic book, *Heaven*, Randy Alcorn dresses down those who think that way: "Our belief that Heaven will be boring betrays a heresy—that God is boring. There's no greater nonsense." He goes on to list all of the categories of human pleasure, every one of which came straight from our Creator's hand.

Then he wraps up his pro-heaven argument with this: "We think of ourselves as fun-loving, and of God as humorless killjoy. But we've got it backward. It's not God who's boring; it's us. Did we invent wit, humor, and laughter? No. God did. We'll never begin to exhaust God's sense of humor and his love for adventure. The real question is this: How could God not be bored with *us*?"[6]

And yet he's not. He delights in us, and he wants us to delight in him. For all eternity. Harps are optional.

Think Heaven

In my Father's house are many mansions. If it were not so, I would have told you. John 14:2 KJV

If you could print out an exact record of your thoughts for the past twenty-four hours, you would probably discover that you haven't spent much time thinking about heaven. How could you, when there's so much else to think about?

There's work, church, school, chores, sporting events, grocery shopping, and children to care for. How can you possibly find time to think about a place that seems so infinitely far away? And why should you, when you sincerely hope you're not going there anytime soon?

Yet heaven should shape the way we think and act on earth, reminding us that we're not living for the here and the now. We're living for something more.

Keeping heaven in mind can encourage us when life on earth seems too challenging to bear. We can find comfort remembering the loved ones who've gone before us.

Step outside and look into the sky. Think about all the galaxies beyond our own—and another world we cannot see but that is just as real, a place called heaven, where Jesus right now is making room for you. If it were not so, wouldn't he have told you?

Heaven Changed Him

[A]s far as the east is from the west,
so far has he removed our transgressions from us.   Psalm 103:12

During his time in heaven, Dale Black saw countless angels and people, all suffused with light. Drawing near to the gate of the city, he noticed a crowd that had gathered to welcome him. Everyone was dressed in soft, white robes. Though he didn't know anyone's name, everyone seemed to know his and to be overjoyed that he was there.

Part of Dale's joy, he says, came not just from all the wonderful things he encountered in heaven "but from the absence of everything terrible. There was no strife, no competition, no sarcasm, no betrayal, no deception, no lies, no murders, no unfaithfulness, no disloyalty, nothing contrary to the light and life and love.

"In short, there was no sin.

"And the absence of sin was something you could feel."[7]

As God would have it, Dale Black was not allowed to pass through the gates to the magnificent city he had seen. Instead, he returned to earth to begin the slow and painful process of recovery. Almost immediately he began telling people about God's love.

Dale went on to become a commercial airline pilot, dedicating his career to improving aviation safety. As a volunteer on nearly one thousand flights, he has helped with efforts to build churches, orphanages, and medical clinics in more than fifty countries around the world.

Forty years after that terrible day when the plane in which he'd been riding crashed, Dale Black is still amazed at how heaven changed him.

Don't Over-Spiritualize Heaven

*For he [Abraham] was looking forward to the city with
foundations, whose architect and builder is God. Hebrews 11:10*

What if you and your spouse were planning a trip to Hawaii
in a year's time? Wouldn't half the fun come from anticipat-
ing your journey? But how can you anticipate something you
can't possibly imagine?

Perhaps you've lived all your life in Ohio, never once
stepping beyond its boundaries. You have never dipped your
toe into the ocean, never seen a palm tree nor marveled at a
volcano. Strangely, you've never even watched a television
show about Hawaii or looked up images of it on the Internet.
Instead, you've contented yourself with the vague longing
you feel for a land that everyone says is a tropical paradise even
though you can't possibly imagine what it might look like.

This far-fetched example is not so far-fetched when it
comes to heaven. Randy Alcorn says most of us have only the
vaguest notion of what heaven is like not because there's nothing about it in Scripture but because we ignore what the Bible
says about it, things like this:

Heaven is a city (Hebrews 11:10; 13:14). How can you have
a city without people, art, music, work, buildings? *Heaven is
a country* (Hebrews 11:16). Countries have an identity, geography. They have leaders and citizens. *There will be a new earth*
(Revelation 21–22). Why shouldn't there be beaches, oceans,
mountains, rivers, forests, meadows, rocks, cliffs, animals,
plants?[8]

Let's not make heaven vague and surreal, something our
hearts can't delight in because our minds can't imagine it.
Instead let's focus on heaven. Let's study it, look forward to it,
and bend our lives toward it like Abraham did so that the hope
of heaven will guide our lives on earth.

Too Fancy?

And the twelve gates are twelve pearls, each of the gates is a single pearl, and the street of the city is pure gold, transparent as glass.   Revelation 21:21 NRSV

Does the biblical image of heaven enclosed by pearly gates and crisscrossed with streets paved with gold appeal to you? Or does it seem way too dressed up and fancy for your tastes? Perhaps shabby chic is more your style. Or maybe you prefer sleek, modern lines. Never fear. Heaven will appeal to you, no matter what.

John's vision in Revelation is symbolic. Gates of pearl and golden streets, crystal seas and gem-filled walls seem outdated in the twenty-first century. The point really is that heaven is beyond our imagination—filled with great splendor and over-the-top magnificence.

It does not matter how you want to envision heaven. Don't worry—you will like it, whatever it looks, feels, smells, and sounds like.

Beyond Imagining

No eye has seen, no ear has heard, and no mind has imagined what God has prepared for those who love him. 1 Corinthians 2:9 NLT

What is heaven like?

- It's more delightful than a bed made in crisp, cotton sheets.
- More comfortable than a zero-humidity day.
- More peaceful than the first fresh snowfall.
- Sweeter than the sugar-ice flowers on a birthday cake.
- Calmer than the stillness after everyone's fallen asleep.

Heaven is far more and far better than we can describe or imagine. Everything good we have ever experienced is only a taste of what God has waiting for us.

Heaven is the place where God lives, a land where joy runs rampant and where the bright love of God overflows all hearts so there never can be any darkness at all.

Good Shepherd

Then Jesus said to them again, "Most assuredly, I say to you, I am the door of the sheep. . . . I am the door. If anyone enters by Me, he will be saved, and will go in and out and find pasture. John 10:7, 9 NKJV

In Bible times, shepherds had outdoor sheep pens that were near the pasturelands. They were simple enclosures made of piled rocks, with one narrow opening that served as both entrance and exit. At night, the shepherd slept in the opening in order to protect the sheep from predators, and in the morning he would usher them through the opening one by one. His own body was the sheep gate, and the only ones allowed to use the door were the sheep the shepherd counted as his own.

You are a sheep. So am I. Every person, peasant to queen, is a sheep. And Jesus himself is our door to the pasture. He is the Good Shepherd. He nurtures and protects his flock, searches for the lost lambs, carries the weak ones, guiding every one of us every day.

The Good Shepherd himself is the only way through the impassable wall between heaven and earth. If you are part of the Shepherd's flock, he is caring for you. Just keep paying attention to his voice. That's all you need to do.

God Is on Your Side

If God is for us, who is against us? He who did not spare His own Son, but delivered Him over for us all, how will He not also with Him freely give us all things? Romans 8:31–32 NASB

You may have enemies. Circumstances may be arrayed against you. But take heart because you have a huge advantage. The biggest person in the universe is on your side. One of the reasons we know that is because God took the initiative to save us. He reached down into our dark world so that he could deliver us. He loves us and wants us to be with him in heaven forever so he devised a plan to bring us there.

Perhaps that sounds like a too-easy, one-sided path to heaven. Maybe you've grown up believing that God only helps those who help themselves. Or maybe you suspect God of being an ogre, always eager to punish your faults. But that's not what Scripture says.

When we finally discover the humility to accept our need for God's grace, that's when confidence will come flooding in. We will know in our hearts the truth of Paul's words. The one who did not spare his own Son—this is the God who will give us everything we need. Even heaven.

Unwreckable

*For I am convinced that neither death nor life, neither angels
nor demons, neither the present nor the future, nor any powers,
neither height nor depth, nor anything else in all creation, will be
able to separate us from the love of God that is in Christ Jesus our
Lord. Romans 8:38–39*

Ann Voskamp says that our lives are unwreckable because
Christ's love is unstoppable. That's one way of saying that
nothing can ultimately rob us of the happy ending God has in
store for us. Remember that the next time you are tempted to
think you are facing circumstances that will sink you.

Take a moment now to envision yourself with the word
"Unwreckable" written over you. Then read this beautiful
poem, titled "Heaven Over Us," by the English poet Christina
Rossetti. As you live out your day, imagine heaven overarch-
ing everything you do.

Heaven overarches earth and sea,
    Earth-sadness and sea-bitterness.
Heaven overarches you and me,
A little while and we shall be—
Please God—where there is no more sea
    Nor barren wilderness.
Heaven overarches you and me,
    And all earth's gardens and her graves.
Look up with me, until we see
The day break and the shadows flee.
What though to-nigh wrecks you and me,
    If so tomorrow saves?

                                        CIRCA 1893

Crossing Over

"I tell you the truth, whoever hears my word and believes him who sent me has eternal life and will not be condemned; he has crossed over from death to life." John 5:24

Wayne Herring is a Presbyterian pastor in Memphis, Tennessee. Several years ago, his aunt, Kate Lewis, lay dying in a hospital bed. This good woman, who had prayed for so many others, now needed prayers herself.

Her breathing was slow and agonized, and she had been semi-comatose for days. At one point medical staff attempted to revive her, initiating heroic measures to do so. Suddenly Aunt Kate sat straight up in bed. Looking around her, she addressed everyone in the room: "Why on earth did you bring me back?" she scolded. "It's been wonderful. I've been with the angels and I didn't want to leave!"[9]

After that she sank back down on her pillow and never spoke another word. A few days later Aunt Kate was gone.

For most of us, death is a question mark. We wonder what will happen after we die. For others, it's a period—a definitive end to life. But Aunt Kate's words, combined with countless testimonies from people with near-death experiences, point to the truth of the Scripture, which says that those who believe in Christ will not die. Instead, they will cross over from death to life.

Put Earth in Your Rearview Mirror

But they that wait upon the Lord shall renew their strength; they shall mount up with wings as eagles; they shall run, and not be weary; and they shall walk, and not faint.   Isaiah 40:31 KJV

Earthly trials keep us earthbound. They root us only in what we can see, hear, taste, smell, and feel. Too often, it never even occurs to us to cast a glance upward toward heaven. But when we do, as countless people have discovered, a very real heavenly strength flows into our souls and spirits, renewing and fortifying what's left of our own determination, and supplying fresh vigor for whatever we are facing.

Joni Eareckson Tada, a quadriplegic since a diving accident when she was a teen, has discovered that "God is our refuge and strength, a very present help in trouble" (Psalm 46:1 KJV). She has tested her "eagle's wings" many times. Here is what she says about it:

Looking down on my problems from heaven's perspective, trials looked extraordinarily different. When viewed from its own level, my paralysis seemed like a huge, impassable wall; but when viewed from above, the wall appeared as a thin line, something that could be overcome. It was, I discovered with delight, a bird's-eye view. . . .

Eagles overcome the lower law of gravity by the higher law of flight, and what is true for birds is true for the soul. . . . If you want to see heaven's horizons, as well as place earth in your rearview mirror, all you need to do is stretch your wings (yes, you have wings . . .) and consider your trials from heaven's realms. . . . [By doing that,] you are able to see the other side, the happier outcome.[10]

Being Sure of Heaven

Jesus looked at them and said, "For mortals it is impossible, but not for God; for God all things are possible."   Mark 10:27 NRSV

Our limited minds struggle to comprehend a God who loves. We can't fathom how God can love us when we find it so difficult to love ourselves. But the truth is that God loves everyone. After all, it was love that motivated him to create the universe in the first place. He loves the world and every single person in it, even those of us who haven't yet begun to love him.

Perhaps you think that entering heaven is an impossible task, far beyond your ability. You know you're not good enough to get there. If that's what you're thinking, you'd be right. You can't get to heaven on your own. Only God can take you there.

Fortunately, everything is possible for God, which of course means that even impossible people—people like you and me—can make it into heaven.

Don't Be Afraid

*For I am the LORD, your God, who takes hold of your right hand
and says to you, Do not fear; I will help you.   Isaiah 41:13*

As a young pastor, Richard John Neuhaus was a part-time
chaplain at Kings County Hospital in Brooklyn, a medical
center that cared for the poor before Medicare or Medicaid
had even been invented. When people were dying, they were
simply sedated, their beds lined up next to each other, fifty to
a hundred at a time. Food was brought for those who could
eat. Neuhaus estimated that a day wouldn't go by without him
accompanying at least one or two people to their deaths. One
of these, he would never forget.

"His name was Albert, a man of about seventy and (I don't
know why it sticks in my mind) completely bald. That hot
summer morning I had prayed with him and read the Twenty-
third Psalm. Toward evening, I went up again to the death
ward—for so everybody called it—to see him again. Clearly
the end was near. Although he had been given a sedative, he
was entirely lucid. I put my left arm around his shoulder and
together, face almost touching face, we prayed the Our Father.
Then Albert's eyes opened wider, as though he had seen something in my expression. 'Oh,' he said, 'Oh, don't be afraid.' His
body sagged back and he was dead. Stunned, I realized that,
while I thought I was ministering to him, his last moment of
life was expended in ministering to me."[11]

Where did Albert get the strength to comfort someone
who was trying to comfort him? Most likely from the same
God who repeatedly says to us: "Don't be afraid."

Heaven's Escorts

*You have come . . . to countless thousands of angels in a joyful
gathering. Hebrews 12:22 NLT*

Every few years, Jeremy's dad received a promotion. Then
the family would pack up and move to a new city, and Jeremy
would have to adjust to a new school.

Here he was again. Entering the front door of his new
school, Jeremy wondered how he would find his classrooms
or make friends. As the principal of the school welcomed him,
Jeremy noticed that someone was with her. "Jeremy," the
principal said, "this is Sam. He'll be your escort for the next
few days." Suddenly, Jeremy's racing heart calmed down. A
friendly escort would make this transition an easy one.

New experiences and new environments leave many of us
apprehensive and nervous. Perhaps even the thought of entering heaven frightens you, not knowing what it will be like,
who will be there, or where you should go.

Several people who have had near-death experiences have
mentioned finding a friendly escort in heaven. Earl Foster was
greeted by his brother Robert.[12] A terminally ill patient told
his nurse, "There's an angel at my window, Trudy, can you see
him?"[13] Marv Besteman spoke of being greeted by the Apostle
Peter.[14]

Hold My Hand

*Yet I still belong to you; you hold my right hand. You guide
me with your counsel, leading me to a glorious destiny. Psalm
73:23–24 NLT*

"Hold my hand, Mommy!" You may have said this more
than once when you were young, looking for a little security.
When your mother said the same to you, she turned it into a
safety instruction: "Hold my hand, honey, while we cross the
street."

Holding hands is a time-honored way of showing affection. Sometimes, though, we forget about holding hands. It
embarrasses us. Teenagers, for instance, wouldn't be caught
dead holding a parent's hand.

But God is a hand holder. It says so in his word. With his
mighty hand he takes hold of our small hands to keep us safe,
show his love, and lead us home. Those who belong to him are
never too old to take hold of his hand.

Animals in Heaven?

Are not two sparrows sold for a penny? Yet not one of them will fall to the ground outside your Father's care. Matthew 10:29

I have a friend who loves dogs. More than a trainer, he's a kind of dog whisperer who's capable of helping incorrigible dogs discover their better selves. When this man gets to heaven, I wouldn't be surprised if, in addition to the usual crowd of family and friends, he's greeted by a big pack of dogs, all barking their heads off with joy.

But do dogs really go to heaven? Are there any animals in heaven?

Some theologians say no, pointing out that unlike human beings, animals don't have immortal souls, nor were they created in the image of God. They say that Jesus died to save human beings, not animals. Others contend that God can do whatever he wants. So if you and I aren't happy unless Fido is in heaven with us, then he can bring Fido to heaven.

We've already seen that the Bible speaks of a new heaven and a new earth. It's hard to conceive of a new earth devoid of either vegetation or animals. Disputing the "no animals in heaven" point of view, writer Anthony DeStefano says, "the Bible makes it clear that there is going to be lush vegetation in heaven. Well, Christ obviously didn't die on the cross to redeem vegetation....

"Do you think God is going to let some shrub experience life everlasting and refuse the same gift to a puppy?"[15]

Nobody knows for sure. But if I were a betting woman, I'd put my money on that puppy making it there.

More on Animals in Heaven

The wolf will live with the lamb,
the leopard will lie down with the goat. . . .
They will neither harm nor destroy
on all my holy mountain. . . .
Isaiah 11:6, 9

Not everyone likes animals as much as I do. To my friend Jeanne, the prospect of a no-animal policy in heaven probably sounds downright heavenly. When she was a little girl, Jeanne was so afraid of robins that she would run from them. All that twittering, flying, and hopping around must have been truly terrifying. Plus robins are always pulling worms out of the ground and gobbling them up. Uggh!

I admit there are some scary things about animals here on earth. Ever watch a wildlife show focused on predators? Lucky for us that human beings are located at the top of the food chain.

Fortunately, heaven won't have any food chains, nor will there be gory television shows showing animals chewing on each other. Come to think of it, I'm convinced we won't be eating steak or pork chops or chicken nuggets once we get to heaven. Why not? Because doing so would inevitably involve suffering. And there's not going to be any suffering in all God's heaven.

What! you say. No lobster in heaven? Don't worry. There will be food you will love even more. Better yet, you'll be able to eat without a twinge of guilt, knowing that no animal has had to suffer to give you a little bit of pleasure.

So what will all those animals be doing? Maybe they'll be romping around, playing with each other and us. Imagine sharing the streets of the heavenly Jerusalem not only with people but with lions and tigers and bears, oh my!

Is Someone Watching Over You?

"See that you do not despise one of these little ones. For I tell you that their angels in heaven always see the face of my Father in heaven." Matthew 18:10

Several years ago, I moved into a lovely old home with a large unfinished attic, which I planned to transform into office space. One night after my children had gone to bed, I went up to the attic to survey the renovations. While I was roaming around, admiring what had been accomplished that day, I nearly pitched forward off the edge of the steep stairwell. I had forgotten that one of the railings had been removed earlier in the day. One more step and I might have sent myself straight to heaven. Fortunately, I looked up in the nick of time.

What made me look up? Was it instinct, luck, or prompting from my guardian angel that prevented me from showing up in heaven prematurely?

Some believe in guardian angels whose assignment is to help us on our earthly journey and then guide us home to heaven when the time comes. In addition to watching over us, part of the angel's job description, according to one commentator, is to "tempt us to do good." I like the sound of that. When it comes to being good and doing good, I need all the temptation I can get.

As you go about your day, be mindful that there is more to the world than you can see. Ask God to help you to be open to new insights, good impulses, and fresh inspirations because they just might be coming to you from an angel who's watching over you.

White Light

God is light; in him there is no darkness at all. 1 John 1:5

Many years ago when my aunt, who was not particularly religious, was close to death, she had a vision, which she later confided to her physician and to my mother. In the vision or dream she was walking toward a being who was radiating light. While many people with near-death experiences report similar visions, my aunt felt no peace, but only terror. She lived for a couple of months after that, during which time she prayed a prayer surrendering her life to God. Later, I wondered if her fear might have stemmed from the fact that she wasn't yet ready to meet God. Perhaps she had been given the time she needed to make her peace with him.

Mary Neal is an orthopedic surgeon who had her own near-death experience several years ago, except she believes she died and was brought back to life. Here's what Neal says about the "white light," of which so many have spoken.

She describes "traveling down a path that led to a great and brilliant hall, larger and more beautiful than anything I can conceive of seeing on earth. It was radiating a brilliance of all colors and beauty. I believe that when people with near-death experiences describe 'seeing the white light' or 'moving toward the white light,' they may be describing their moving toward the brilliance of this hall."[16]

Today as you think about eternal realities, join me in considering whether Christ may be calling you into a deeper relationship with him. If you are ready to say yes, simply tell God you are sorry for your sins and that you want to surrender your life to him. Ask him to deliver you from evil and fill you with his Spirit and he will.

A Heavenly Surprise

We look not at what can be seen but at what cannot be seen;
for what can be seen is temporary, but what cannot be seen is
eternal.   2 Corinthians 4:18 NRSV

Many of us have lost the joy of surprises. In an effort to avoid them, we provide loved ones with birthday lists and Christmas lists (lest we have to pretend to be thankful for something we don't want). Brides register for specific items for their homes. Expectant moms work out color schemes and themes for their layette gift lists. The wrapping paper or gift bag proclaims where we made each purchase. It's all very practical, but whatever happened to the element of surprise?

Though God has promised us many things, he's not asked for a list of things we want in heaven. But whatever you think you want, rest assured that whatever God supplies will be even better. Get ready, then, to be delighted, to be wonderfully and joyfully surprised by the goodness, and power, and love of God that will be finally and fully revealed in heaven!

Heaven's New Song

And I heard a sound from heaven like the roar of rushing waters and like a loud peal of thunder. The sound I heard was like that of harpists playing their harps. And they sang a new song before the throne and before the four living creatures and the elders. Revelation 14:2–3

Several years ago, my children and I visited Niagara Falls. To savor the experience we donned blue plastic ponchos and boarded the *Maid of the Mist*, a boat that takes you as close to the falls as safety allows. The thundering water drowns out every other sound. You have only to stand in amazement.

Charles Spurgeon, the great nineteenth-century preacher, tried to help his listeners imagine an even more amazing scene, the one that will take place when every lover of God will be gathered into heaven and all will be joined in thunderous praise of God. "It is not," he says, "the voice of one ocean, but the voice of many, that is needed to give you an idea of the melodies of heaven. You are to suppose ocean piled upon ocean, sea upon sea,—the Pacific piled upon the Atlantic, the Arctic upon that, the Antarctic higher still, and so ocean upon ocean, all lashed to fury, and all sounding with a mighty voice the praise of God."[17]

Take a moment now to imagine the scene. Listen as your own voice blends with that of many others to proclaim the faithfulness and might of the one we call the King of Kings and Lord of Lords.

The End of Hurt

"He [God] will wipe every tear from their eyes." *Revelation 21:4*

Theologian and pastor R. C. Sproul remembers the comfort his mother provided whenever he was hurt. "When tears spilled out of my eyes," he says, "I sobbed with uncontrollable spasms, my mother took her handkerchief and patted the tears from my cheeks. Often she would 'kiss away the tears.'

"There are few more intimate human experiences than the physical act of wiping away another person's tears. It is a tactile act of compassion. It is a piercing form of nonverbal communication. It is the touch of consolation.

"My mother dried my tears more than once. Her consolation worked for the moment and the sobbing subsided. But then I would get hurt again, and the tears would flow once more. My tear ducts still work. I still have the capacity to weep.

"But when God wipes away tears, it is the end of all crying."[18]

The end of all crying, the end of all pain, the end of all that is and ever has been wrong with the world, that's what heaven will be.

Linked Together Through a Dream

If one part [of the body] suffers, every part suffers with it. 1 Corinthians 12:26

Many years ago, I had a dream that an acquaintance of mine had died. I didn't think much of it and soon forgot the dream. Two months later, I had a similar dream, though this time it was more vivid. Feeling a strong urge to pray, I interceded especially for the man's wife, asking God to give her strength for whatever lay ahead. I kept praying for the next few weeks.

Two months later, a mutual acquaintance called me with the news that the man I had been praying for had been diagnosed with lung cancer. His doctors thought he might live another eighteen months. Would I pray for him and his wife, she asked, not realizing I had already been praying for them for several weeks.

Then, nineteen months after I had my first dream, he passed away.

Once his diagnosis was made public, people all over the world began to pray for him. Why I had been given a head start puzzled me. But then I reread the words of Paul to the Corinthians. Speaking of the body of Christ, he told them: "If one part suffers, every part suffers with it; if one part is honored, every part rejoices with it. Now you are the body of Christ, and each one of you is a part of it." Indeed the souls of those who believe are linked together in mysterious ways. Even our dreams tell us this is so.[19]

Making It to Heaven

The Lord our God is merciful and forgiving, even though we have rebelled against him.   Daniel 9:9 NLT

"I'll never make it to heaven. I'm not good enough." Have you ever heard anyone say or imply that? Have you wondered how to reply?

Understandably, we don't want to judge others, or even ourselves. Who will make it to heaven and who won't? It's best to leave ultimate judgment to God especially since we often judge more harshly than he does. Plus our judgments are based on only partial and distorted knowledge. How can you judge rightly if you don't know everything? Only God can see with perfect clarity into a person's heart.

We do know one thing, however. Jesus has promised to save anyone who believes in him and repents of their sins. With the psalmist we can rejoice, proclaiming the truth that God "has removed our sins as far from us as the east is from the west" (Psalm 103:12 NLT). With that kind of distance between us and our sins, nothing can keep us from heaven.

Where Is Heaven?

But Jesus said, "Let the little children come to me, and do not stop them; for it is to such as these that the kingdom of heaven belongs." Matthew 19:14 NRSV

One day a grandmother asked her three-year-old grandson, Jason, "Where is heaven?" She had no idea if her daughter had told him about heaven or if he had heard anything about it in Sunday school. She expected the usual childish answer, something about beyond the clouds, up in the sky, or a place far away. But Jason surprised her by saying, "Heaven is in your heart, Grandma, don't you know that?"

I thought the story was cute when I first heard it. Then, I realized Jason was on to something. In terms of human geography, heaven really *is* located in our hearts and not our minds, because our minds can't comprehend what heaven is like. But heaven is all our hearts have ever wanted—to experience the presence of God forever. When we get to that place of perfect bliss, we will never want to leave.

The Promise of Heaven

"Arise, shine, for your light has come,
*   and the glory of the* LORD *rises upon you.*

See, darkness covers the earth
*   and thick darkness is over the peoples,*
but the LORD *rises upon you*
*   and his glory appears over you." Isaiah 60:1–2*

Isaiah's prophecy was delivered during a very difficult time for God's people. If ever anyone had a right to sing the blues it was these people during this period of their history. And that is exactly when God broke in with a dazzling promise of future greatness.

In many ways, our own lives are often lived under an oppressive kind of darkness. The world seems to move from one disaster to another. Our children stray, our spouses disappoint, the stock market collapses, another war breaks out.

But then God breaks into our gloom. Like a father encouraging his children to stand beside him on tiptoe, peering over the fence to see what's on the other side, he paints a picture of a dazzling future that only he is tall enough to see. Instead of looking down, we begin to look up. Instead of giving up, we decide to stand up, energized by the realization that life will turn out better than we think. Not because of anything we've done but because of everything he's done.

As we take hold of heaven, our picture of reality will begin to change, not because our lives are suddenly easy, but because we realize that we are not living a mistake. Even in the midst of difficulty, we are aiming toward a future that is altogether bright, living toward a dream that God himself has planted in our hearts.

Remember Your Future

*Then I saw a new heaven and a new earth, for the first heaven
and the first earth had passed away, and there was no longer any
sea. Revelation 21:1*

Hundreds of years after the vision proclaimed in Isaiah, the
Book of Revelation picks up the theme again. Now peering
even further into the future, the Bible speaks of a new and glorious Jerusalem that will descend from heaven at the end of the
ages. This shining Jerusalem, a city of pure gold, like transparent glass, is a picture of our true home, the one for which we
are destined. It is a portrait of our bliss, painted in symbolic
language.

When life on earth is difficult—and when isn't it?—we
need to remember who God is and what his ultimate intentions
for our world are. Thousands of years ago, God encouraged
his people, nearly broken by the weight of their difficulties,
with a luminous vision of the future, one that is still unfolding. Today he assures us that we, too, are destined to live with
him in this new and glorious world, where there will one day
be no more mourning, crying, or pain, no more disappointment, anxiety, or tears, a world in which we will see him, no
longer through a glass darkly, but now face-to-face.

The Things Heaven Won't Have

Nothing will hurt or destroy in all my holy mountain.
Isaiah 11:9 NLT

In heaven there will be no arguments, confusion, embarrass-
ment, harassment, pain, tears, failure, hurricanes, toothaches,
lawsuits, traffic tickets, computer viruses, car breakdowns,
nightmares, misunderstandings, hunger, asthma, diabetes, or
death. Nor will there be doctors, psychologists, police, soldiers, lawyers, or IRS agents. We won't need them anymore.
If you were one of these things on earth, you'll be something
else in heaven. Oh, and of course there will be no politicians,
glory halleluiah! Let us thank the Lord for all the things
heaven won't have.

Your True Self

To the one who is victorious, I will give some of the hidden manna.
I will also give that person a white stone with a new name written
on it, known only to the one who receives it.   Revelation 2:17 NIV

When you arrive in heaven, you can expect to fit in perfectly.
At last, you will have arrived at your true home, the place you
have been longing for since the day you were born. As a part of
your homecoming, you will receive your true name. This will
be the case for each person who makes it to heaven.

George MacDonald read the Scripture above and wrote
this: "God's name for a man must be the expression of his own
idea of the man, that being whom he had in his thought when
he began to make the child, and whom he kept in his thought
through the long process of creation which went to realize the
idea. To tell the name is to seal the success."[20]

Peter Kreeft comments: "Heaven means not just a pleasant
place but *our* place. . . . We fit there; we are fully human there.
We don't turn into angels (that's why there has to be a resurrection of the body; we don't change species). . . . It is our home
because we receive there our true identity."[21]

A Table for Two

You prepare a table before me in the presence of my
enemies. Psalm 23:5

"Mommy, I just had the best dream." Seven-year-old Kelly
went on to describe the dream to her mother. She was in a
restaurant sharing a table for two with Jesus. Though others
were dining nearby, theirs was the only table that was bathed
in light. Recounting the dream, she concluded by saying, "I
feel so close to God."

A year earlier, at the age of six, Kelly had undergone surgery to remove a malignant brain tumor. After that she had
soldiered on through months of radiation and chemotherapy.
Despite her family's hopes for a full recovery, two weeks after
her eighth birthday a routine test revealed that the cancer had
returned. She had only weeks to live.

Months later, her mother found a journal in which the little
girl had written a letter to Jesus shortly after her dream. "Dear
Jesus," she wrote, "I am so excited to come to your kingdom
someday! I don't know anything about what heaven looks
like, I know it's going to be the best place I have ever been! It
feels so good to know that I'm in your arms, safe and sound! I
couldn't have gotten through last year without you, Jesus!!!"

Tears streaming down her face, Kelly's mother knew that,
she, too, would not be able to get through the year without
Jesus. But her discovery of her daughter's letter seemed like a
promise that God would help her. For she was sure that her little girl knew something most of us do not—she knew exactly
what heaven looks like—the best place any of us could ever
be.[22]

Together Again

*Since we believe that Jesus died and then came back to life again,
we can also believe that when Jesus returns, God will bring
back with him all the Christians who have died. . . . So comfort and
encourage each other with this news.* 1 Thessalonians 4:14, 18 TLB

The best way to think about death is as an interruption rather
than a conclusion. To put it in grammatical terms, death is a
parenthesis rather than a period. It interrupts our relationships here on earth, but only for a while. Fortunately, we have
God's promise that we will one day be reunited with family
and friends who belong to him. And what better symbol of
joyous intimacy than sitting down together at a feast—which
is exactly what Jesus promised his disciples during his last meal
with them (Matthew 8:11).

In addition to reuniting with cherished loved ones, we will
get to know people who died long before we were born. Imagine talking with Moses or David or Mary Magdalene or any
of the great figures of history who belonged to God. We will
have all eternity to take pleasure in each other's company as
we praise the Lord who makes heaven possible.

Last Impressions

O death, where is thy sting? 1 Corinthians 15:55 KJV

Charlene Baumbich is a writer who lost her mother several days after a massive stroke. As soon as she heard the news, Charlene flew to Albuquerque, New Mexico, to be with her. Though she steeled herself for the worst, she was shocked when she walked into her mother's hospital room. The limp figure lying unconscious on the bed, hooked up to various machines, seemed the antithesis of the beautiful, vibrant woman she had always known.

"Sadly," she says, "my last vision of my mother was a tragic one. Colorless, an oxygen mask covered her mouth, and she lay with one eye open and the other closed. What a horrible last impression of my smiling, joyous, large-hearted mother! The memory haunted me."

Then one night she had a dream. "I saw my mother standing in a glass telephone booth filled with light. The background was smoky gray and misty, somewhat ethereal. But a bright light surrounded my mother. I couldn't talk to her or touch her, and she didn't talk to me. But we communicated. Her face was absolutely at peace, and she was smiling at me with a brilliance I had never seen before. I can only say she looked beatific. Healed, whole, and utterly happy. It was as though she were saying, 'Charlene, I'm well and you are going to be all right. You need to know this.'"

Charlene's dream was a privileged gift that brought her complete peace. So often our own last impressions of those we love are haunted by the memory of pain and disfigurement they've suffered prior to their passing. Perhaps the story of Charlene's dream will serve as a reminder that death is never the end of the story. For those who love God it's the beginning of a life of absolute peace and joy.

Something to Sing About

*For God so loved the world that he gave his only Son, so that
everyone who believes in him may not perish but may have eternal
life. John 3:16 NRSV*

One thing the Bible is clear about is that in heaven, there will
be a whole lot of singing going on. Pastor and writer Calvin
Miller spoke about how after the death of his older brother,
his mother would often sing a particular hymn. "I don't know
why she sang," he says. "Perhaps grief can't quit hurting until
it starts singing."[23]

Today, why not join me in singing a couple of verses of
"What Wondrous Love Is This," a hymn that reminds us of all
the singing we will be doing in eternity.

> *What wondrous love is this, O my soul, O my soul!*
> *What wondrous love is this, O my soul!*
> *What wondrous love is this*
> *That caused the Lord of bliss*
> *To bear the dreadful curse for my soul, for my soul,*
> *To bear the dreadful curse for my soul!*
>
> *And when from death I'm free, I'll sing on, I'll sing on;*
> *And when from death I'm free, I'll sing on.*
> *And when from death I'm free*
> *I'll sing His love for me,*
> *And through eternity I'll sing on, I'll sing on,*
> *And through eternity I'll sing on.*
>
> ATTRIBUTED TO ALEXANDER MEANS,
> CIRCA 1811

Let the Party Begin

On this mountain the Lord Almighty will prepare a feast of rich food for all peoples, a banquet of aged wine—the best of meats and the finest of wines. Isaiah 25:6–10 NIV

Now that's a party!

The prophet Isaiah envisioned a massive gathering: a feast with everyone from all times, places, and nations gathered around a great big table to celebrate with the Lord of Heaven and Earth. "But how will that work?" your literal mind might ask.

Some people don't eat meat, some don't drink wine. I happen to love pepperoni pizza. My sister prefers veggies, fruit, and no meat—ever. My uncle likes headcheese (ewww!), and my aunt has never touched a drop of wine. My nephews, on the other hand, would be elated with a great big plate of Oreo cookies with a little ice cream on the side.

But, really, we don't need to overthink this. Isaiah is portraying the idea of the grandest, most elegant celebration possible. The food isn't the focus; the gathering is.

The best party ever will welcome all of us forever into God's feast of love.

God's Great Compassion

The Lord is merciful and gracious, slow to anger and abounding in steadfast love.   Psalm 103:8 NRSV

Some of us may wonder if we'll get into heaven when the time comes. We've done too many things we're ashamed of and left too many good things undone. How could God possibly welcome us into heaven when we die? We're simply not good enough.

While it's true that none of us are good enough for heaven, God is good enough to bring us there. His mercy is greater than our greatest fault, our worst sin, our most pathetic weakness. Like a loving parent, he doesn't stay angry forever. Nor does he hold a grudge, drag up the past, or rub our noses in all the things we've ever done wrong. Full of compassion and loving-kindness, he does what we would never be able to. He forgives us, forgetting our sins completely.

Because of Jesus, we can become pure, clean, holy, whole, and perfect in God's sight. That's the state in which we'll enter heaven if we entrust our lives to Christ. Because of him, God will throw open the gates and say to us, "Enter in!"

Heavenly Joy

You are looking forward to the joys of heaven, and have been ever since the Gospel first was preached to you. Colossians 1:5 TLB

We equate heaven with joy, and for good reason. Any joy that we experience on earth comes from heaven's overflow. As Peter Kreeft puts it, "The home of joy is God. We are God's colonies, and he visits his colonies. The fire of God descends into the air of our spirit and even into the waters of our soul and the earth of our body. Feelings of joy are like the hot crater made by a meteor that has burst through the atmosphere, parted the seas, and come to rest on the sea bottom."[24]

Throughout the Bible, particularly in the New Testament, "joy" and "heaven" often crop up in the same sentence.

So we do not look at what we can see right now, the troubles all around us, but we look forward to the joys in heaven which we have not yet seen. (2 Corinthians 4:18 TLB)

Since you became alive again, so to speak, when Christ arose from the dead, now set your sights on the rich treasures and joys of heaven where he sits beside God in the place of honor and power. (Colossians 3:1 TLB)

Need more joy in your life? Take a few moments to soak in these words of God's Spirit to impress them on your heart.

Out of Sight

Look at the heavens, and see; and behold the clouds, which are higher than you. Job 35:5 ESV

When you are driving along a road in mist and fog, the road disappears ahead and you can't see where you are going. You may drive cautiously, a little more slowly than usual, but you keep going anyway, fairly sure that the road will take you where you want to go.

In the same way, you are unable to see heaven from your current location on the road of life. But you know you'll reach your destination if you keep going and stay on the road. You may get tired of driving and the fog may get thicker. Darkness may fall and other travelers may get in your way. But a careful driver can keep moving with a minimum of concern.

So we do not lose heart. Though our outer self is wasting away, our inner self is being renewed day by day. For this light momentary affliction is preparing for us an eternal weight of glory beyond all comparison, as we look not to the things that are seen but to the things that are unseen. For the things that are seen are transient, but the things that are unseen are eternal. (2 Corinthians 4:16–18 ESV)

A Father in Heaven

"People judge by outward appearance, but the LORD looks at the heart." 1 Samuel 16:7

Connie Neal describes her father as a "tornado of a man," someone with endless moneymaking ideas and schemes who experienced repeated failures. Looking back, she realizes that today he would probably be diagnosed with attention deficit disorder.

Toward the end of his life, he cashed in his insurance policies, sold everything, and then lost his home. Then one night he suffered a serious heart attack. Sadly, his last moments were spent not saying goodbye but worrying aloud about where the money would come from to pay for his funeral.

Disturbed by the manner of his passing, Neal prayed, asking God what kind of legacy she could possibly draw from his life. The night after his funeral, she had a dream. Suddenly she saw her father standing in front of her. "Dad, what are you doing here?" she asked.

Smiling widely, he replied: "Well, I had to show you people. I had to come and tell you that I finally found a place where I am appreciated."

"But Dad, don't you know you're dead?" Connie asked.

"Of course I know I'm dead," he replied, still grinning. "You see these tools? The Lord gave me these, and I'm up there working on the mansions right now. Well, that's all I wanted to say. I finally found a place where they know what I'm worth."

"When I woke up," Connie explains, "I couldn't help but think that his lifelong dream had finally been realized; He had at last found acceptance and real appreciation. He was cherished as he never had been on earth."

Though Connie doesn't claim to understand the inner workings of dreams, she felt this one came in reply to her prayers. It comforted her to realize that God sees through our individual difficulties to the true kernel of every person. While we're here on earth, some of us are burdened with far more challenges than others. But when we get to heaven, we'll discover we are finally valued not for what we can do but for who we are.[25]

Crown of Boasting

For what is our hope or joy or crown of boasting before our Lord Jesus at his coming? Is it not you? 1 Thessalonians 2:19–20 NRSV

Most of us dislike boasting. But Paul suggests there may be boasting in heaven. It won't be about who's the most attractive, the richest, or the most powerful, but about who has laid down their lives so that others might know him. Loving God through humble service is what will make a person great in heaven.

You may be one of those people. Laying down your life for your children, for elderly parents, for the poor. You may be sharing the gospel with people who seem far from God. There are a thousand and one ways to put others first and all of them are costly, sometimes so costly that you may wonder if it's worth all the trouble.

If that's how you're feeling right now, remember that you can't do it on your own. You need grace daily to do what God is calling you to do. Ask him now to refresh you with a sense of his presence so that you will have the strength to go on. And remember that one day you will have a crown that will last forever.

The Patchwork of Heaven

Now I know in part . . . 1 Corinthians 13:12

When the national quilt show came to town, I knew I had to be there. Though I'm not a quilter, I admire those who "paint" with textiles. In order to step up my appreciation for the craft itself, I asked an expert quilter if she'd like to attend the show with me. I wanted her to school me on the details so I could better appreciate the intricate stitches and patterns.

It occurs to me that we can do something similar when it comes to learning more about heaven. Instead of just standing back and appreciating the broad brushstrokes of heaven, we can begin to study heaven by reading what Scripture has to say about it and by reading books about it. But be careful; though there are many books about heaven, not all of them are trustworthy. Two of the best I've found are Randy Alcorn's *Heaven* and Peter Kreeft's *Heaven, the Heart's Deepest Longing*.

As we learn more about heaven, a deeper, more beautiful picture may begin to emerge, much like a beautiful quilt that has been stitched together by God's own hand.

Premixed

And the building of the wall of it was of jasper: and the city was
pure gold, like unto clear glass.   Revelation 21:18 KJV

A recent home decorating project reacquainted me with the
wacky world of paint color names. Apparently "heaven" is a
popular motif right now. Marketers would like you to create a
snapshot of paradise by rolling a gallon of "heaven" onto your
four walls—if you believe, that is, that heaven is largely done
up in white whites and light brights such as these:

Heavenly White, White Heaven, Heaven ("an ethereal
shade of palest grayed lavender"), Gateway to Paradise (lilac),
Heaven Sent (light violet), Heavenly Song (pale pink), Simply Heaven (light aqua), Heavenly Blue (pale blue), Heaven on
Earth (light blue, "timeless," and "elegant"), Jewel of Heaven
(muted green), Heavenly (pale yellow), Heavenly Sand ("but-
tery"), and Heaven's Light ("perfect, soft yellow").

I think they missed some options. When the Apostle John
saw the jewel-spangled heavenly city, the gemstones flashed
rich colors such as red-brown (sardonyx), orange-red (sar-
dius, or carnelian), an array of dazzling greens (emerald, jasper, chrysolite, and chrysoprasus), blue-green (aquamarine
beryl), gold (ancient topaz), topped off with shades of purple
(amethyst). Truly heavenly!

"Kill Me or Cure Me"

*"And the smoke of their torment will rise for ever and
ever." Revelation 14:11*

Ronald Reagan (not the one you're thinking of) was bleeding
to death after a brawl outside a neighborhood market. A drug
addict and convicted criminal, he arrived at one hospital only
to be taken by ambulance to another. As they were speeding
away from the first hospital, the paramedic who was caring for
him leaned down and said, "Sir, you need Jesus Christ."

Reagan responded with curses. But instead of taking
offense, the paramedic simply told him again that he needed
Jesus.

Before Reagan could reply, it seemed to him as though
the ambulance had suddenly exploded. He felt as though he
were being drawn through a tunnel of smoke. Then came the
screams. Looking down, he witnessed a horrifying scene.
Beneath him was a volcanic opening with human beings
inside, burning but not being burned up. He recognized people he had known in the past.

They were in agony, he says. But "the most painful part
was the utter loneliness. The depression was so heavy, that
there was no hope, no escape, there was no way out of this
place. The smell was like sulfur, like an electric welder, the
stench was terrible."

Fortunately, Reagan woke up in the hospital. When he was
released, he tried to resume his former lifestyle. But it didn't
work. He just couldn't forget what he'd seen.

One morning he took a chance and went with his wife to
church, listening intently as the minister read from the Bible:
"Behold the Lamb of God who takes away the sins of the
world."

Intending to leave, Reagan surprised himself by walking down the aisle to the front of the church and praying: "God, if you exist, and Jesus, if you are God's lamb, please, please kill me or cure me. I don't want to live anymore, I'm not a husband, I'm not a father, I'm no good." In that moment, Reagan says, "the darkness and the blackness left my life... The guilt left my life, the violence, anger and the hatred left my life. And Jesus Christ became Lord and Savior."[26]

Ronny Reagan is no longer haunted by his glimpse of hell. "God," he says, "healed my mind, my memory, the drug addiction; the alcoholism was instantaneously gone, delivered." From that moment, he knew he had to tell the story so that others might be spared the consequences of a life without of God.

Traffic Calming

I'm asking God for one thing, only one thing:
To live with him in his house my whole life long.
I'll contemplate his beauty; I'll study at his feet.
That's the only quiet, secure place in a noisy world,
The perfect getaway, far from the buzz of traffic. Psalm 27:4–5 MSG

Recently the city installed speed bumps on my suburban street. There is an elementary school a few blocks away, and cars were driving too fast for the safety of the children. The official reason for the speed bumps is for "traffic calming," a term that everyone (except the traffic department) finds amusing. Wouldn't you know, one of the unintended effects of the "calming" has been to attract some of the skateboarding boys right into the street. When school's out, they like to compete with each other to see who can "catch the most air," using the bumps for the opposite reason from which they were intended.

Those speed bumps made me think about how I have installed a few traffic-calming measures in my busy life. I have found that having regular times for quiet prayer, worship, and Bible reading calms my spirit and keeps me safely on the road to heaven.

God Can Sing!

For the LORD your God is living among you. He is a mighty savior. He will take delight in you with gladness. With his love, he will calm all your fears. He will rejoice over you with joyful songs. Zephaniah 3:17 NLT

The idea that there will be great singing in heaven isn't new. "Sing ye, choirs of angels," says the old Christmas carol. The Bible pictures saints and angels gathered around God's throne, all singing his praises. So there are saints singing, angels singing, choirs singing. In heaven there will be a whole lot of singing going on.

But how about God singing?

The prophet Zephaniah announced that God sings joyful songs. He sings praises. Amazing as it may seem, he sings *our* praises. He sings both *about* and *over* his people!

I wonder what God's voice sounds like. Is it tenor, bass, or something altogether different? Does he have an extensive repertoire of songs to suit the diversity of the heavenly saints? Whatever God sings, it will be glorious. Take a moment now to think about how much he loves you. God takes delight in you. He rejoices over you with joyful songs.

Don't Try This with Teenagers

And the glory of the LORD *will be revealed.   Isaiah 40:5*

It's a curious fact that people of a particular age seem incapable of appreciating certain classic works of literature. Take *Winnie the Pooh*. Though many young children and adults love reading stories about Pooh Bear, Piglet, Christopher Robin, and friends, most teenagers would not be caught dead reading them.

I think the same can be said about hymn singing. There's a decidedly uncool factor when it comes to the old hymns. Take the song variously titled "Do Lord" or "I've Got a Home in Glory Land." Fortunately, those of us that are beyond worrying about cool can have a lot of fun with this hymn. If you don't know the tune, why not look it up on YouTube. Then get up out of your chair and start clapping your hands, stomping your feet, and singing along. Just see if it doesn't warm your heart. For you really do have a home in Glory Land.

> *I've got a home in glory land that outshines the sun*
> *I've got a home in glory land that outshines the sun*
> *I've got a home in glory land that outshines the sun*
> *Way beyond the blue*
>
> *Do Lord, O, do Lord, O do remember me*
> *Do Lord, O, do Lord, O do remember me*
> *Do Lord, O, do Lord, O do remember me*
> *Way beyond the blue*

Your Longer-Term Future

Store up for yourselves treasures in heaven.   Matthew 6:20

One of my favorite financial phrases is the "magic of com-pounding." I like it because it conjures images of large heaps of money, growing fatter each year, simply because you have saved and invested. You started early and kept at it because you believed in your long-term future. Now you can look for-ward to a lovely retirement.

But this dream-come-true scenario is nothing more than a daydream for those of us who got started late. Perhaps we were so enamored with the present that we forgot to invest in the future.

Jesus, the wisest man who ever lived, counsels us not to make the mistake of storing up "treasures on earth, where moth and rust destroy and where thieves break in and steal." Instead he says we should lay up for ourselves treasures in heaven (Matthew 6:19–20 NKJV).

I don't think Jesus was telling us not to save money for our old age. Rather, he was indicating where the big money really is, directing us to invest everything we have in what God is doing now. The work we do in, through, and for God is the only thing that will have lasting value.

Want to be rich? Begin today by thinking about your longer-term future, the one that starts the moment you leave earth, headed toward heaven. Ask God to show you how to invest yourself in a way here that will build up treasure there.

Happy Ending

They will enter Zion with singing; everlasting joy will crown their heads.   Isaiah 51:11

I suppose you will think me conceited if I tell you I'm gifted. Let me assure you I'm not talking about natural gifts but about the gift of faith, which enables me to believe that the biggest, most important story in the universe, the one about Jesus saving the world, is true. No matter how many ups and downs there have been or will be, God has already told us how the story will end. He has also assured us that our own stories will end happily if we belong to him, even though that happiness may not become apparent until we go to heaven.

Ann Spangler tells the story of a friend who believed she had witnessed one of those happy endings. "Patti had been reading the newspaper," she explains, "when the music began. It was exquisite—strange but beautiful. Certain the music wasn't coming from a television, radio, or DVD player, Patti walked through the house trying to locate the source. But a thorough search revealed nothing. Then she opened the front door, but all was quiet....

"Shortly after that Patti heard a siren and noticed the flashing red light of an ambulance as it pulled into the driveway next door. Though her neighbors hadn't lived there long, Patti knew the wife had been suffering from Lou Gehrig's disease. She watched as paramedics carried her out on a stretcher.

"The woman's suffering, she learned, had ended that night. At the exact time Patti had been hearing the music, it seems that her neighbor had been passing from this life to the next."[27]

The experience was so vivid that she later told the woman's husband about it, saying she felt certain she heard angels overhead as they were carrying his wife to heaven.

Someday Heaven

Eye hath not seen, nor ear heard, neither have entered into the heart of man, the things which God hath prepared for them that love him. 1 Corinthians 2:9 KJV

The trouble started last night. Before the snow began flying, I hired a plow for the season to clear the driveway. To my dismay, most of my driveway is still covered in snow despite a large storm. When I called to talk to the contractor, he informed me that his plow is too wide for the drive. Oh, and no, he said, there would be no refund because his contract stipulated "no refunds." I was steamed. I'm sure he felt the heat through the phone. With any luck it was fused to his ear.

Well, at least I could clear the sidewalks with my small snowblower. Trouble is, the snowblower wouldn't start. More shoveling. And what about my elderly neighbor's sidewalks? My youngest had promised to clear them for her for the rest of the winter. Have you ever tried getting a snowblower fixed in the middle of December? Oh well. More shoveling.

Then I walked back into the house. What's that smell? It seems the cat had gotten trapped in the bathroom and had pooped in the sink. Good thing I hadn't eaten breakfast yet or that might have gone into the sink as well.

Please, Lord, nothing more today, okay? Then I grabbed a late breakfast and went into my office to get some writing done. I opened the file I had been working on only to discover that I had lost every letter of every word I had written yesterday. Argh!! And it wasn't even noon.

I don't know what the rest of my day holds, but I do know one thing. I need to find a way to refocus. Instead of stewing over a thousand and one things that threaten my peace, I need to think about what God has planned for me. I need to think about heaven.

In heaven there will be no shady contractors (at least no unrepentant ones), no broken snowblowers, no lost files, and no cats! Sorry, I didn't mean that about the cats. In heaven there will be love, peace, and joy unending. Thank you, God!

Enjoy the Journey

Lead a life worthy of God, who calls you into his own kingdom and glory. 1 Thessalonians 2:12 NRSV

Every summer the Beck family traveled to New Jersey to visit Susan's parents. During the fourteen-hour drive from Michigan to the Jersey shore, the family spent hours talking about what was to come: Grandma's welcome hugs and warm kisses, pancakes for breakfast, long, hot days on the beach spent jumping the ocean waves, and making things with Grandpa in his woodshop. They just couldn't wait to get there.

After a while, Susan decided to change the focus of the trip, realizing it was just as important for her family to enjoy the journey as the destination. The promise of what was ahead was great, but they also needed to relax a little, enjoy the journey, and check out the sites along the way. And so began another tradition—the getting there.

After a predawn start, they stopped for breakfast at McDonald's. The two boys opened small presents in the backseat to keep them entertained. They stopped for a picnic at lunchtime. Sometimes they stopped to view the scenery or an historic site or to eat ice cream cones. The journey became almost as fun as the promised destination.

Our anticipation of heaven is something like going to Grandma's house—we know the welcome will be great and the fellowship warm. It sounds marvelous. But we can't hurry the process of getting there, so we might as well enjoy the journey.

> *"No eye has seen, not ear has heard*
>   *and no mind has imagined*
> *what God has prepared*
>   *for those who love him."* 1 Corinthians 2:9b NLT

Kay Warren, wife of California pastor Rick Warren, was once in an airport with a friend, waiting for a flight. They heard patriotic music and noticed a group of people dressed in red, white, and blue and waving little American flags. Evidently they were there to greet some returning U.S. troops as they disembarked from an international flight.

The weary men began to file through the doorway. "We appreciate you! Thank you! Welcome home!" Many of the soldiers were visibly moved. None of them had expected such a welcome.

The experience made Kay think of how it will be when we first enter heaven. Who will be part of the welcoming committee? "As believers in Christ," she says, "we are all soldiers in the Lord's army. We, too, take oaths of fidelity, sacrifice, and service...

"Scripture teaches us about the welcome and rewards we will receive when our battle on earth is over. Artists, writers, and theologians have all taken stabs at imagining what those moments of heavenly welcome will look like. That afternoon, we were visualizing the very moment when we would step into eternity."[28]

Heaven to the Max

*Yes, we are fully confident, and we would rather be away from
these earthly bodies, for then we will be at home with the Lord.*
2 Corinthians 5:8 NLT

From the accounts of those who claim to have visited heaven,
the people who are there now seem to be filled with joy. Even
so, they aren't yet experiencing heaven to the max, because
ultimately, the new heaven and the new earth will be both
spiritual and physical, meant to be experienced by both
our bodies and our souls. Justin Martyr, an early Christian
apologist who wrote a little more than a century after Jesus'
resurrection, said, "If God has called humans to life and resurrection, he has called not a part, but a whole—and this is the
soul and the body."[29]

If that is so, why do so many accounts of heavenly encounters include visions of people and places that seem to be physical in nature?

I like the way author Anthony DeStefano explains it.
"Everyone knows," he says, "what it feels like to be separated
from our bodies, because everyone knows what it feels like to
dream. Think about this for a moment. When you are sound
asleep in bed, your body motionless, you know that in your
mind you can be a thousand miles away....

"The colors you're seeing are just as vibrant, the sounds
you're hearing just as clear, the emotions you're feeling are just
as genuine. Best of all, the 'you' that is living in the dream is
really you....

"The same God who gave us the power to see, hear, and
feel things as we sleep will also give us the power to 'sense'
things as we await the resurrection."[30]

So, don't worry. You are not destined to become a disembodied soul aimlessly floating around in heaven. Your spirit

will experience delight as you reunite with family and friends in a place where everyone is full of joy. Best of all, you will experience the complete happiness of seeing God and living in his presence forever.

Why Heaven Is a Happy Place

But seek first his kingdom and his righteousness, and all these things will be given to you as well. Matthew 6:33

Life on earth doesn't make sense unless you understand that every person on the planet is facing the same fundamental problem. We're broken, busted, bent out of shape. Doesn't matter how old, smart, or rich you are, nor whether you've grown up in a healthy or a dysfunctional family. It has nothing to do with your racial identity or your national affiliation. Something isn't working right inside you. Because of sin, the relationship between your body and your will has been fundamentally altered so that your bodily cravings often trump your good intentions.

One of the wonderful things about heaven is that everything broken will be completely healed and repaired. There will be no more cravings we can't control. No more struggling to do the right thing. No more saying one thing and doing another. We will be perfectly in sync, our bodies taking orders from our wills, which will be perfectly aligned with God's intentions.

That's one reason why heaven is such a happy place. In heaven there are no social problems, no dysfunctional families, no dysfunctional people. Everything and everyone works perfectly because all have been perfected.

So should we just wait for heaven to straighten things out? Not according to Jesus. While we're here on earth, we're called to build up his kingdom, and we do that by sharing the gospel and by surrendering ourselves to God over and over, until every square inch of us is transformed. Even though the job won't be finished until heaven, let's not waste another moment. Let's get started now.

He's in Heaven Now

Brothers and sisters, we do not want you to be uninformed about those who sleep in death, so that you do not grieve like the rest of mankind, who have no hope. For we believe that Jesus died and rose again, and so we believe that God will bring with Jesus those who have fallen asleep in him. 1 Thessalonians 4:13–14

Last night, I went to the funeral home, hoping to comfort friends whose father had just passed away. But I was the one who ended up being comforted.

What took me by surprise was their joy. Even though they were grieving the loss of a man they loved, they were absolutely certain he was in heaven. One of Bob's daughters told me that as the family gathered around his bed just prior to his death, they sang hymns and prayed. As they were praying and praising God, she said she caught a glimpse of him crossing into heaven. His eyes were sparkling, and he looked so young and happy. In that sacred moment, she felt the joy of belonging to the saints on earth just as her father was joining the saints in heaven.

Later, as I said my goodbyes, her brother-in-law confirmed how good their time of prayer together had been. Throughout it, family members had taken turns encouraging Bob, telling him that his suffering was about to end and that he would soon be in heaven.

"We feel the grief. We're sorry to lose him. But we're so happy he's in heaven now. And I can't wait until I go there myself!" I could tell by the joy on his face that he meant it.

Do Not Be Afraid

Be strong and courageous; do not be frightened or dismayed, for the
Lord your God is with you wherever you go. Joshua 1:9 NRSV

God spoke these reassuring words to Joshua, the leader of the
Israelites, as he was about to cross the Jordan River and enter
into the land that God had promised his people. The land held
the promise of peace and prosperity. It overflowed with an
abundance of food. Above all, it was a place where they could
finally end their wandering lives, settle down, and rest.

The biblical language about this journey to the Promised Land echoes today in our language about heaven. Just
as the Israelites crossed the Jordan, we speak of crossing over
to the other side when we die. Certain songs speak of crossing the Jordan River to enter heaven, clearly connecting this
Bible story with our passage into heaven.

While the crossing is an important part of the story, the
most important part is what God told Joshua right before he
entered the land: "No matter what happens, I will be with
you. You must be strong and courageous. I will help you; I
will guide you. And when you make it, I will give you rest."

The same words God spoke to Joshua are given to us today.
Don't be afraid—when the time comes to cross over, God will
be with you, and he will bring you safely home.

Dust

Your hands fashioned and made me. . . . Remember that you have made me like clay; and will you return me to the dust? Job 10:8–9 ESV

Ever seen people walking around with a big black smudge on their foreheads? If so, you have probably just spotted someone who has attended an Ash Wednesday service. During the liturgy on this first day of Lent, people line up to be reminded of a depressing truth. The person administering the ashes, dips his thumb into a bowl of ashes, makes a cross out of it on people's foreheads, and then says, Remember, thou art dust and unto dust thou shalt return.

But why would anyone line up to receive such gloomy news? Christians do it, because they believe that death is not the end of the story. Though they admit to being dust, they know they are beloved dust. So they begin Lent by humbling themselves so that when this season of penance ends, they can celebrate the joyous hope of Easter.

Many Jewish people also believe in God's power to bring the dead to life. Here are four lines from an ancient prayer spoken during every Jewish service:

> *You are mighty, eternally, O Lord*
> *You bring the dead to life, mighty to save.*
>
> *Who can compare with Your might, O Lord and King?*
> *You are Master of life, and death, and deliverance.*[31]

Specks of dust that we are, let us rejoice today because God is far more powerful than the processes that will eventually render our bodies into dust. The One who is called "Master of life, and death, and deliverance," he is the One who loves us and has promised to bring us back to life so that we can live in his presence forever.

Heavenly Moneybags

Fear not, little flock, for it is your Father's good pleasure to give you the kingdom. Sell your possessions, and give to the needy. Provide yourselves with moneybags that do not grow old, with a treasure in the heavens that does not fail, where no thief approaches and no moth destroys. For where your treasure is, there will your heart be also. Luke 12:32–34 ESV

We hang on so tightly to our treasures, don't we? Pleasure, success, family, health, and money—all these and more. Perhaps we instinctively realize that such gifts come from heaven. They are like cherished souvenirs, small tastes of heaven, and so we clutch them tightly. But too much clutching will inevitably cause trouble. Why? Because while we're here on earth, heaven's most important treasures are things that take shape within our hearts.

Have you ever noticed that the words "heaven" and "heart" start with the same three letters? That's useful to remember because the language of heaven is a heart-spoken one. Its treasures, few but essential, include faith, hope, and love, blessings that are found within the human heart.

Ask yourself today how well your treasures align with your heart. Is your heart looking forward to heaven while you are still here on earth? If so, it will be true to say of you: "Her heart is in the right place."

Satellite View

Those who believe in the Son have eternal life, but those who do not obey the Son will never have life. John 3:36 NCV

Every summer, friends invite my husband and me for a barbecue at their house on a lake. Whenever we visit, I think how nice it would be if we, too, could afford to live on that lake. The water is clear, good for swimming and waterskiing. Many residents have boats, and the lake is big enough for everyone.

The only time we have access to the lake is when our friends invite us, because every inch of shoreline is privately owned, and each owner has a private dock. Once I looked online for a public-access park and discovered a satellite view of the area. The image reminded me of a circular gear turned inside out, ringed as it was with stubby docks all pointing toward the middle. It was obvious that lake access is restricted to owners only.

Heaven is a little like that lake. There's no such thing as public access. People can't just push in because they caught a glimpse of its beauty and feel like sightseeing.

Unlike property on the lake, nobody is rich enough to buy a place in heaven. That's not how it's done. The Father owns it all, and the only way to get your foot on the shore is by inheritance: "You have received the spirit of sonship. . . . and if children, then heirs, heirs of God and fellow heirs with Christ" (Romans 8:15, 17 RSV).

Even so, the good news about heaven is that there's always room for one more.

What About Hell?

They [those who do not know God] will be punished with
everlasting destruction and shut out from the presence of the Lord
and from the glory of his might. 2 *Thessalonians 1:9*

In the twenty-first century, hell has fallen decidedly out of
fashion. It's become merely a word we let slip whenever we
get frustrated or upset. The idea that hell could be a real place
offends our sensibilities. How could a good God ever send
someone to a place that the Bible speaks of as "outer darkness,"
"eternal fire," or the "second death"? Surely a loving God
would do no such thing.

But what if hell isn't a place God sends us to but a destination we choose? Listen to what C. S. Lewis says: "There are,"
he says, "only two kinds of people in the end: those who say to
God, 'Thy will be done,' and those to whom God says, in the
end, 'Thy will be done.' All that are in Hell, choose it. Without that self-choice there could be no Hell. No soul that seriously and constantly desires joy will ever miss it. Those who
seek find. To those who knock, it is opened."[32]

I think Lewis and the Bible are right. There is a place called
"hell," and only people who reject God and his ways will go
there. Hell is a place of outer darkness, of total separation and
alienation—where human beings exist apart from goodness,
light, beauty, strength, and love, not because God has sent
them there but because, in the end, they have chosen to go
there.

Let us pray today for ourselves and others to find the grace
to choose heaven, entrusting our lives to God as we say "not
mine, but thy will be done."

"Keep Me Out of Hell!"

*If you declare with your mouth, "Jesus is Lord," and believe
in your heart that God raised him from the dead, you will be
saved. Romans 10:9*

Charles McKaig, a fifty-seven-year-old mail carrier, was on
a treadmill undergoing a stress test when he stopped breathing and collapsed on the floor. Maurice Rawlings, the attending cardiologist, immediately began efforts to resuscitate him,
alternating between compressing his chest and reaching for his
instruments to install a pacemaker.

Each time the patient was resuscitated, he would scream,
"I am in hell!" "Don't stop!" he would say. "Don't you understand? I'm in hell! Each time you quit I go back to hell. . . . How
do I stay out of hell?"

Finally, in an effort to assuage the man's panic, Rawlings
told him to repeat this prayer: "I believe Jesus Christ is the Son
of God. Jesus, save my soul. Keep me alive. If I die, please keep
me out of hell!" It wasn't the kind of advice you would expect
from an atheist, which Rawlings was.

After that, everything changed.

McKaig later explained that he no longer felt afraid. When
he faded out, he had the pleasant experience of seeing his
mother and stepmother and then of walking down a lane with
brilliant colors painting both sides. "Nobody," he said, "not
even Rembrandt could reproduce those colors, they were so
bright. . . . It surrounded me and took care of me. I've never felt
so good and so safe in my whole life."[33]

That day something remarkable happened. Four times a man
who had stopped breathing and whose heart was no longer beating was brought back to life. Even more remarkable, God used a
"make-believe" prayer suggested by an atheist doctor as the cata-

lyst for a double conversion. Because of what happened in that clinic, both the patient and the doctor who treated him came to believe that Jesus is real.

We Need Encouragement

> *"For all those words which were written long ago are meant to*
> *teach us today; that when we read in the scriptures of the endurance*
> *of men and all the help God gave them in those days, we may*
> *be encouraged to go on hoping in our own time."* Romans 15:4
> PHILLIPS

The Puritans used to name their children, especially their daughters, with "virtue names" such as Charity, Joy, Temperance, Prudence, Faith, Grace, Constance, Hope, and Patience. Some of these names are still used today, although many, like Silence, Diligence, Repent, or Tribulation, never seem to have caught on. Too bad because a lot of teachers would love to have a classroom full of Silence and Diligence.

Interestingly, Heaven and Neveah ("Heaven" spelled backward) are two names that have risen in popularity. Though many of the virtue names sound quaint, they serve as personal reminders of spiritual realities.

Unsurprisingly, Scripture itself, from which these names are taken, offers the best reminder of heavenly realities. Like the parents of one young Puritan named Safe-on-High, we can draw courage and strength from the Word of God, which will enable us to stay the course as we steer straight for our heavenly home.

Headlines

No temple could be seen in the city, for the Lord God Almighty and
the Lamb are worshiped in it everywhere. . . . Nothing evil will
be permitted in it—no one immoral or dishonest—but only those
whose names are written in the Lamb's Book of Life. Revelation
21:22, 27 TLB

We see similar headlines so often they appear to have been
recycled: "California Firm Recalls Chicken Products." Poten-
tial contamination with *E. coli* bacteria. "Lettuce Recall
Blamed an Outbreak of Listeria." Even labels such as "free
range," "organic," or "FDA approved" hold no guarantees.
Chemicals, bacteria, and toxins compromise food safety so
frequently that we've gotten used to impurities in our food
supply. That's just the way things are.

We feel something similar about the world we live in.
The world is broken. We are broken. Nothing and no one is
quite safe or pure, including us. That's just the way things are.

In heaven, the reverse will be true. Everyone will be
safe. Everything will be pure. No evil or brokenness will
be allowed because in heaven everything broken will be fixed,
everything bent will be straightened out. Even stubbed toes
and sprained ankles will become a thing of the past.

Sick of the steady stream of bad news? Rejoice, because one
day soon only the good news will survive.

Carry Us Up

*As [Jacob] slept, he dreamed of a stairway that reached from
the earth up to heaven. And he saw the angels of God going
up and down the stairway. At the top of the stairway stood the
Lord.   Genesis 28:12–13 NLT*

Jacob was on the run. He was leaving everything behind to
escape his brother's wrath. Exhausted and afraid, he lay down
to rest under the open sky. That's when he had the dream
about a stairway connecting heaven and earth.

Many see in that stairway a prefigurement of Christ—who
is the one who bridges the gap between heaven and earth. He's
the one who makes it possible for us to escape punishment
for our sins so that we can have a relationship with God and a
home in heaven.

I like how Ann Voskamp puts it. "Jesus," she says, "doesn't
show you the steps to get to heaven—Jesus *is* the steps to
heaven.

"Jesus doesn't merely come down to show you the way
up—Jesus comes down to make Himself into the Way to carry
you up."[34]

At a vulnerable moment in his life, Jacob discovered that
heaven is not merely a wish or a dream but something real
and vivid. Because of what Jesus has done, we can rest in the
knowledge that when the time comes, Jesus will carry us up.

The Stairway

He had a dream in which he saw a stairway resting on the earth, with its top reaching to heaven. Genesis 28:12

The night before Jeff died, he kept telling his younger brother Wayne: "There's a staircase in my room. What's a stairway doing here?" Wayne couldn't see anything, but Jeff insisted he saw stairs.

After that, his brother's death weighed heavily on Wayne. The two had been so close.

A diabetic since the age of fourteen, Wayne suffered from high blood pressure and kidney damage. The disease had worn him down so that he had little energy after returning home from work. One night he came into the kitchen and told his wife about a dream he'd just had. He was shaking as he told the story.

"I heard the doorbell ring. When I answered it, Jeff was right there, standing on the other side of the door. He didn't say anything. We just hugged each other. It was so good to see him again.

"It was real," he insisted. "It was just like you and I are talking right now. I saw Jeff."

Six months later, shortly after Wayne kissed his wife good-bye and left for work, Terri Youngsma got the call. It was from the San Bernardino County Medical Center. Her husband had suffered a heart attack on his way to work, dying instantly when his car rolled over at high speed. A driver behind him had seen him slumped over the wheel before the accident.

Recalling the dream Wayne had about his older brother the night before Jeff's death, Terri says, "I know our lives lead somewhere. No one can convince me that everything ends when our hearts stop beating and we take our last breath. I like to think about Jeff heading up those stairs with Wayne right behind him. It helps me to know they are together again."[35]

Growing Up in Heaven

"I will turn their morning into gladness; I will give them comfort and joy instead of sorrow." Jeremiah 31:13

The Bible doesn't tell us everything we want to know about heaven. For instance, it doesn't say whether children will still look like children or whether the elderly will have gray hair. I like what J. Vernon McGee has to say on the topic of children.

"Will our children be as we last saw them? I do not know nor can I prove it from Scripture (for Scripture is silent on this point), but I believe with all my heart that God will raise the little ones as such and that the mother's arms that have ached for them will have the opportunity of holding them. The father's hand that never held the little hand will be given that privilege. I believe that the little ones will grow up in heaven in the care of their earthly parents...there are no children in hell.... Referring to children Christ said, 'Of such is the kingdom of heaven.' "[36]

Losing children is one of life's most painful traumas. But imagine holding them in heaven one day, and helping them grow up. Wouldn't that be fantastic? One thing for sure—you would be a far better parent in heaven than you would have been on earth.

In heaven there will be no shadows, no anger, and no disappointment. There will never even be a misunderstanding or mistake.

Ever-Increasing Love

Many waters cannot quench love;
rivers cannot sweep it away.   Song of Songs 8:7

D. L. Moody was a famous nineteenth-century evangelist. In 1898, he received a telegram that conveyed heartbreaking news. His one-year-old grandson, Dwight, had died. Trying to console his son and daughter-in-law, he wrote:

> I know Dwight is having a good time, and we should rejoice with him. What would the mansions be without children? He was the last to come into our circle, and he is the first to go up there! So safe, so free from all the sorrow we are passing through! I thank God for such a life. It was nearly all smiles and sunshine, and what a glorified body he will have, and with what joy he will await your coming! God does not give us such strong love for each other for a few days or years, but it is going to last forever, and you will have the dear little man with you for ages and ages, and love will keep increasing.[37]

Truly the love that God gives a father and mother for their children is strong. Fortunately, for those who love him, that love will keep increasing for all eternity.

Babies in Heaven

Jesus said, "Let the little children come to me, and do not hinder them, for the kingdom of heaven belongs to such as these." Matthew 19:14

Marvin Besteman was a self-described Dutch Calvinist. An army veteran and bank president, he seemed more comfortable with concrete facts and figures than heavenly visions. Yet in April 2006, while recovering from surgery at the University of Michigan Medical Center in Ann Arbor, he was visited by two clean-cut-looking angels who seemed to carefully detach him from a tangle of tubes that were connected to his body and transported him to heaven. For the next half hour, he spent time in heaven, marveling at sights that surprised and delighted him.

One of these was a vision of babies—countless babies of every age and description. "Believe me when I tell you," he said, "there were millions of babies from the tiniest unborn baby, about the size of my pinkie finger, to babies who were preterm to babies who were born full term, and every age on up from there.

"I felt a physical jolt of shock at the sheer numbers of babies, babies upon babies upon babies, each one cherished and loved. They seemed to be grouped by age, from the earliest stages of development on up."

Though Marv didn't catch sight of his own babies, one lost just after birth and three that had miscarried, he felt certain they were in heaven. Like the little ones he saw as he peered through heaven's gate, he was sure his own were "perfectly safe, entirely happy, and wholly loved."

Marvin didn't claim to know whether the babies he saw would grow up and become adults in heaven. He only knew that "all God's children, no matter the age they died, are with him, safe and loved."[38]

More About Babies in Heaven

For you created my inmost being;
you knit me together in my mother's womb.   Psalm 139:13

Whenever Marvin Besteman spoke publicly about his half hour in heaven, people wanted to know more about the babies he'd seen. What he had to say seemed to comfort those still grieving the loss of their own little ones.

The babies he saw seemed completely peaceful and happy. No one was hollering, fussing, or crying. "None of them," he said, "wore diapers, although the older babies had some kind of simple clothing on, nothing elaborate. They just didn't have to be fed, burped, changed, or bathed like babies here do."

Marv went on to describe the scene. "I imagine the grass they were lying close to was softer than any blanket that ever swaddled a baby down here. I say lying 'close to' because there was a layer of space between the babies and that green grass. You could almost say they were resting on air pillows.... They were also cradled in the perfect love of God, wholly joyful and basking in the warmth of his light and presence."[39]

Though Marv caught only a glimpse of heaven, it's interesting that God gave this father, who had lost four of his own children, a vision that has comforted so many. If you or someone you know has suffered the loss of a child, remember that every soul God has ever made, whether it perishes before or after birth, is precious in his sight.

At Last!

"As the deer longs for streams of water,
*   so I long for you, O God*
I thirst for God, the living God.
*   When can I go and stand before Him?*
Day and night I have only tears for food,
*   while my enemies continually taunt me, saying,*
*   'Where is this God of yours?' "*   Psalm 42:1–3 NLT

If you saved all the tears you will shed during the course of your lifetime, I wonder whether they would fill a thimble, a glass, a bathtub, or a river. Even the most stoic among us will usually break down and cry at some point in our lives.

. . . Tears of grief over the loss of someone dear.

. . . Tears of pain, even if only from a speck of dust in your eye.

. . . Tears of frustration when your computer crashes once and for all.

. . . Tears because of a touching moment in a movie.

. . . Tears of despair over a wayward child in a hopeless situation.

. . . Tears of relief and joy when reunited at last with a loved one.

. . . Tears of earnest concern. Even the Apostle Paul wept at times. Listen to what he says to a group of Christian leaders: "Remember that for three years I never stopped warning each of you night and day with tears" (Acts 20:31 NIV).

In heaven, you will shed no tears. Some bright day God will wipe away every last tear, and from that moment on, your eyes will sparkle with joy.

Suffering and Heaven

I consider that our present sufferings are not worth comparing with the glory that will be revealed in us. Romans 8:18

No one anticipates spring like those who live in frigid climates. When the first thaw comes and the air starts warming, when the buds begin to sprout and then flower, there are no happier people on earth than those who have endured the harshness of winter. Living through winter increases our capacity for joy when spring finally arrives.

Living through any kind of suffering can do something similar. I like what Joni Eareckson Tada says about the relationship between suffering and heaven. "It's not merely that heaven will be wonderful *in spite* of our anguish; it will be wonderful *because* of it. Suffering serves us. A faithful response to affliction accrues a *weight* of glory. A bounteous reward."

Joni ought to know. As a teenager she was paralyzed in a diving accident and has spent the rest of her life in a wheelchair. But when you meet her, you're struck, not by her incapacity, but by the humility and grace that mark her. Because of her suffering, she's become a wonderful advocate for other disabled people. She hasn't wasted a moment of the life God's given her nor of the suffering he has allowed.

"Why else," Joni asks, "would God meticulously chronicle every one of your tears?...God will give you indescribable glory for your grief....

"Whatever suffering you are going through this minute, your reaction to it affects the eternity you will enjoy. Heaven will be more heavenly to the degree that you have followed Christ on earth."[40]

You Will Be with Me in Paradise

Then Jesus said, "Father, forgive them, for they do not know what they do." . . . Then one of the criminals . . . said to Jesus, "Lord, remember me when You come into Your kingdom."

And Jesus said to him, "Assuredly, I say to you, today you will be with Me in Paradise." Luke 23:34, 39, 43 NKJV

Jesus did it first, so the rest of us can know what to do.

First he forgave everyone, even those who condemned him to death and the soldiers who were standing around the cross, still wiping the blood from their hands.

Having heard the bitter interchange between the two criminals, he turned his face toward the one who addressed him. To this least likely candidate for sainthood, he promised, "Today you will be with me in Paradise." Taking the man's honest confession as repentance, he assured him (just in time) that his name was in fact written in heaven.

Though you and I may never be condemned for crimes we have committed, we can at times feel guilt-ridden, unable to forgive ourselves. When that happens, remind yourself of what Jesus said to the thief on the cross next to his.

He is right there next to you, willing to forgive any sin you have ever committed. Only ask and he will forgive. And when you're forgiven, do what he did by forgiving those who have ever offended you.

A Pilgrim's Progress

But Jesus turning unto them said, "Daughters of Jerusalem, weep not for me, but weep for yourselves, and for your children." Luke 23:28 KJV

Jesus was full of mercy even to the end. On his way to be crucified, he spoke to the onlookers, many of whom were weeping. He paused long enough to tell them not to weep so much for him as for themselves and for their children, for he could foresee the suffering that lay ahead for the many who had rejected him as well as for those who had believed and who would suffer for their faith.

Centuries later, in 1688, a dying, sixty-year-old John Bunyan quoted Jesus' words. He went on to console the friends who surrounded his bed, saying, "Weep not for me, but for yourselves. I go to the Father of our Lord Jesus Christ, who will, no doubt, through the mediation of his blessed Son, receive me, though a sinner, where I hope we ere long shall meet, to sing the new song, and remain everlastingly happy, world without end."[41]

He told everyone that his chief desire was to be with Jesus Christ. As he lay dying, he raised his hands to heaven and said, "Take me, for I come to thee!" And then he was dead.

Bunyan left behind many published works, including *The Pilgrim's Progress,* an allegory in which the main character is a man named "Christian." The book has never gone out of print and is considered a classic. It traces Christian's extensive journey through life until he reaches heaven, which he called "the Celestial City."

He Didn't Stay Dead

*That I may know him, and the power of his resurrection, and
the fellowship of his sufferings, being made conformable unto his
death; if by any means I might attain unto the resurrection of the
dead. Philippians 3:10–11 KJV*

I remember my first trip to Mexico. There were so many
churches and cathedrals I wanted to explore. But as I stepped
into some of them, I encountered a spiritual atmosphere that
seemed to focus more on Jesus' death than on his resurrection.
Some of them were downright scary, featuring thick red blood
dripping down the face of an agonized figure nailed to a cross.

While I think it's important to remember the agony of the
crucifixion, it's vital to remember the joy of the resurrection;
we worship someone who is not dead but *alive.*

It's interesting that the New Testament hardly ever mentions Jesus' death by crucifixion without also stating that he
rose from the dead. "The apostles preached powerful sermons
about the resurrection of the Lord Jesus" (Acts 4:33 TLB). "[This
healing] was done in the name and power of Jesus from Nazareth, the Messiah, the man you crucified—but God raised
back to life again" (Acts 4:10 TLB). "Jesus Christ our Lord, who
came as a human baby . . . and by being raised from the dead he
was proved to be the mighty Son of God" (Romans 1:2–4 TLB).

It may sound obvious, but no one can have a relationship
with a dead man. Fortunately for us, Jesus is alive. As we get to
know our Savior, we too will come alive and stay alive.

Will We Eat in Heaven?

And I confer on you a kingdom, just as my Father conferred one on me, so that you may eat and drink at my table in my kingdom and sit on thrones, judging the twelve tribes of Israel. Luke 22:29–30

I'm not sure I could live without coffee or dark chocolate in heaven. I'm mean, really? How could a body—even a heavenly one—get out of bed without a cup of coffee, steaming hot with a good kick to it? That's the way to start the day.

Well, good news. Though the Bible doesn't talk about chocolate or coffee, it does talk about eating in heaven. Jesus himself spoke about tables, banquets, and eating and drinking in his kingdom. Randy Alcorn wonders why we always conclude that he was speaking figuratively about such things, especially since he ate with his disciples while in his resurrected body. If I remember correctly, Jesus even cooked after the resurrection.

Like Jesus, we, too, are promised a new body, and it is likely that it will be a body that takes pleasure in food.

Though the Bible contains a lot of symbolic language about heaven, not everything it says should be taken figuratively. Over-spiritualizing heaven is what makes it sound so boring.

When it comes to eating in heaven, I like what Randy Alcorn has to say: "our resurrected bodies will have resurrected taste buds."[42] Chew on that for a while. While you're at it, thank God, for all the great things you've ever tasted on earth. Don't forget the chocolate and the coffee.

Is Heaven a Cop-Out?

Faith is the confidence that what we hope for will actually happen;
it gives us assurance about things we cannot see. Hebrews 11:1 NLT

Is believing in heaven just a big cop-out—pie in the sky by and by—as many people say it is? Are we distracting ourselves with dreams of a better world so that we don't have to face the troubles of this one? Is heaven merely a crutch we're leaning on?

Well, consider this: if heaven is only a dream that weak people hide behind, why is it that some of the greatest advances in human history were made by those with a strong belief in heaven? The hope of heaven, as C. S. Lewis points out, is not a form of escapism but rather something that empowers us to do all that we can to live well in this world.

"If you read history," he says, "you will find that the Christians who did most for the present world were just those who thought most of the next. The Apostles themselves, who set on foot the conversion of the Roman Empire, the great men who built up the Middle Ages, the English Evangelicals who abolished the slave trade, all left their mark on Earth, precisely because their minds were occupied with heaven."

Lewis goes on to say that it is only since Christians have stopped thinking about the next world that they have become so ineffective in this one. "Aim at heaven," he says, "and you will get earth 'thrown in': aim at earth and you will get neither."[43]

Let's aim high today. Rooted in the hope of heaven, let's take the risks we need to in order to live purposefully on earth.

Rest for Now, Rest for Later

Six days shall work be done, but on the seventh day you shall have a holy Sabbath of solemn rest to the Lord.   Exodus 35:2 NRSV

God had a plan. He wanted his people to experience a taste of paradise before they ever got there. So he mandated that one day out of every seven would be reserved as a day for rest, a day in which all work was pushed into the background so that God could take the foreground. In fact, he felt so strongly about his people's well-being that he made it one of his top ten rules for living (see the Ten Commandments in Deuteronomy 5).

Like the Israelites, we, too, need time to slow down, regroup, and refocus. We need time to think beyond the immediate demands of the day so that we can turn our hearts toward God and deepen our relationship with him and others.

You and I may find it difficult to set aside an entire day for rest. But giving ourselves a few short hours a week will begin to give us a taste of that heavenly, restorative rest.

Secrets of Heaven

*The secret things belong to the Lord our God, but the revealed
things belong to us and to our children forever, to observe all the
words of this law.*   Deuteronomy 29:29 NRSV

Most of us don't like secrets we're not privy to. We'd much
rather be in the know. We love knowing things.

But even people with multiple degrees are ignorant about
many things. Though explorers, scientists, and inventors
study the natural wonders of the universe and though theologians and philosophers analyze the rest, there is still a lot we
don't know and many things we will never know.

Fortunately, God has revealed everything we really need
to know. He's revealed his Son. He's revealed his love. And
he's revealed his plans to give us a future full of hope.

Will we know everything once we get to heaven? Surely
not, because only God knows everything. But we may know
many things that are mysteries to us now. Who knows? Maybe
we will even be able to look back on all the hard things in our
lives and know exactly why God allowed them.

Until then, let's be content with the things God has already
revealed.

Surprising Peace

Precious in the sight of the LORD
is the death of his faithful servants.   Psalm 116:15

Sixty seconds—that was the gift God gave in answer to my prayer.

My father had been ill for several months. Despite major surgery to remove a tumor, he continued to decline. My mother, brothers, and I began keeping vigil at his hospital bed. We wanted to make sure he wasn't alone in the last days and hours of his life. With that in mind, we set up a rotation so that one of us would be with him through the night. "Please, God," I prayed. "Let me be with my father when he dies."

When it was my turn to spend the night, I was late getting to the hospital. Sending up another quick prayer that God would allow me to be with my dad when he died, I hurried to get there. My mother and brothers were already present. "He's passing," they said as I entered the room. I walked to the bed, caressed his forehead, and told him I loved him. Then I whispered the words of the Lord's Prayer in his ear. Just that quick he was gone. I had been given a precious sixty seconds to say goodbye.

Under the sheets, I could see the frame of a body ravaged by cancer. My father's face, gaunt and sallow, registered the long months of suffering. Even though the scene was grim, I found it difficult to leave. Strangely, just being in the room seemed like a privilege because I was flooded with an incredible sense of peace.

God was there. He was with my father. With my mother and my brothers. And he was right there with me. At that moment, I didn't want anything to disturb us. I felt certain that God had just enfolded my father in his arms, carrying him to heaven. It was enough and more than enough.

Rewards in Heaven

Rejoice and be glad, for your reward is great in heaven. Matthew
5:12 NRSV

While it's true that none of us can earn our way to heaven, it's
also true that some of us will receive extraordinary rewards
once we get there. How do I know? I read the Bible. Jesus
spoke about heavenly rewards on at least three different occa-
sions. He wanted people to know that the good we do on earth
will someday be recognized.

Is it so hard to imagine that the God who knows when
even a tiny sparrow falls to the ground also knows everything
about us, including the good we do?

For those who believe in God, good deeds are motivated
not primarily by the rewards they will receive but by the
profound gratefulness they feel for his love.

God's love is a change agent. It transforms us into his likeness so that we begin to do what comes naturally to him—
showing kindness, feeding the hungry, loving justice. By
doing good, we are simply "passing it forward."

What opportunities do you have today to do something
good, something that will bless others and catch the notice of
your Father in heaven?

Sketchy Outlines

Yours, O LORD, are the greatness, the power, the glory, the victory, and the majesty; for all that is in the heavens and on the earth is yours; yours is the kingdom, O LORD, and you are exalted as head above all. *1 Chronicles 29:11 NRSV*

In her book *Heaven: Your Real Home*, Joni Eareckson Tada states, "Even the most beautiful displays of earth's glory—towering thunderheads above a wheat field or the view of the Grand Canyon from the south rim—are only rough sketches of heaven. Earth's best is only a dim reflection, a preliminary rendering of the glory that will one day be revealed."[44]

When I visualize all the best I know and love about this world, as Joni did, I think of family and friends—the laughter, the sharing, the inside jokes, the celebrations, the memories that make me laugh.

What about you? Perhaps your family memories are the opposite of wonderful. In that case, think about other great things—the kindness of friends, the best meals you've ever enjoyed, the music you've loved, the great books you've read. Whatever is best to you about this world, which is passing away, is still only a "rough sketch" of heaven, a dim reflection of "the glory that will one day be revealed."

Tomb Talk

The LORD is my strength and my shield. Psalm 28:7 ESV

Until it happened to me, I thought it might be pleasant to be confined to bed, unable to work, because of illness. Cushioned with many pillows, sick people seem to have all the time in the world to sip water, read books, and rest.

Then, suddenly, I fell ill with pneumonia....My youngest was only five months old, and I couldn't even get out of bed long enough to change her diaper. My husband, mother, and friends had to take care of everything.

That's how I found out that when you're that sick, you're too sick to enjoy anything. You're so far gone, you can't even pray for yourself. Instead of reveling in bed rest—an unheard-of luxury for any mother of young children—I was just a feverish lump under the covers. And my faith and expectations were lumped there, too.

I came out of that time weakened in body but not in spirit, because I discovered something valuable: how little my own efforts could accomplish. My job was not to direct my own recovery, or even to "rest up" and "think positive."

A little like Lazarus in the tomb, I was unable to lift a little finger of faith for healing. Like him, I had to wait until I heard the equivalent of "Lazarus, come forth!" spoken by the One with all authority in heaven and earth.

All initiative and all power lie on *his* side of any bed or any tomb.

The Hope of Heaven

You wove me in my mother's womb. Psalm 139:13 NASB

Gwen Ellis had begun labor prematurely. Her twins were coming three months early. In the hospital, she felt herself suddenly transported from the delivery table to a green meadow framed by the most vivid blue sky she had ever seen. Everything was sharp and crisp. Even the grass had a quality of brittleness to it. In the midst of all that beauty, she felt complete peace.

Then she heard a voice, saying, "Go back. Ed and Wendy need you." She thought of her husband and three-year-old daughter. In an instant, she felt herself traveling backward through a long, dark tube toward earth. Then she awoke on the delivery table.

Unfortunately, she lost her twin girls. As hard as that was, Gwen says that she could sense God's care. "He seemed to be standing behind me holding me up, like when you put your arms under someone whose legs have turned to jelly. His presence was so palpable that I almost felt like we were one. The truth is, we were so close that it would have seemed like a distraction to pray."[45]

Years later, Gwen still cherishes her experience of traveling to heaven or its outskirts that day. "I always felt," she explains, "as though God gave me that experience to comfort me and give me a glimpse of the beautiful place he would provide for my girls—a place where I will one day hold them in my arms and tell them how much I've missed them." Though Gwen lost her children, she knows the separation is only temporary. In his mercy, God has given her the imperishable hope of heaven.

A Place Called Home

For this world is not our home; we are looking forward to our everlasting home in heaven.   Hebrews 13:14 TLB

Home—it's a place where happiness and laughter abound.

Where uniqueness is celebrated and friendship encouraged. Where the door is always open and everyone can stay forever.

It's a place where our joys are shared and our sorrows defeated, where peace and confidence grow strong.

This is the place we call *home*—a place where we are always loved, and where we always love.

Home—it's another word for heaven.

St. Peter's

*Simon Peter answered, "You are the Christ, the Son of the
living God." And Jesus said to him, "Blessed are you, Simon
Barjona, because flesh and blood did not reveal this to you, but
My Father who is in heaven. I also say to you that you are Peter,
and upon this rock I will build My church; and the gates of Hades
will not overpower it. I will give you the keys of the kingdom of
heaven; and whatever you bind on earth shall have been bound in
heaven, and whatever you loose on earth shall have been loosed in
heaven." Matthew 16:16–19 NASB*

Cartoonists customarily portray St. Peter, suitably bearded,
white-robed, and haloed, standing behind a podium like
a maître d' at a fine restaurant. Quill pen in hand (perhaps
plucked from an angel wing?) he is checking his big book to
see if the poor soul sinking to his knees in a puffy cloud in
front of him has a reservation for heaven.

How did rough-and-ready Peter get picked for that role?
Not just in modern cartoons, of course, but in serious Renais-
sance paintings and sculpture. How did he become heaven's
chosen gatekeeper?

Simply because of how Jesus spoke to him. Whether or not
Peter is really the head security officer of paradise, the words
of his confession will serve as keys to heaven for any one of us:
"You are the Christ, the Son of the living God."

Preview of Heaven

"My purpose is to give them a rich and satisfying life."
John 10:10 NLT

Preview, preschool, preteen, pre-op, premature, prehistoric . . . The *pre* part of each of these words lets us know that this is something that comes *before.* We see a preview of a movie before the full-length feature is released. Our young children attend preschool before they are ready for kindergarten. Our eleven- and twelve-year-old children are called preteens.

Along those lines, perhaps we should add a new word to our vocabulary: "pre-life." It identifies our present life, the life that occurs before our life in heaven. The good things we experience now in this pre-life are a preview of the full-length feature of our life in heaven!

To see your own preview, roll up all the joys and laughter, mountaintop experiences, gorgeous sunsets, cool drinks of water on hot days, warm welcomes from friends and family. For that is just a sneak peek of all that awaits you in the life to come.

Kingdom Come

*In my vision at night I looked, and there before me was one like
a son of man, coming with the clouds of heaven. He approached
the Ancient of Days and was led into his presence. He was given
authority, glory and sovereign power; all nations and peoples of
every language worshiped him. His dominion is an everlasting
dominion that will not pass away, and his kingdom is one that will
never be destroyed.   Daniel 7:13–14*

The prophet Daniel spent most of his life as a Jewish captive in
a heathen nation. Although he became a powerful leader, he
remained faithful to the God of Israel, despite various attacks
against him. As he aged, Daniel was comforted by dreams and
visions of the heavenly world. He saw dramatic scenes that
disturbed him, but he also watched God's triumph over all
the evil powers of the world. "Then the sovereignty, power
and greatness of all the kingdoms under heaven will be handed
over to the holy people of the Most High. His kingdom will
be an everlasting kingdom, and all rulers will worship and
obey him" (Daniel 7:27 NIV).

Today as you read the paper or watch the evening news,
remind yourself that despite appearances God is going to pre-
vail over all the evil in our world. Then take a few moments
to pray for the difficult situations you've just learned about.
As you close your time of prayer, echo the words that Jesus
spoke to his disciples when he taught them how to pray, saying, "Thy kingdom come, thy will be done on earth as it is in
heaven.

Take Me to Heaven

I will trust and not be afraid.   Isaiah 12:2

Joann Kruse's young cousin, Catherine, suffered from leukemia. Raised by parents who had left the church, Catherine was frightened of dying and her parents felt helpless to comfort her.

Fortunately, a family friend began talking with her about God and his love. He spoke of angels who watched over her and would take her to heaven when the time came.

When Catherine was ten, she was so ill that she didn't even have the strength to sit up. One afternoon, however, she shocked everyone by sitting straight up and pointing. "Can't you see the angels? They're all around us! They're laughing and one of them is stretching out his arms and asking me if I would like to go with them."

As Kruse tells it, Catherine's father responded by asking his daughter if she wanted to go with them.

"If it's all right with you and Mom," she replied. After her parents said yes, Catherine stretched out her arms, reaching for someone they could not see. Then she died.

According to Kruse, "Catherine's vision and the peace and joy that accompanied her death marked the beginning of their return to faith."[46]

You Can't Take It with You

Set your minds on things that are above, not on things that are on earth. Colossians 3:2 NRSV

Little Clara and her sister Madeline loved to have tea parties in the afternoon with their mother, Jenny. The three of them would sit around the tiny table in the playroom, sipping "tea" from tiny plastic cups.

One day Clara noticed a pretty set of teacups in the china cabinet. "Momma," she asked, "can we use those pretty teacups this afternoon when we have tea?"

Her mother replied, "I'll think about it." And the matter was dropped.

But as the day passed, Jenny realized something. As a little girl she had often asked her own mother to use those same grown-up teacups that had been handed down from Grandma, but she was never allowed to sip from one until she was an adult. By then it was no longer exciting and special. "What am I saving them for?" Jenny asked herself. "I certainly can't take them with me."

That afternoon Jenny took out three of the cups and their saucers when she joined the girls for teatime. "Oh Momma," Clara squealed with delight. "This is wonderful!"

Take a look at your own possessions. Your joy in sharing them will far exceed your pleasure in saving them. You certainly can't take them to heaven with you. Decide today what event or special person you are saving them for.

Beyond the Farthest Star

God is so great—higher than the heavens, higher than the farthest stars. Job 22:12 NLT

We have trouble wrapping our heads around great distances. Distances between countries on earth are hard enough to understand, still less the space between the earth and the moon or the light-years that separate the Milky Way from other galaxies.

Remember Peter Pan and Neverland? The only way to get to this magical land was to take the second star to the right and then travel "straight on till morning." Wonderful as Neverland is, it's still a far cry from heaven, full as it is of snapping crocodiles and kidnapping pirates.

Unlike Neverland, heaven is a real place, more real than the world in which we currently live. Even though the world's most advanced GPS will never be able to map its coordinates, God knows the way. And that's all that matters.

Restless Hearts

You will seek me and find me; when you seek me with all your heart, I will be found by you, says the Lord, and I will restore your fortunes and gather you from all the nations and all the places where I have driven you, says the Lord, and I will bring you back to the place from which I sent you into exile. Jeremiah 29:13–14 RSV

Always on the hunt for happiness, our longings can lead us toward God or away from him. Centuries ago, Augustine wrote words that still fit us: "You have made us for yourself, O Lord, and our hearts are restless until they rest in you."[47] Unfortunately our restless hearts can become confused about what they really want. Our inner motives hide themselves. And so we chase things that deliver only momentary happiness rather than joys that will endure. What *do* we seek, really?

"Until they rest in you" implies permanence, not a fleeting, momentary experience that depends on just the right constellation of circumstances. Resting in the Lord implies heaven.

C. S. Lewis wrote: "There have been times when I think we do not desire heaven, but more often I find myself wondering whether, in our heart of hearts, we have ever desired anything else."[48]

Like Little Children

I tell you the truth, you must change and become like little children. Otherwise, you will never enter the kingdom of heaven. The greatest person in the kingdom of heaven is the one who makes himself humble like this child. Matthew 18:3–4 NCV

Who hasn't heard a sermon about Jesus' statement regarding the little children?...

"He meant 'child*like*,' not 'child*ish*'...."

"You don't have to be smart and savvy to get into heaven...."

"Every child is precious to Jesus...."

Yes, and if you're a grown-up, the only way to become like a little child is to ask God to teach you how to be humble. You can start today, cooperating with his grace by doing something about your self-sufficient pride, your strongly held opinions, your vested interest in being right, your so-called maturity, your underlying fears of missing the boat.

Stop trying so hard to take care of everything. Just go to Jesus and let him work in you. You don't have to do anything to catch his attention because he has already summoned you to come. Look into his eyes; he's looking at you.

Then Jesus called the children over to him and said to the disciples, "Let the little children come to me! Never send them away! For the Kingdom of God belongs to men who have hearts as trusting as these little children's. And anyone who doesn't have their kind of faith will never get within the Kingdom's gates." (*Luke 18:15–17 TLB*)

What's It All About?

I wanted to see what was good for people to do under the heavens during the few days of their lives. I undertook great projects. . . . Ecclesiastes 2:3–4

Nobody sets out to live a meaningless life. Even those of us who don't think very deeply about things wonder at times, "What's it all about?"

People immerse themselves in one thing after another: education, career, marriage, family. Religion often gets a fair share of attention, along with doing "good works." But at the end of the day, what is it worth? What will last? Will our achievements just fade away? The writer of Ecclesiastes declares, "All is vanity." Is our innate desire for significance merely self-serving?

Quite likely this desire springs from being created in the likeness of God. Being "chips off the old block" implies that we are part of something bigger than ourselves, something eternal that will last longer than the most monumental granite tombstone. Jesus shows us the way to eternal significance when he speaks of humility and obedience: "Many who are first will be last, and many who are last will be first" (Matthew 19:30).

Think about it. Jesus must have looked like a failure when he died on a cross and his followers were scattered. His short life would have seemed insignificant, wasted. Yet he managed to change the world. His success wasn't measured by public acclaim but by simple obedience to the Father's will. Similarly, if we want to lead lives that mean something, we're going to have to follow his example by living with humble, faith-filled obedience to the Father who loves us.

Great Storms of Hope

"Where, O death, is your victory? Where, O death, is your sting?" 1 Corinthians 15:55 NRSV

John Chrysostom was an early Christian who was known as "golden-mouthed" (Greek: *chrystostomos*) because of his eloquent and persuasive preaching. In the year 387, he was serving as a deacon in his Roman-ruled hometown of Antioch, in what is now modern-day Turkey. Living during a time of great upheaval, the people of his congregation were under severe pressure, and many despaired that their situation would ever improve.

On Easter Sunday of that year, he spoke passionately to his struggling congregation: "Your resignation assumes God is dead. Do not be so certain. He who embraced death has defeated its power over us. He who went down to hell liberated every city held captive by hell's despair. Christ is risen! Open the doors of your comfortable despair, that the great storms of hope may blow life into us again."

To this day, we give death too much power, allowing it to frighten us and weaken our hope. Yet we should know that death itself has been dealt a fatal blow. Because of that we can open the doors and let great storms of hope blow life into us again.

Doorway to Heaven

Now there was a man named Joseph from the Jewish town of
Arimathea. He was a member of the council, a good and righteous
man, who had not consented to their purpose and deed, and he was
looking for the kingdom of God.   Luke 23:50–51 RSV

At great expense to his reputation as well as his pocketbook,
Joseph of Arimathea went to Pontius Pilate to request the dead
body of Jesus, which still hung on the crossbeam, bloody and
limp in the setting sun. For a high price, Joseph had purchased
a new private tomb that was carved into solid rock, and he
intended to bury Jesus there.

Of course he was burying his own hope, too. Little did he
know how well things would turn out a mere three days later.
When he found out, he must have gone to see the empty tomb
for himself; even soldier-guards could not have kept him
away.

Alive again! Now *that's* a game-changer! Joseph's tomb had
become a doorway to heaven. Because we belong to Christ,
our graves, too, will become like Joseph's—a doorway to
heaven.

Too Many Harps?

When He had taken the book, the four living creatures and the twenty-four elders fell down before the Lamb, each one holding a harp and golden bowls full of incense, which are the prayers of the saints.   Revelation 5:8

Listening to the stories of so many who've tasted the reality of heaven, you may wonder why some people make fun of heaven, describing it as a place of ultimate boredom. Where did this idea originate? Perhaps from the Bible itself—or from a misunderstanding about how it describes heaven. I like what C. S. Lewis has to say about this.

"There is no need to be worried," he says, "by facetious people who try to make the Christian hope of heaven ridiculous by saying they do not want 'to spend eternity playing harps.' The answer to such people is that if they cannot understand books written for grown-ups, they should not talk about them. All the scriptural imagery (harps, crowns, gold, etc.) is, of course, a merely symbolic attempt to express the inexpressible.

"Musical instruments are mentioned because for many people (not all) music is the thing known in the present life which most strongly suggests ecstasy and infinity. Crowns are mentioned to suggest the fact that those who are united with God in eternity share His splendor and power and joy. Gold is mentioned to suggest the timelessness of heaven (gold does not rust) and the preciousness of it. People who take these symbols literally might as well think that when Christ told us to be like doves, He meant that we were to lay eggs."[49]

Thank you, C. S. Lewis, for putting a smile on my face today and for reminding me that heaven will be better than the best things we can imagine.

One Last Visit

For he shall give his angels charge over thee, to keep thee in all thy ways. Psalm 91:11

"Please, God, don't take Kenny from me—not yet."

This was Kathryn Hillis's constant prayer, as though saying it enough times might make her wish come true. Her three-year-old son, Kenny, had been born with a serious heart defect. Whenever Kenny's lips would turn blue just from the effort of climbing into her lap, she would pray—one more year, one more Christmas, please, Lord.

One day her son overheard her talking to her husband about a four-year-old who had died from the same condition. "No, no, I don't want to die!" Kenny cried, running into the kitchen and gasping for breath.

Gathering him in her arms, she tried to chase the fear away. "Not you, not you, darling. I was talking about another boy. Mommy's going to take care of you."

That night, as she tucked Kenny into bed, she asked God to comfort him.

The next morning, Kenny woke up smiling. "Mommy, I had a dream about a lady. She was this big," he said, lifting his arm high above his head. "She had a long white dress and wings like the one in our picture [a painting of an angel in his parents' bedroom]. She picked me up to take me on a ride. Then I woke up. I love you, Mommy," he said as he reached his arms around her neck.

"I love you, too, my snuggly bear." Suddenly, Kenny's body stiffened. Then he fell limp in her arms. Though Kathryn and her husband rushed him to the hospital, the doctors couldn't save him.

When Christmas approached, she didn't feel like celebrating. Everything reminded her of Kenny. Besides, how could she rejoice at the birth of God's son, when her own son had been taken from her?

Then, on Christmas Eve she dreamed about Kenny. He was walking toward her, holding an angel's hand. "Kenny let go of her hand and ran to me. Ran! He wasn't breathless at all, and his lips were a healthy red." Holding him on her lap, she stroked his curly blond hair and kissed his cheeks.

"When I awoke," she says, "the air felt warm, almost electric. The dream, instead of fading, grew more vivid in my memory. It was like a touch from God, guiding me back to the one thing that could fill the emptiness inside me—His love, the love He'd shown me by giving me Kenny for a few precious years."[30]

Ultimate Comfort

*All praise to God, the Father of our Lord Jesus Christ. God is
our merciful Father and the source of all comfort. 2 Corinthians
1:3 NLT*

Comfort: a fluffy down comforter on a cold winter's night.
Cuddling on the couch with your favorite someone. A slice
of hot apple pie. Receiving a doggy-welcome as you open the
door.

Comfort is something we all want—and advertisers know
how to play into our emotional need for it—yet ultimate comfort eludes us. Pillows get lumpy, comforters get stained, candles burn down. Everything and everyone is temporary.

There's only one place to find the comfort we long for, and
that's in heaven. Our God is the God of *all* comfort. One day
his home will become our home—the ultimate comfortable
place.

Suck in Your Stomach

Strive to enter by the narrow door [force yourselves through it], for many, I tell you, will try to enter and will not be able. Luke 13:24 AMP

Never mind your hair appointment. Forget about your nails. Let your gym membership lapse. Cancel the carpet cleaning. Throw away those sale catalogs. Turn your family picture to the wall. Forfeit the blue ribbon. Disregard all the stuff in your two-car garage that forces you to park your cars in the driveway. Never mind any of it.

Having lots of prestige and possessions may be the ticket to the American way of life, but it will not gain you entrance at heaven's narrow gate. In fact, it may well keep you out.

That doorway is so skinny that you can't even bring your purse through. Even one credit card will create too much of a bulge in your pocket. Come empty-handed. You won't need a thing, anyway. Plus, you will want to leave both hands free so you can put them into the hands of your Savior, who is waiting for you on the other side.

Journey to Heaven

Precious in the sight of the L*ORD*
is the death of his faithful servants.   Psalm 116:15

"I'm standing on the seashore. A ship at my side spreads her white sails to the morning breeze and starts for the blue ocean. She's an object of beauty and strength and I stand and watch her until, at length, she hangs like a speck of white cloud just where the sea and the sky come down to mingle with each other. And then I hear someone at my side saying, 'There, she's gone.'

"Gone where? Gone from my sight, that is all. She is just as large in mast and hull and spar as she was when she left my side. And just as able to bear her load of living freight to the place of destination. Her diminished size is in *me*, not in her.

"And just at the moment when someone at my side says, 'There, she's gone,' there are other eyes watching her coming, and there are other voices ready to take up the glad shout, 'Here she comes!' And that is dying."[31]

"They Carried Daddy to Safety"

*Now to him who is able to do immeasurably more than all we
ask or imagine, according to his power that is at work within us,
to him be glory in the church and in Christ Jesus throughout all
generations, for ever and ever! Amen.   Ephesians 3:20–21*

Several years ago, when Alex Malarkey was just six years old,
he and his father were in a devastating accident, and Kevin
was thrown from the car. After regaining consciousness, he
stumbled toward the car, looking for his son. To his horror,
he found Alex sitting in the backseat, unconscious with blood
running down his forehead and his head dangling to the side.
The boy's eyes were bloodshot and staring—as though no one
was looking out from behind them.

Unbeknown to Kevin and others present at the scene, Alex
was acutely aware of what had just happened to him and to his
father. Here's how the boy describes what he saw:

"For just one second before all of the 'action' began, there
was a moment of calmness. I remember thinking someone was
going to die. When the calm ended, I heard the sound of glass
breaking, and I saw Daddy's feet going out of the car.

"Now I thought I knew who was going to die. But then I
saw something unbelievably cool. Five angels were carrying
Daddy outside the car. Four were carrying his body, and one
was supporting his neck and head. The angels were big and
muscular, like wrestlers, and they had wings on their backs
from their waists to their shoulders. I thought Daddy was
dead, but that it was okay because the angels were going to
make him okay."[52]

The boy was right. Aside from minor injuries and a grief-
stricken heart, his daddy was okay. As for Alex, that's a story
for another day.

"He's Not Going to Die"

"If you believe, you will receive whatever you ask for in prayer." Matthew 21:22

Beth Malarkey rushed to the hospital after she heard that her husband and son were in an accident. When she spotted a paramedic named Dave Knopp in the parking lot, she asked if he had been on the helicopter that had just transported her son Alex to the hospital. Dave said a quick yes and then then went on to say, "You're going to go in the trauma room and you're going to hear some horrible things. In fact, they're going to tell you your son's going to die. But I laid hands on your son and prayed for him in the name of Jesus. I'm telling you, he's not going to die."

Later, Dave expressed his surprise at the faith he felt in that moment. He was certain Alex would live and that it was vital that his mother not give in to fear. But after he spoke to her, his confidence suddenly vanished and he thought to himself: *"What did I do? I'm in trouble now."*[53] Still he kept thanking God for what he intended to do in the life of this young boy.

Some people think miracles will happen if only we have enough faith to believe they will. But I don't think that's how it works. Instead, I think God sometimes gives a special gift of faith when he wants us to know that he intends to do something extraordinary. At such times, that kind of faith can help us make the right decisions and spur us and others to more powerful prayer. In the case of Alex Malarkey, God seemed to telegraph his intentions to his mother through the faith of another believer, one of many links in a chain of people God would use to help save Alex's life.

Between Heaven and Earth

Yes, only God knows whether I was in my body or outside
my body. But I do know that I was caught up to paradise and
heard things so astounding that they cannot be expressed in
words. 2 Corinthians 12:3–4 NLT

Alex Malarkey should not have lived. Suffering from an internal decapitation as a result of an automobile accident, the only thing fastening his head to his body were ligaments, muscles, and skin. After reviewing the X-rays the doctor warned his parents that injuries like the one their son had sustained virtually always ended in death.

Yet years later, Alex tells a remarkable story about spending time in heaven while his body was struggling to survive on earth. Here's his view of what was happening in the emergency room, right after he was admitted:

"When we got to the hospital, I was watching everything that happened from the corner of the emergency room, near the ceiling. Jesus was standing there beside me.

"I was not afraid. I felt safe.

"The doctors were very busy, working on my body, which by this time was kind of blue. . . .

"While everyone was talking about my not living, Jesus said to me that I would survive the accident. He also told me I would breathe on my own after some time had passed."[54]

Alex remained in a coma for two months. When he finally woke up, he told an incredible story of traveling to heaven and spending time with Jesus. He also recalled details of the accident and its immediate aftermath with remarkable accuracy. How could someone in his condition be aware of what had been happening around him unless God had been right beside him, holding him tight as he hovered between heaven and earth?

Glimpse of Glory

After six days, Jesus took Peter, James and John with him and led them up a high mountain, where they were all alone. There he was transfigured before them. His clothes became dazzling white, whiter than anyone in the world could bleach them. And there appeared before him Elijah and Moses, who were talking with Jesus. Peter said to Jesus, Rabbi, it is good for us to be here." Mark 9:2–5

Not long before his crucifixion, Jesus took three of his disciples up on a mountaintop to witness an amazing transformation. As he was transfigured before their eyes, they saw him in all his greatness. That vision must have steeled them for the difficult days that lay ahead.

The Transfiguration of Jesus is still a window through which we can catch a glimpse of heaven, revealing realities that can strengthen us for our own difficult days. A sacred space and time in which heaven was revealed on earth, the Transfiguration of Jesus reveals important realities we humans cannot normally perceive.

Someday soon, when Jesus comes for us, that small window to heaven will open up to become a great big door through which we will pass with all the saints. On that day we will echo the words of Peter, saying: "How good it is that we are here!" That will become our refrain for all eternity.

Rehabilitating Heaven

Turn to us, Almighty God!
  Look down from heaven at us;
  come and save your people! . . .
Preserve and protect the people you have chosen,
  the nation you made so strong.
We will never turn away from you again;
  keep us alive, and we will praise you.
Bring us back, Lord God Almighty.
  Show us your mercy, and we will be saved.
Psalm 80:14, 17–19 GNT

The headlines appeared in the midst of a brutal winter. Someone in New Jersey had rescued an abused puppy named "Heaven," delivering her to the local animal hospital. Sick and drastically underweight, she was so skinny she barely dented the special dog cushion she was given to sleep on. Little Heaven seemed to have been delivered from a literal hell.[55]

In our own times, heaven has often been neglected, too. Mocked by hardened cynics and trivialized by many others, heaven has often been reduced to a slogan for greeting cards. Phrases like "What a heavenly scent!" or "Cut it out, for heaven's sake!" are symptoms of the fact that our culture doesn't take heaven all that seriously.

After plenty of TLC from the hospital staff, the poor little puppy called Heaven will recover her strength and start living up to her name. Before next winter, she will probably be sheltered in the bosom of a loving family somewhere.

Likewise, we can hope that the biblical meaning of heaven will be restored one day soon, finding its way into the hearts of people everywhere.

Sex in Heaven?

"At the resurrection people will neither marry nor be given in marriage; they will be like the angels in heaven."   Matthew 22:30

Depending on your experience of marriage, you may find Jesus' words either consoling or disappointing. But why no marriage in heaven?

Despite our culture's extreme emphasis on personal pleasure and fulfillment, Christianity has always viewed marriage not as an end but as a means. Through marriage, human beings participate with God in creation, bringing new human beings into the world and then nurturing the lives they helped to create. Another purpose of marriage is to help lead two people to heaven. At least that's what happens in a truly good marriage.

Once those purposes have been achieved, marriage becomes unnecessary. But even though there will be no marriage in heaven, nothing in Scripture indicates that we will have exactly the same relationship with everyone there. Surely those close to us on earth will also be close to us in heaven. That means we may still feel especially close to a former spouse despite the fact that we are no longer married.

But what about the pleasures of the sexual relationship? Won't a lot of people be disappointed if there's no sex in heaven? According to what we know of heaven, disappointment won't be part of the picture because heaven wouldn't be heaven in that case.

When I was a child, one of my favorite "foods" was cotton candy. Now I prefer crème brûlée. Maybe it's something like that when it comes to sex. One thing we do know. If there's no sex in heaven, God will provide something better.

Closer to Heaven

Be kind and compassionate to one another, forgiving each other, just as in Christ God forgave you. Ephesians 4:32

Ever find yourself avoiding someone? Someone who cheated you or judged you or lambasted you for not holding the same political views they do? Or maybe the offense was worse. Perhaps someone abused you, broke up your marriage, or hurt your children, leaving you with emotional or physical scars than run deep.

It is hard to imagine having a relationship with someone like that in heaven. In some cases, you may wonder how such people could even make it to heaven. But Jesus tells us that anyone who repents and believes will be saved. That's why we can expect to encounter all kinds of formerly rotten people in heaven—thieves, child predators, murderers, as well as people who have hurt us while we were on earth.

If that sounds like bad news, the good news is that their presence in heaven won't bother you, not for a minute. Why not? For one thing, you will understand them better. You will have God's eyes to see the hurts and frustrations that may have caused them to inflict harm on others. For another, you will understand your own failings more clearly. And your understanding of yourself and others will be bathed in the light of God's love.

Just as God sees Christ when he looks at us, we will see Christ in those who have offended us. Perfectly forgiven, we will be able to perfectly forgive.

But forgiveness doesn't need to wait until heaven. In fact, refusing to forgive while we are still on earth can become a barrier to heaven. Why not take time today to pray for people who have hurt you? Bring each one to God in prayer. Tell God that you release them from your judgment because he, and not you, is their judge. Then ask him to bless each one. Doing that will not only bring you one step closer to heaven; it will also give you greater freedom while you're here on earth.

Will My Dog, Cat, Hamster, or Whatever Go to Heaven?

Aren't two sparrows sold for only a penny? But your Father knows when any one of them falls to the ground. Matthew 10:29 CEV

For many in the West, pets have become part of the family. We grieve when they die and wonder if we will ever see them again. Whenever my children ask about whether one of their pets will go to heaven, I say that I don't know but I hope so.

Let me share a strange experience I had many years ago. I had just pulled into my driveway, managing to startle a rabbit that had been hiding in the underbrush near the road. I watched with dismay as it jumped straight into the wheels of a semi-truck. In a split second, I saw the rabbit crumple in the road as something that looked like its steam image rose into the air and then disappeared. Crazy as it sounds, I wonder if I saw the rabbit's soul, or spirit, separating from its body when it died.

That's not to say that rabbits or other animals have immortal souls as humans do. Still, I like what philosopher Peter Kreeft says about whether our pets will go to heaven. To the question, "Is my dead cat in Heaven?" he replies, "Why not? God can raise up the very grass; why not cats?" Kreeft goes on to say, "We were meant from the beginning to have stewardship over the animals. We have not fulfilled that divine plan yet on earth; therefore it seems likely that the right relationship with animals will be part of Heaven: proper 'petship.' And what better place to begin than with already petted pets?"[56]

Angels in Heaven—And on Earth

*"See that you do not despise one of these little ones. For I tell you
that their angels in heaven always see the face of my Father in
heaven." Matthew 18:10*

Sue had instructed her three-year-old son, Jason Hardy,
to stay in the front yard, away from the backyard pool that
belonged to his cousins. Tragically, his body was found at the
bottom of the pool.

By the time paramedics pulled Jason out, he had no heartbeat and was starting to turn black. In anguish his mother
cried out: "Jesus, Jesus!" begging for the miracle she knew he
could do. Minutes later Jason's heart began to beat. "Immediately, I was filled with peace," Sue says.

A helicopter transported Jason to the hospital, where doctors explained that brain damage begins after a heart is deprived
of oxygen for three to six minutes. But Jason had been without
a heartbeat for far longer. If he survived, he would be paralyzed
and would suffer from profound brain damage.

But his mother's faith told her otherwise, and she assured
them he was going to walk out of the hospital by himself.
Though Jason was in a coma and though he nearly died of
pneumonia, Sue didn't stop praying. She even called a local
church to ask their elders to come pray with him, which they
did. Twenty days after he'd been airlifted to the hospital, Jason
walked out of the hospital. Seven months later his physician
examined him and pronounced him healthy.

A few years later while watching TV, Jason commented on
a scene with a swimming pool. "It was dark underneath the
pool, but the angel stayed with me," he said.

"The angel?" Sue asked.

"Uh-huh. He was there so I wouldn't be afraid."[57]

From a clinical standpoint, Jason Hardy had no heartbeat and no pulse when he was pulled from the pool. Though he never spoke of visiting heaven, it seems that heaven touched him in the shape of an angel who watched over him and kept him safe.

Fragile

All flesh is grass, and all its loveliness is like the flower of the field.
The grass withers, the flower fades, because the breath of the Lord
blows upon it; surely the people are grass. The grass withers, the
flower fades, but the word of our God stands forever." Isaiah
40:6–8 NKJV

"Life is fragile; handle with care."

In the 1970s, that was Dow Chemical Company's mantra, part of a massive safety awareness campaign. Posters appeared in schools and workplaces, with the tagline displayed on a simple green and black icon featuring a silhouetted child backed up by his mother and father.

Before long, preachers co-opted it, changing it to "Life is fragile; handle with prayer."

Care and prayer. Both make sense because life *is* fragile. One moment everything is normal and then the phone rings with a dreaded diagnosis or unthinkable news. It doesn't take much—a slip on an icy sidewalk, a blood clot, a traffic accident.

But life as we know it in Christ is robust. It's so robust, in fact, that it will survive death itself. For now, as Paul tells the Corinthians, "we have this treasure in jars of clay to show that this all-surpassing power is from God and not from us. We are hard pressed on every side, but not crushed; perplexed, but not in despair; persecuted, but not abandoned; struck down, but not destroyed. We always carry around in our body the death of Jesus, so that the life of Jesus may also be revealed in our body" (2 Corinthians 4:7–10 NIV). Fragile and strong— earthly bodies that have been filled with the Spirit of Christ.

Circle of Love

Your trust can be in God who raised Christ from the dead and gave him great glory. Now your faith and hope can rest in him alone. Now you can have real love for everyone because your souls have been cleansed from selfishness and hatred when you trusted Christ to save you; so see to it that you really do love each other warmly, with all your hearts.   1 Peter 1:21–22 TLB

"My favorite definition of heaven," writes Kathleen Norris, "comes from a Benedictine sister, who told me that as her mother lay dying in a hospital bed she had ventured to reassure her by saying, 'In heaven, everyone we love is there.' The older woman had replied, 'No, in heaven I will love everyone who's there.'"[58]

Or maybe both.

With the help of God's ever-loving Spirit during our earthly sojourn, our circle of loved ones will expand in every direction. We will learn to love even our enemies, turning the other cheek as Jesus taught us to do.

Heaven Sings Praise

Praise the Lord. Praise God in his sanctuary; praise him in his mighty firmament. Praise him for his mighty deeds; praise him according to his surpassing greatness! Psalm 150:1–2 NRSV

I remember visiting a friend's church one Easter Sunday. I'll never forget the nonstop singing, which climaxed in the Hallelujah Chorus. Anyone familiar with that famous piece of music was invited to join in. With double the voices, the choir's rendition nearly raised the roof. It was spectacular.

Worship in heaven will be like that, only better. Thousands upon thousands of voices—all blending in perfect pitch and harmony. Even now angels and saints are raising their voices in heaven to praise God. Why not join in by singing the first and last verses of Handel's famous chorus.

Hallelujah! Hallelujah! Hallelujah!
Hallelujah! Hallelujah!

For the Lord God Omnipotent reigneth.
Hallelujah! Hallelujah! Hallelujah! Hallelujah!

And He shall reign forever and ever,
King of kings! and Lord of lords!
And He shall reign forever and ever,
King of kings! and Lord of lords!
Hallelujah! Hallelujah! Hallelujah! Hallelujah!
Hallelujah!

Called to Serve

He sat down, called the twelve, and said to them, "Whoever wants to be first must be the last of all, and servant of all." Mark 9:35 NRSV

Many years ago while traveling in Texas, Dan and a few business associates decided to dine at a local steak house. The restaurant featured a "cook your own steak" dinner. As the waiter began describing this option, instructing the group about how to cook their steaks, Dan looked up and said, "You've got to be kidding!"

It wasn't that Dan didn't know how to cook; he just didn't want to. After a long day of work, he had been looking forward to relaxing as someone served him a meal.

Noting Dan's reluctance, the server quickly added, "Or we can cook it for you," to which Dan enthusiastically agreed.

Being served makes us feel special. It's also a sign of our faith because we are called to be Christ's servants. What better way to serve God than to show his love to others in concrete acts of service?

Though serving isn't held in high esteem in our culture, it's something that God highly esteems. Why else would he have enshrined it in heaven, saying "the throne of God and of the Lamb will be in the city, and his servants will serve him" (Revelation 22:3 CJB).

In heaven our service will be a joy, a delight, and a privilege, something we do without failure, pain, fatigue, or boredom because of the greatness of the God we serve.

Heaven's Poetry

"God saved you by his grace when you believed. And you can't take credit for this; it is a gift from God. Salvation is not a reward for the good things we have done, so none of us can boast about it. For we are God's masterpiece. He created us anew in Christ Jesus, so we can do the good things he planned for us long ago." Ephesians 2:8–10 NLT

I like the way Ephesians 2:10 is translated in one version of the Bible. It calls us not "God's masterpiece" but "heaven's poetry." Exquisite poetry is memorable, thrilling, thought-provoking. We are meant to be a display of God's virtuosity.

The poet's artistry is something to be celebrated and enjoyed. The most stunning poem in the world can't compare to the poetry God wants to write through our lives.

But how does poetry get written in a life? Isn't it through trust and obedience, through doing the hard things God sometimes asks? Isn't it through lifting up the lowly and showing kindness to strangers? Isn't it through believing that what God says is true? Isn't it through remaining open as God pours his grace into you and then out through you?

As you go about your day today, try to think of yourself, not as an ordinary person, but as a poem God is writing to express his love to the world.

Only a Shadow

"Where, O death, is your victory?"   1 Corinthians 15:55

Donald Grey Barnhouse, the former pastor of Tenth Avenue Presbyterian Church in Philadelphia, once told a story about how he tried to help his children at the loss of their mother. Though he knew the anguish they were experiencing, he wanted to comfort them by easing their fear of death.

After the funeral, he noticed an enormous moving van that was passing their car, its shadow sweeping over them. Barnhouse turned to his children and asked a question: "Would you rather be run over by a truck or run over by its shadow?"

"By its shadow, of course," they replied. "A shadow can't hurt us at all."

Then Barnhouse replied, "Two thousand years ago the truck of death ran over the Lord Jesus . . . now only the shadow of death can run over us!"[59]

Angels Attend Us

Then I saw another angel flying directly overhead.   Revelation 14:6

In January 1956, five young Americans made headlines after dying in the jungles of Ecuador. They were missionaries who had gone to Ecuador to share their faith with an isolated tribe in the Amazon jungle.

When the young missionaries finally made contact with the tribe, they were speared to death. Later, Dawa, one of the women present at the attack, said that as the men were being killed she had seen *cowodi* (their term for foreigners or strangers) above the trees singing. Two other Indians confirmed that they, too, had heard the singing, and one described seeing something like a multitude of lights moving around and shining in the sky. Later, Dawa said that her encounter with the supernatural was what had encouraged her to believe in God when she finally heard about him.

Were the *cowodi* she had seen above the trees angels? At first Dawa didn't know how to describe the strange music she had heard that day. It was only after she was exposed to Western music brought in by later missionaries that the term "choir" seemed to fit.[60]

You may wonder if angels attend us when we die. Dawa's story would seem to indicate they do.

The Rest of Heaven

*Do not be anxious about anything, but in everything, by prayer
and petition, with thanksgiving, present your requests to God.
And the peace of God, which transcends all understanding, will
guard your hearts and your minds in Christ Jesus. Philippians
4:6–7*

One of the reasons many of us think heaven will be boring can
be traced to the phrase "rest in peace" or to prayers like "eternal rest grant unto him, O Lord." They sound dirgelike, con-
juring pictures of someone laid out stiff and solemn in a casket,
with hands folded peacefully in front. Fortunately that's not
the kind of rest or peace that's meant.

Anthony DeStefano points out that heavenly rest will
be like the restorative rest an athlete enjoys after enduring a
grueling competition. After all, most of us get to heaven only
after running the marathon we call life. In heaven we will get
to rest up, to recover from living in a world of nonstop stress,
anxiety, frustration, and strife.

What about the word "peace"? *Shalom* is the Hebrew word
translated as "peace" in English translations of the Old Testament. But biblical shalom involves far more than simply experiencing a state of calm or an absence of conflict. The Bible's
idea of peace involves enjoying good relationships with God
and others. It also means wholeness, satisfaction, perfection,
safety, healing, success, and wellness. This is the kind of robust
peace that was meant to characterize our lives when God first
made the world. Unfortunately the peace was violated when
humans strayed. Though we still catch hints of it here on
earth, in heaven it will become the atmosphere we breathe.

The next time you feel frazzled, empty, confused, hurt, or
insecure, ask God to fill you with his shalom so that you can
rest in the peace that only he can give.

What Will We Do in Heaven?

*God blessed them [Adam and Eve] and said to them, "Be fruitful
and increase in number; fill the earth and subdue it. Rule over the
fish of the sea and the birds of the air and over every living creature
that moves on the ground."   Genesis 1:28*

I have a friend who is always stressed out because of nonstop
demands at work. Year after year, the expectations ramp up,
and she has to run harder and faster just to do her job. Unfortunately, her experience has become the norm in corporate
America.

It may come as either good news or bad to learn that there
will still be plenty of work to do in heaven. But wasn't work
part of the curse that ensued after human beings disobeyed
God? A careful reading of Genesis indicates that work itself
was never a curse. What was cursed was the way in which we
would experience it after we sinned and fell away from God.
Rather than being a source of blessing and joy, work devolved
into something that often causes difficulty, anxiety, and
frustration.

In heaven this curse will be lifted and we'll be given work
that we love. What kind of work will we do in the new earth?
Randy Alcorn points out that "God created Adam and Eve to
be king and queen over the earth. Their job was to rule the
earth, to the glory of God."[61] But they failed and ceded their
kingdom to an usurper, to Satan, who now rules. But this des-
pot will fall from power the moment God establishes the new
heaven and the new earth and restores our rightful reign.

Instead of sitting on thrones, perhaps many of us will exercise our calling as architects, chemists, businesspeople, artists,
foresters, pilots, writers, musicians, carpenters, or even inter-
planetary travel agents. What we won't be is policemen, social
workers, forensic scientists, IRS agents, lawyers, doctors,

or therapists. But don't worry, if you're working in a term-limited occupation right now, God will give you something even better to do in heaven. Whatever we do will be an extension of our commission as human beings to rule the earth for the glory of God.

I Might Miss Something

We have waited for You eagerly; Your name, even Your memory,
is the desire of our souls. At night my soul longs for You, Indeed,
my spirit within me seeks You diligently.   Isaiah 26:8–9 NASB

Every parent knows the drill at bedtime. "But I'm not sleepy."
"First read me a story." "I need to finish this game." "Please,
can I have a glass of water." Underlying all the ploys is one
great concern: "If I close my eyes, I might *miss* something!"

Perhaps our children worry that once they're asleep we'll
be rolling up the rug and partying. Friends. Excitement.
Music. Snacks. At the very least, they're sure we'll be watching something thrilling on TV.

We grown-ups aren't much different. We hate missing
out. But the truth is that some of us are missing out big-time.
We've become so spiritually sleepy, so preoccupied with other
things, that we've forgotten how important it is to seek God
on a regular basis. Together let's ask the Lord for the grace to
build regular times of prayer, devotion, and study into our
lives. May we aspire to be like the psalmist who prayed: "At
night my soul longs for You, Indeed, my spirit within me
seeks You diligently."

You'll Get Your Ticket Just in Time

Therefore do not worry about tomorrow, for tomorrow will worry about itself. Matthew 6:34

Corrie ten Boom and her family were members of the Dutch underground during World War II. A survivor of the notorious death camp Ravensbrück, she later wrote a bestselling book titled *The Hiding Place*. In it she tells the story of her first encounter with death. She saw a baby lying still and cold in a crib. That night she could neither eat nor sleep.

"I need you! You can't die! You can't," she cried out as her father entered her room to say good night.

Calmly, he sat down on the edge of her bed and asked, "Corrie, when you and I go to Amsterdam—when do I give you your ticket?"

Sniffing, she replied, "Why, just before we get on the train."

"Exactly," her father continued. "And our wise Father in Heaven knows when we're going to need things, too. Don't run out ahead of Him, Corrie. When the time comes that some of us will have to die, you will look into your heart and find the strength you need—just in time."[62]

The Father Is on Your Side

*Blessed be the God and Father of our Lord Jesus Christ! By his
great mercy we have been born anew to a living hope through the
resurrection of Jesus Christ from the dead, and to an inheritance
which is imperishable, undefiled, and unfading, kept in heaven for
you, who by God's power are guarded through faith for a salvation
ready to be revealed in the last time. 1 Peter 1:3–5 RSV*

You may be someone blessed with the rock-solid confidence
that you're going to heaven. Or you may be a person with
secret doubts. After all, it's a minefield out there, with endless
temptation, frustration, evil, and confusion. What if you flub
up big-time?

The hazards are real. Battles lie around every corner. But
do you really think God would send his Son to save you, only
to stand back and watch you fail?

Fortunately, the Father has set up a personal security detail
for you and for everyone else who has ever said yes to him. It's
not exactly a safety belt, and it might not protect you from
crashes. But his divine power is available to strengthen your
faith no matter what you are facing.

Faith is a gift God gives to enable us to remain faithful to
him while we're here on earth. He is capable of strengthening
our faith whenever we waver.

Nobody knows this better than Peter, who denied Jesus the
night before the crucifixion. Jesus had already foreseen this,
telling him, "I have prayed for you, that your faith may not
fail" (Luke 22:32 RSV). Peter's faith did waver, but only for a
moment. Then God strengthened him, and he spent the rest of
his life spreading that faith to others.

Eternal Inheritance

[Christ] is the one who mediates a new covenant between God and
people, so that all who are called can receive the eternal inheritance
God has promised them.   Hebrews 9:15 NLT

Imagine that you have just received a large inheritance. It's
from an uncle you hardly remember. Astonished, you send
up a prayer of thanks for his generosity, for this unexpected
windfall that you know you don't deserve. When the check
comes in the mail, it's so large that you can't imagine ever running out of money. But as the years pass and expenses mount,
you realize your bank account is quickly emptying. Soon the
inheritance that had arrived so unexpectedly will be completely spent.

Heaven is a little like but a whole lot unlike that inheritance. First of all, just like your imaginary inheritance, the
gift of heaven is totally undeserved. You couldn't earn it if
you tried (and perhaps you have). Second, it's totally different,
because heaven will never run out. It will never fade away.
The Bible calls it an "eternal inheritance."

So what are you worrying about? God has promised you
untold riches that will never run out.

God's gift of heaven—let us thank him for it!

A Suitcase and a Box

By faith Moses, when he was grown up, refused to be called the son of Pharaoh's daughter, choosing rather to share ill-treatment with the people of God than to enjoy the fleeting pleasures of sin. He considered abuse suffered for the Christ greater wealth than the treasures of Egypt, for he looked to the reward. Hebrews 11:24–26 RSV

Tricia McCary Rhodes, pastor's wife and devotional author, writes about an experience that highlights the old saying "You can't take it with you."

"Recently," she says, "I helped my ninety-one-year-old grandmother, who could no longer live alone, sort through her things. It was a sobering experience. In one day, Grandmother's life was narrowed down to a suitcase and a box.

"Ever since, as I look around my own house with personal touches and meaningful memories, I am reminded that there will come a time to pare down until all that's left fits in a suitcase and a box. And even that will not enter eternity.

"If our hope is in this life alone, we must despair. But Grandmother's inheritance is not in a suitcase and a box."⁶³

Take a moment now to look around at all the treasures you've amassed thus far. Look for something to give away. Let this gesture be a small sign that you're not interested in storing up treasure on earth but only in heaven.

Never Assume

Trust God from the bottom of your heart; don't try to figure out everything on your own. Listen for God's voice in everything you do, everywhere you go; he's the one who will keep you on track. Don't assume that you know it all. Run to God! Proverbs 3:5–7 MSG

My husband will eat anything I put in front of him. He never criticizes a meal, which makes it easy to cook for him. One day he came through the kitchen as I was slicing tomatoes. "What are you making?"

"A tomato salad for dinner."

"Oh . . . you know what?" he said. "I never told you before, but I really don't like tomatoes."

That was news to me. How many hundreds of times in the course of our marriage had I served him tomatoes? I had simply assumed that because I liked them he did, too. But I was operating on a false assumption.

I wonder if we sometimes make unfounded assumptions about heaven, too. For example, we may assume that getting baptized or joining a church or doing good deeds is the same as signing a binding contract with God. Now surely we will go to heaven when we die, right? Perhaps nobody ever told us otherwise.

Fortunately, we can learn a lot about heaven through the pages of the Bible. Though God has kept some things secret, he has told us everything we really need to know.

What Does Heaven Sound Like?

Shout for joy, Daughter Zion! Shout out, Israel!
Be happy and boast with all your heart, Daughter Jerusalem!
The Lord has removed the judgment against you; he has turned
back your enemy.
Israel's king, the Lord, is in your midst!
You no longer need to fear disaster. Zephaniah 3:14–15 NET

In the middle of a recent cross-country flight, I couldn't help but notice how loud the engine was. Frequent flyers must become experts at lipreading. Yet the unending drone of the engine also serves as "white noise," allowing people to slumber peacefully in their seats from takeoff until landing.

It made me think about one of heaven's mysteries—how a place that is bursting with joyful shouts and unrestrained worship can at the same time be a place of true peace and rest. Both appear in the scriptural picture:

Yes, says the Spirit, they are blessed indeed, for now they shall rest . . . (Revelation 14:13 TLB)

I heard the shouting of a vast crowd in heaven. . . . Again and again their voices rang. . . . Then I heard again what sounded like the shouting of a huge crowd, or like the waves of a hundred oceans crashing on the shore, or like the mighty rolling of great thunder. . . . (Revelation 19:1, 3, 6 TLB)

With God

We are made right with God by placing our faith in Jesus Christ.
And this is true for everyone who believes, no matter who we
are. Romans 3:22 NLT

The question popped up on the online Bible forum: "How can I 'get right with God'?" The questioner was worried about making it to heaven.

Quotes from Romans 3 helped answer the question. To figure out how to "get right," a person must first recognize that something has gone very wrong, and then surrender this impossible-to-resolve state of affairs into the hands of Someone big enough and loving enough to take care of it:

For everyone has sinned; we all fall short of God's glorious
standard. Yet . . . God presented Jesus as the sacrifice for sin.
People are made right with God when they believe that Jesus
sacrificed his life, shedding his blood. [He] declares sinners to
be right in his sight when they believe in Jesus. (Romans 3:23,
25–26 NLT)

The heavier emphasis falls on "with God" than "get right." Because getting right comes only from being with God.

Laughter in Heaven

An angel from heaven appeared to him and strengthened him. Luke 22:43

Nine-year-old Rebecca had just been admitted to the hospital. With bright red hair that fell in waves to her waist, she was a force to be reckoned with. Leanne Hadley was surprised by her first meeting with the unsinkable Rebecca. Standing in front of her parents and her nurse, the young girl was belting out the lyrics to a song from the hit musical *Annie*. Everyone smiled and clapped as the song ended while the indomitable Rebecca held her arms to the sky in triumph and then bowed deeply to her fans.

One day Rebecca began confiding in Leanne. She wasn't afraid to die. It was just that heaven sounded so boring to a girl who loved having fun. "It will be worse than this stupid, boring hospital," she blurted out.

Rebecca's illness continued to worsen. One night she surprised Leanne by whispering, "Leanne, remember how I told you my wish, how I told you I didn't want to die? Remember how I told you heaven would be boring? It isn't.... They told me...you know...the people, but you know they aren't really people...but they tell you and show you heaven. And they showed me, and it isn't boring. It's beautiful, and you can laugh there and have fun, and there are kittens...oh, and the rainbows are so pretty. I just wanted to tell you it isn't boring at all there. I'll laugh when I get there and play with kittens and climb on rainbows if I want to.... I just wanted you to know."

The young girl who was all about fun died a few months later. Now, whenever Leanne sees a rainbow, she can't help but think how happy her young friend must be.[64]

The End of the Story

For I know the plans I have for you, declares the Lord, plans for
welfare and not for evil, to give you a future and a hope. Jeremiah
29:11 ESV

These words were first spoken to exiles. The Hebrews—
whole families of them—had been dragged off to Babylon
by King Nebuchadnezzar. Their beloved city, Jerusalem, had
been destroyed.

In the midst of their bitter tears, the prophet Jeremiah
gave them God's startling advice: they were supposed to settle
down and make a new life, not bitterly but cheerfully: "Build
houses and live in them; plant gardens and eat their produce.
Take wives and have sons and daughters; take wives for your
sons, and give your daughters in marriage, that they may bear
sons and daughters; multiply there, and do not decrease. But
seek the welfare of the city where I have sent you into exile,
and pray to the Lord on its behalf, for in its welfare you will
find your welfare" (Jeremiah 19:5–7 ESV).

God wasn't finished with them yet. The last chapter of
their story would lead them back out of exile and their children would reap the good graces that their parents had sown.
If they obeyed, all of them would possess the ultimate "future
and hope"—a place in the heavenly Jerusalem.

It will be the same for us.

Built for Eternity

Yet God has made everything beautiful in its own time. He has planted eternity in the human heart, but even so, people cannot see the whole scope of God's work from beginning to end. Ecclesiastes 3:11 NLT

My nephew loves archaeology. He spends hours in museums, fascinated by ancient pots and bowls, wondering how they have managed to survive relatively intact for thousands of years when so many others have been destroyed by wars, earthquakes, scouring winds, treasure seekers, or natural processes. Perhaps in some cases the potter or sculptor crafted something special into his object to make it endure beyond a thousand generations.

When God created humans in his likeness, he built us to endure. We were not meant to last for a mere seventy, eighty, or even a hundred years. We were sculpted with eternity in our hearts, with the desire to be connected to an eternal God.

But this desire, Scripture tells us, can only be fulfilled in one way: "You must remain faithful to what you have been taught from the beginning. If you do, you will remain in fellowship with the Son and with the Father. And in this fellowship we enjoy the eternal life he promised us" (1 John 2:24–25 NLT).

In your prayers today, thank God for placing eternity in your heart and ask him to deepen your fellowship with him so that you can enjoy the eternal life he has promised.

Life Assurance

And this is what God has testified: He has given us eternal life,
and this life is in his Son. Whoever has the Son has life. 1 John
5:11–12 NLT

Insurance companies bombard us with advertisements, constantly reminding of us of the need to protect our loved ones by purchasing life insurance.

No doubt, a life insurance policy is important. But there's something else that is even more important—a life *assurance* policy. A classic hymn by Fanny J. Crosby includes these words: "Blessed assurance, Jesus is mine! O what a foretaste of glory divine! Heir of salvation, purchase of God, born of His Spirit, washed in His blood."

Our blessed assurance is our assurance that after this life (when our life insurance has paid out) our life assurance begins. Our life assurance from God provides us with a permanent place in heaven. Life assurance is different from life insurance in more ways than the two-letter spelling difference, but they have one thing in common: we "cash them in" when we die. Our life insurance pays out in cash. Our life assurance pays out in eternal life.

God Knows the Day and the Hour

You have decided the length of our lives.
You know how many months we will live,
and we are not given a minute longer. Job 14:5

Erwin Lutzer, former senior pastor at Moody Church in Chicago, tells a remarkable story about a young girl who was close to death. Her pastor, A. D. Sandborn, visited her one day in her home, where she was propped up in bed with pillows. "Now just as soon as they open the gate I will go in," she whispered.

Then she sat up straight and said in a disappointed voice, "They have let Mamie go in ahead of me, but soon I will go in."

Moments later, she said, "They let Grampa in ahead of me, but next time I will go in for sure."[65]

A little while later she died.

When Sandborn inquired about the identities of Mamie and Grampa, he learned that the former was a young girl who had moved to New York. The latter was a family friend who had also moved away. Curious, Sandborn wrote to both. The answers he received surprised him.

It seems that both Mamie and Grampa had both died the morning of September 16, during the same hour that the young girl had passed away.

How Much Happiness Can You Stand?

As a deer longs for flowing streams, so my soul longs for you, O God.
My soul thirsts for God, for the living God.
When shall I come and behold the face of God? Psalm 42:1–2

In heaven, our greatest joy will be to see God face-to-face. Theologians have called this the beatific vision. No longer will we catch only glimpses of God in the beauty of creation or catch the shadow of his passing. Instead, we will be filled to the brim with God himself.

As Anthony DeStefano points out, "Scripture doesn't just say that God is the creator of beauty, power, truth, and life. It says that he *is* beauty, power, truth, and life. That's a difficult concept to understand. It means that when we see material objects on Earth that possess those characteristics, they are really only reflecting different qualities of God. You might say that they're like photographs of God from different angles."[66]

What's the most beautiful place, the most attractive person, the greatest truth, the most powerful aspect of nature you've ever observed? Great as these are, they are merely tiny reflections of God's glory, photographs of him from different angles. But how will we be able to take it all in? According to DeStefano, some of us will have a greater capacity for God than others. What he means by that is that those of us who have loved God to the max while we're here on earth will have a larger capacity to enjoy him in heaven. But won't that make the rest of us feel bad, knowing that we have less of God than someone else?

The answer is no. We will enjoy God to our capacity. We will be filled with his truth, his beauty, his power, and his love. Some of us will be thimble-full while others will be bathtub-full or lake-full or even ocean-full, depending upon our capacity. Being filled with God, we will be as happy as we can stand to be.

Jigsaw Puzzle

And we know that in all things God works for the good of those
who love him, who have been called according to his purpose.
Romans 8:28

I'm not good at jigsaw puzzles. Whenever one of my children asks me to help put one together, I start by turning over all the pieces. Then I pick out all the straight-edged ones so that I can construct the border. Once the border is done, I'm done. That's my big contribution. My children know I'm handicapped when it comes to doing puzzles because I can't envision how all the remaining pieces fit together.

Perhaps that's why I'm not an artist or an engineer or a math professor. It's certainly why I'm not God—because I am stumped when it comes to figuring out how all life's pieces fit together.

When close to death, some people report having flashbacks. In an instant, they see their life unfolding. There they are as a fifth grader listening as their parents inform them they are divorcing. They see themselves falling in love. They watch themselves receiving an award or reacting to bad news. Moments of celebration, understanding, failure, hurt, loneliness, and delight all pass across the screen, telling the story of their life.

I think we may be able to look at our lives like that in heaven, not so that we can relive every moment on earth but so that we can reach a deeper understanding of all that's happened. Like pieces in a jigsaw puzzle that come together to form a whole, we will see how the disparate pieces of our lives fit together, finally making sense. The failures, sins, betrayals, successes, joys, and triumphs—everything haphazard or planned—all will come together to form a picture, and we will understand how God in his faithfulness has used everything to shape us toward heaven.

An Angel's Hand Is There

*Not only so, but we also glory in our sufferings, because we know
that suffering produces perseverance; perseverance, character; and
character, hope. And hope does not put us to shame, because God's
love has been poured out into our hearts through the Holy Spirit,
who has been given to us.*   Romans 5:3–5 NIV

Most of us are oblivious to heaven during times of content-
ment and abundance. It's only when we suffer that we begin to
think of going home to heaven. To the extent that it leads us to
heaven, suffering should be considered a gift.

Not all hardships automatically translate into a desire for
heaven. Not until we begin to talk to God about our difficulties, seeking answers, does heaven enter the picture. Faith is
a matter of the heart, and heartbreak makes us pour out our
cares to God. He sends the help we need, strengthening our
wobbly spirits and giving us new reasons to press on.

The Italian friar and painter Fra Angelico (circa 1400)
wrote in a letter: "Everything we call a trial, a sorrow, a duty,
believe me, [an] angel's hand is there, the gift is there, and the
wonder of an overshadowing Presence....Life is so full of
meaning and purpose, so full of beauty beneath its covering,
that you will find earth but cloaks your heaven.

Vision of Heaven

Then I saw a Lamb. . . .   Revelation 5:6

The Apostle John was one of Jesus' closest disciples, perhaps his best friend. As an old man, he was exiled to the island of Patmos, off the coast of modern-day Turkey. In a cave on this island paradise he was granted a stunning vision. Take a moment to imagine yourself with John, looking on in heaven as this scene unfolds.

Then I saw a Lamb, looking as if it had been slain, standing at the center of the throne, encircled by the four living creatures and the elders. The Lamb had seven horns and seven eyes, which are the seven spirits of God sent out into all the earth. He went and took the scroll from the right hand of him who sat on the throne. And when he had taken it, the four living creatures and the twenty-four elders fell down before the Lamb. Each one had a harp and they were holding golden bowls full of incense, which are the prayers of God's people. And they sang a new song, saying:

> *"You are worthy to take the scroll*
> *and to open its seals,*
> *because you were slain,*
> *and with your blood you purchased for God*
> *persons from every tribe and language and people and nation.*
> *You have made them to be a kingdom and priests to serve*
> *our God,*
> *and they will reign on the earth."*

Then I looked and heard the voice of many angels, numbering thousands upon thousands, and ten thousand times ten thousand. They encircled the throne and the living creatures and the elders. In a loud voice they were saying:

> *"Worthy is the Lamb, who was slain,*
> *to receive power and wealth and wisdom and strength*
> *and honor and glory and praise!"*

Then I heard every creature in heaven and on earth and under the earth and on the sea, and all that is in them, saying:

> *"To him who sits on the throne and to the Lamb*
> *be praise and honor and glory and power,*
> *for ever and ever!"*

The four living creatures said, "Amen," and the elders fell down and worshiped. *(Revelation 5:6–14)*

"Isn't She Beautiful?"

*For he will command his angels concerning you
to guard you in all your ways. Psalm 91:11*

Four-year-old Tommy suffered from leukemia.

One day a student chaplain by the name of Leanne Hadley entered his hospital room and suggested that Tommy's mom take a break. Knowing that whenever his mother left him the little boy became anxious, often ripping out IV lines or pulling the sheets off his bed, Leanne promised to stay until his mother returned. Both women were surprised by Tommy's response. "Why don't you take a break together?" he suggested.

"Tommy, whenever you're alone you get into trouble, so I need to stay with you while your mommy goes out," the chaplain explained.

"No, you should go together," the little boy insisted.

"Why?" she asked.

"Because *she* is here," Tommy replied. "Isn't she beautiful?"

Neither woman could see anyone. Still, they left the room. When they returned, they were surprised to see that his sheets and the IV lines were still in place. The same thing happened repeatedly.

One day he started asking questions, looking not at the people in the room but to the lady no one else could see: "Will it hurt when I die? Will my dog be with me in heaven? Do little children miss their mommies when they go to heaven?"

Not long after that, Tommy began to fade. Once again, he asked everyone to leave so that he could be alone with the beautiful lady. A few moments later a nurse checked on him, only to discover that he had died. No one spoke until his mother broke the silence: "I'm so happy that she was with him," she said. Tommy's mother knew that when his time came to pass from this world to the next, Tommy had been blessed with an angel to comfort him.[67]

We Will Be Changed

*For the trumpet will sound, the dead will be raised imperishable,
and we will be changed.* 1 Corinthians 15:52 NRSV

The Bible speaks to us of transformation. One of the most
remarkable of its many promises is that we will one day have
a brand-new body. No longer subject to death, it will be
imperishable.

Take a moment to think about your body, especially things
that aren't working so well. I'm thinking right now about
allergies, sinus infections, sore feet, and a bad back. Your list
may be better or worse than mine. Now take several minutes
to read and ponder these passages from the Bible. Imagine
what it will be like to have a body that always works perfectly
and that will live forever. Thank God for giving you the body
you have now and then thank him for the beautiful, marvelous body he will give you in the life to come.

*So it is with the resurrection of the dead. The body that is
sown is perishable, it is raised imperishable; it is sown in dishonor, it is raised in glory; it is sown in weakness, it is raised in
power; it is sown a physical body, it is raised a spiritual body. If
there is a physical body, there is also a spiritual body. (1 Corinthians 15:42–44 NRSV)*

*What I am saying to you brothers is this: flesh and blood cannot
inherit the kingdom of God, nor does the perishable inherit the
imperishable. Listen, I tell you a mystery: We will not all die,
but we will all be changed—in a moment, in the twinkling of
an eye, at the last trumpet. For the trumpet will sound, the dead
will be raised imperishable, and we will be changed. (1 Corinthians 15:50–52 NRSV)*

How Do I Get to Heaven?

"Apart from me you can do nothing." John 15:5b NRSV

Do you have to be good to get to heaven? Most of us would probably answer an unqualified yes. But here's what philosopher and author Peter Kreeft has to say about that important question. "I have repeatedly taken polls and surveys in college classrooms and adult education classes, and the percentage of people who believe the world's most pervasive superstition, that good guys go to Heaven and bad guys go to Hell, is always well over 50 percent, often over 90 percent. This popular religion is really legalism, though none of its believers call it that. . . .

"Jesus tells us two shocking things about getting to Heaven. We often hear the second without the first. The second shock is the good news that Heaven's door is open; that only accepting the gift by faith, hope and love is required; that the gift is Christ, who takes the whole scraggly, clownish, ragamuffin, confused and bickering crowd of sinner-saints piggyback to Heaven. But the first shock is the bad news that all other ways are absolutely impotent, whether good works or good intentions or meditation or mystical enlightenment or asceticism or social service or any kind of spiritual athleticism."[68]

What's your strategy for getting to heaven? Choosing to rely on good deeds is like choosing to ride a bicycle to the moon when someone has offered you a ride on an Apollo rocket. If you want to land safely in heaven, entrust your soul to Christ because only he can take you there.

Heaven's Hospitality

Do not neglect to show hospitality to strangers, for by doing that some have entertained angels without knowing it.   Hebrews 13:2 NRSV

Julie enjoys entertaining in her home. Everyone in the neighborhood loves being invited to her festive celebrations: the annual picnic in the summer, the pumpkin-carving party in the fall, and the celebration to ring in the New Year. Gathering people together is Julie's gift. She enjoys decorating, buying gifts and party favors, designing "tablescapes," and creating activities for friends and family to share. Her home is a welcoming center for those who don't have family of their own or who need a change from the one they have. She can mix personalities and people of varying backgrounds together with such ease that everyone feels comfortable.

We humans are by nature sociable. We form groups and societies of people with similar interests; we join together around a common cause or event; we plan reunions of family and classmates. Now we can also stay connected to people via telephone, email, and social media.

The need for and joy of such togetherness is sure to be fulfilled in heaven. Ask someone what they think heaven will be like, and they'll probably say something about gathering with friends and loved ones. We eagerly await the great gathering and reunion in heaven with those we long to see again. We won't be disappointed.

The View from the Throne

Our God is in the heavens, he does whatever he pleases.   Psalm
115:3 NRSV

...And what exactly does God find pleasing to do? From
his throne in heaven, as he views his creation, what does he
choose to do?

As the Almighty Creator of the universe, he is capable of
doing anything. That thought can frighten people who think
God is aloof and uncaring. The idea is too much for those who
think he is a genie who makes magical things happen whenever people pray, or for the people who see him as a punishing
dictator who wags his finger in disdain, tormenting the ones
who do not follow his rules.

Scripture, however, tells a different story. It openly states
that God is "merciful and gracious, slow to anger and abounding in steadfast love and faithfulness" (Psalm 86:15). According
to theologian John Calvin, God chooses "to renew us into a
firm, perfect, incorruptible and heavenly glory."[69] He creates,
loves, and chooses us to be his.

The overall story of the Bible is that God lovingly creates
us humans out of a desire to have a relationship with us. He
chooses to live in loving relationship with us and to help us
thrive and flourish. From his heavenly throne he chooses, protects, and guides us so that he can welcome us into his home.

Wishful Thinking?

Whoever has ears, let them hear what the Spirit says to the churches. To the one who is victorious, I will give the right to eat from the tree of life, which is in the paradise of God.   Revelation 2:7 NIV

Wish I may, wish I might, have this wish I wish tonight. Is that what heaven is all about, just a matter of fantasizing about a future that will never happen? Is heaven a fairy tale humans have concocted to help themselves feel better about death and suffering? Does the fact that heaven matches up with human desire so well mean that it's nothing but a fantasy?

Listen to what Anthony DeStefano has to say on the matter. "Is it wishful thinking," he asks, "to believe in hell, the devil, and demons? Is it wishful thinking to believe we're going to be judged and held accountable for every sin we've ever committed? Is it wishful thinking to believe the best way to live our life is to sacrifice our own desires for the sake of others? Is it wishful thinking to believe that we should discipline our natural bodily urges for the sake of some unseen 'kingdom'?"[70]

Those who argue that heaven is a matter of wishful thinking, he says, are advancing a ridiculous argument. Wishful people would never have dreamed up Christianity in the first place. They would never have concocted a religion that humbles human beings by confronting their pride and then challenging them to be like Christ by loving their enemies.

We believe in heaven not because we need to fantasize a happy ending but because the One who died for us and who calls us to die to ourselves and live for him assures us that heaven awaits us.

Where Are the Angels?

All the angels are spirits who serve God and are sent to help those who will receive salvation.   Hebrews 1:14 NCV

Four-year-old Maddy was excited. She was flying for the very first time, on her way to visit her grandmother. Eagerly she took her seat by the window, fastened her seat belt, and prepared for takeoff. For this little girl, every part of the experience was new and exciting. As the plane reached a cruising altitude of thirty thousand feet, Maddy looked down at the clouds. Then she turned to her mother and asked, "Where are the angels? I thought there would be angels up here."

Maddy was thinking of the pictures of heaven that include winged angels strumming small harps and sitting on white, fluffy clouds against a sky-blue background. (Obviously she had seen too many advertisements for toilet tissue.)

In reality, angels do exist, though they don't usually live down to our stereotypes. Though Maddy was mistaken in her view of angels, I love the freshness of her spirit. She was open and eager to see angels, confident that they exist. Let's imitate that openness today by thanking God for the angels around us. Whether we see them or not, they are there.

Dreaming the Future

For God speaks again and again,
though people do not recognize it.
He speaks in dreams, in visions of the night,
when deep sleep falls on people
as they lie in their beds. Job 33:14–15 NLT

Rita and Dennis Bennett were active in a renewal movement within the Episcopal Church. A pastor, Dennis had suffered for many years from serious heart problems.

One night Rita dreamed that an exhausted Dennis was sitting in the garden, washing the leaves of a beautiful plant. There were three or four flowers at the end of its branches. The fourth flower seemed less distinct than the other three. Oddly, each could be unscrewed like a lightbulb. In her dream, she walked over to her husband and began praying for him.

Afterward Rita made a note in her journal: "Perhaps this dream means that Dennis has three more years and almost a complete fourth year." She wondered if the plant symbolized Dennis's life and if each flower represented a year of life. Later she forgot about the dream and the note she had made in her journal.

On November 1, 1999, Rita found her husband's body lying on the floor of his office. Shocked at his sudden passing, she realized that God had answered his prayer to either heal him or take him home instead of allowing him to linger painfully in the hospital when the time came.

Still, the shock of his sudden death plunged Rita into a profound sense of grief. Several months later, she came across her journal entry dated January 28, 1988, ten years and ten months prior to his death. As she read the words she had written, she felt profoundly comforted. God had known the moment of Dennis's death with exact precision. The dream had been his way of preparing her—a gift that helped assure her of God's loving care.[71]

Heaven School

"Not that we are competent in ourselves to claim anything for ourselves, but our competence comes from God."   2 Corinthians 3:5

Since heaven is a mystery that will take all of eternity to explore, why should we even think about it while we're here on earth?

Because we're in training. Our lives on earth are like heaven school, meant to prepare each of us for our graduation day. Our everyday existence, filled with tasks, challenges, and trials, gives us plenty of raw material to help us learn to be more like Jesus.

Our instructor in heaven school is none other than God's Spirit, strengthening and encouraging us, revealing God's wisdom as we seek to live for him. Paul tells us, "The Spirit of God not only maintains this hope within us, but helps us in our present limitations" (Romans 8:26 PHILLIPS).

Today, in the midst of your own limitations, ask your heavenly teacher to strengthen the hope within you as you lift up your voice and pray, "Come, Holy Spirit!"

I'll Remember You

Thus says the Lord: "I remember you. . . ." Jeremiah 2:2 NKJV

When the sun shimmers down on the sands of the seashore,
And whitecaps kiss waves in an ocean of blue,
When days run quickly, like bare feet in summer,
Then I'll remember you.

For I know you're with God, touched by hands that are gentle,
As you gaze in His face, oh so great.
With angels you gather, with loved ones sing praise,
And then peacefully rest in this place.

When Death Is Nothing but Hard

"He will wipe every tear from their eyes, and here will be no more death or sorrow or crying or pain. All these things are gone forever." Revelation 21:4 NLT

My mother had a good life. It had its ups and downs, but she knew that God had pulled her through each one. Sadly, the last two years were nothing but hard. Because of advancing dementia she experienced a number of terrifying delusions. No matter how hard we tried, no one in my family could comfort her by assuring her that none of these were real. Though hospice brought some relief, she still had tremendous anxiety.

I will never forget holding her hand and trying to comfort her just minutes before she passed. I could see tears welling in her eyes. I did my best to wipe them away, grabbing tissue from a box in her hospital room. I remember thinking how rough and cheap the tissue felt. I felt awful, scraping it against her parchment-thin cheeks, but it was all I had. That small piece of tissue made me painfully aware that everything I had—whether touch, words, or tissues—was not enough to provide the comfort she needed.

So I prayed for God to comfort her. I knew that some people had visions of heaven when they were close to death. "Please, God, show my mother that you are close." And then she died, the tears still welling in her eyes.

Since then, I've read several obituaries that go like this: "So and so passed peacefully from this life." Each time I read them, I feel a pang. Why wasn't my mother given peace at the moment she died? Why did it have to be so hard?

I have no answer. But I comfort myself with the truth. My mother loved Christ and he loved her. I believe he kept his promise, wiping away her tears in that holy, sacred moment when she passed from this life to the next. I just wasn't given the privilege of witnessing it.

May You Have as Many Happy Birthdays as You Need

A good name is better than precious ointment; and the day of death than the day of one's birth. Ecclesiastes 7:1 KJV

To George MacDonald, death was a familiar theme. He lost his wife, four children, and several grandchildren, many from tuberculosis, a disease that claimed countless lives in the Victorian era.

But to MacDonald, death was not the end; it was a doorway to heaven. In a birthday letter to a friend, he wrote, "May you have as many happy birthdays in this world as will make you ready for a happier series of them afterward, the first of which birthdays will be the one we call the day of death down here. But there is a better grander birthday than that which we may have every day—every hour that we turn away from ourselves to the living love that makes us love, and so are born again. And I think all these last birthdays will be summed up in one transcendent birthday—far off it may be, but surely to come—the moment when we know in ourselves that we are one with God, and are living by his life, and have neither thought or wish but his."[72]

Think Up

Finally, beloved, whatever is true, whatever is honorable,
whatever is just, whatever is pure, whatever is pleasing, whatever
is commendable, if there is any of excellence and if there is anything
worthy of praise, think about these things.   Philippians 4:8 NRSV

The world pulls us in many directions. It distracts our thinking and changes our priorities. It cries out to us for attention,
flashing images before us about the importance of wealth, success, prestige, and position. It drags us into believing that all
that there is on earth is all that there is.

The truth is that we are capable of thinking about so much
more than this world offers.

The roots of heaven are embedded in us. We are capable of
lofty thinking. We are capable of what I call "thinking up"—
of thinking about what is honorable, pure, pleasing to God,
commendable, excellent, and praiseworthy. By thinking up
we can be pulled closer to God and heaven than to the things
of this world.

Let's think up. With our minds and hearts focused up
toward God and his heaven, we will catch a glimpse of heaven
while we are still on earth.

"It Made Me Whole"

*Jesus said, "Let the little children come to me." Matthew 19:14
NRSV*

December 10, 2009—that was the day thirty-three-year-old Crystal McVea died and went to heaven.

Admitted to the hospital with severe abdominal pain, Crystal suddenly stopped breathing. It took nine minutes to revive her. In an especially poignant passage from her book *Waking Up in Heaven*, Crystal tells of approaching the gates of heaven, where she encountered a little girl, wearing a white frilly dress and a small white bonnet. Surrounded by light, the girl was bending over and then dipping a white basket into the golden light, laughing as she scooped it up, like water in a bucket.

"Every time she laughed," Crystal says, "my spirit absolutely *swelled* with love and pride for her. I wanted to watch this little girl play for the rest of eternity. I wanted to run up to her and take her in my arms and tell her how much I loved her. The love just kept building, endless and radiating waves of love so deep and so intense and so unstopping I truly, truly believed my soul was going to explode and I was going to cease to exist."

Suddenly, she says, God made her aware of something he'd been trying to show her all her life. She was that little girl and that was how God loved her.

"Seeing the child," she says, "was the most profound and powerful thing that ever happened to me, because it did something I didn't think was possible.

"It made me whole."[73]

When Crystal told her mother about the experience, the older woman began to cry. Then she showed her daughter a faded color photo of Crystal when she was only three years old. There was the frilly dress and the same white bonnet, exactly as Crystal had seen in her vision. Though there was no basket, her mother remembered that Crystal had loved carrying a small white basket everywhere she went.

That's when they both knew that heaven is real.

Why Do People Go to Heaven and Come Back?

For I am convinced that neither death nor life, neither angels nor demons, neither the present nor the future, nor any powers, neither height nor depth, nor anything else in all creation, will be able to separate us from the love of God that is in Christ Jesus our Lord. Romans 8:38–39

It's no surprise that near-death experiences are life-altering. In Crystal McVea's case, a mere nine minutes in heaven made all the difference. It wasn't simply that she now has a great story to tell. Something deep inside has changed. Here are a few of the ways her life is different.

She no longer holds grudges. Old resentments have faded away.
She is able to forgive even grievous wrongs.
She no longer cares much about material possessions.
She loves everybody, even people who used to infuriate her.
She feels sorry for people who've hurt her and prays for them.
Nothing seems to bother or make her angry.
She feels liberated.

After her experience, Crystal even told friends, "If you ever liked anything in my house, this'd be a good time to ask for it, because I'm ready to give it all away."[74] And she meant it because she realized that she was rich in everything that matters—the love of family, friends, and most of all, God.

Life on earth isn't perfect for anyone, even for those who claim to have gone to heaven and returned to tell the story. But they know that no matter what happens, nothing can separate them from the love of God that is in Christ Jesus.

Experiencing God

"What no eye has seen,
what no ear has heard,
and what no human mind has conceived"—
the things God has prepared for those who love
him— 1 Corinthians 2:9

People who have had a near-death experience often have difficulty describing what it's like to be in heaven because words like "beautiful," "awesome," and "overwhelming" just don't do the job. For Crystal McVea, it wasn't only that her senses were entirely overwhelmed but that she felt God in a way she could never have here on earth.

"In heaven," she says, "we don't have just five senses; we have a ton of senses. Imagine a sense that allowed us to not only see light, but also to taste it. Imagine another sense that allowed us to touch and feel light. Imagine yet another sense that isn't taste or touch but some new way to experience something, creating a more amazing and rewarding connection than any of our earthly senses allow."

"I was," she says, "completely infused by God's brightness and His love, and I wanted to enter into His brightness and intertwine myself completely with it."[75]

No wonder she describes her nine minutes in heaven as the "blessing of all blessings."

Why?

"My ears had heard of you
but now my eyes have seen you." Job 42:5

Do you remember the story of Job? He's the guy in the Bible who had it all—health, family, wealth, prestige—and then lost it all. Job was a good man. The Bible calls him blameless and upright.

When everything fell apart, Job began to question God. Why, he wondered, would God punish a man who was trying to live for him? It didn't seem fair. In the midst of his suffering, he had so many questions.

Crystal McVea had questions, too. She wondered how God could have allowed someone to molest her when she was a child. She thought about all the innocent children who have been brutalized and about all the starving people in the world. Why would God allow innocent people to suffer such grievous hurts? She knew that if she ever met God she would have a thousand questions.

But at the moment her soul slipped from her body and she entered into heaven, her need for answers vanished. Like Job, who had an awe-inspiring vision of the living God, she was given something better than answers—an encounter with a Being so magnificent that she couldn't help but trust him.

"My ears," Job said, "had heard of you but now my eyes have seen you." For Job, seeing God made all the difference.

Like Job and like Crystal, we will one day find ourselves in the presence of the living God, whose love and greatness will be more than enough to satisfy all our questions.

The Upward Call

And the Spirit himself joins with our spirits to say we are God's children. If we are God's children, we will receive blessings from God together with Christ. Romans 8:16–17 NCV

The moment a person starts progressing on the path to heaven, a Spirit-to-spirit exchange happens, in which a person is harnessed to a powerhouse of such mind-boggling capacity that the only way to go is up, up, up.

. . . Until their feet of clay start to drag them down. As veteran pastor Francis Frangipane puts it: "Sadly, many Christians just muddle along, hoping for nothing loftier than a short reprieve from sin and guilt. Yet should the lowliness of our sinful state have veto power over the enormity of God's promises? May it never be! Scripture assures us that, even as lowly as we feel at times, our call is an upward climb that relies upon faith in God and the power of Christ's redemption. We are not harnessed to our flaws and weaknesses; rather, in Spirit-to-spirit fusion we are united to the resurrection power of Heaven! Our call is to walk with the living God and in unfolding degrees of glory be 'conformed to the image of His Son'" (Romans 8:29).[76]

Let's keep aiming ever upward, today, tomorrow, and into the endless future.

Faith Is Rest

We who have believed are able to enter and have God's rest. . . .
Anyone who enters God's rest will rest from his work as God
did. Hebrews 4:3, 10 NCV

Faith at work is not work. It is rest.

It is resting in what we have come to believe in the past,
thereby proving the truth of it. If you have already believed
that the Son of God has won your entrance into his Father's
kingdom, walking in that belief will make you one of the
most well-rested, contented people on the planet. It will also
culminate for you in the haven we call heaven.

Think about it! Your struggles are over before you get
there. Even when urgent needs seem to outstrip your supply,
you do not need to wrestle with God as if you are a deep-sea
fisherman trying to land an impossibly big catch. God's gift to
you is rest. You have only to enter it through the faith he has
given you.

The Book of Life

Everyone whose name is found written in the book—will be
delivered. . . . Those who are wise will shine like the brightness of
the heavens, and those who lead many to righteousness, like the
stars for ever and ever. Daniel 12:1–3

Both the Old and New Testaments speak of a mysterious book
called the "book of life." This book, also called the scroll of
remembrance in Malachi 3:16, is one in which God records the
names of all his faithful.

According to the Bible, to have your name recorded in the
book of life is cause for great rejoicing, while to be blotted out
from it is the greatest tragedy that could befall a person. As
Christians, we know that a life surrendered to Christ is one
that is inscribed in God's book of life.

Take a moment now to imagine yourself in heaven. God
is about to open his great book. Before he does, he gives you
time to prepare by searching your conscience with the help of
his Spirit. Bring whatever you find there to the feet of Christ,
asking his forgiveness. Now picture his response. The Lord
does exactly what Scripture says he will—flinging your sins
so far away that they are no longer visible.

Close your time of prayer by imagining that God is opening his great book. As he scans the pages, looking for your
name, you can see the truth in his eyes. You are loved. You are
safe. You belong to him. With his own hand he has inscribed
your name in the Lamb's book of life.

Epiphany

"Surely the LORD *is in this place, and I wasn't even aware
of it!" Genesis 28:16*

Reggie Anderson had what you might call a reverse epiphany.
After the brutal murders of six of his relatives, who were also
his close friends, he was left with agonizing questions. Why
had God allowed the massacre? Couldn't he have stopped it?
Didn't he care?

Then he had an insight. It wasn't that God was cruel
or uncaring. It wasn't that he was too weak to have prevented the tragedy. God hadn't been there. And he hadn't
been there because he didn't exist. Anderson had stopped
believing in Santa Claus years ago. Now it was time to stop
believing in God. "The epiphany didn't surprise me," he says,
"it only surprised me that it had taken me so long to figure it
out."[77]

Several years later, something happened to change his
mind about God's existence. While camping in the mountains
of Tennessee, he had a dream. Transported to a place more
beautiful and real than anything he'd ever experienced, he
noticed a crowd moving toward him. With a shock he recognized his murdered relatives.

"Jimmy, Jerry, Mary, Ned, Chester, and Aubrey!

"I couldn't believe what I was seeing, but there was no
mistaking them. They looked ecstatic. I'd never seen *anyone* as
happy as they were...."

His friends and relatives were able to assure him that he
shouldn't hold their deaths against God. "Seeing and 'hearing'
from them," he said, "released me from dark thoughts of their
deaths. The weight that had pinned me down for so long had
been removed."[78]

After nearly seven years of wandering in a spiritual wasteland, Reggie Anderson was delivered from all the hate and anger and confusion he had felt as a result of the tragedy. Finally he was free to believe.

"Why Are You Running from Me?"

Jesus looked at him and loved him.   Mark 10:21

Reggie Anderson's dream wasn't over. After encountering his friends, he met someone else—a person who seemed human but more than human, who looked, in fact, like a composite of every race on earth with hair that "was at once silver, golden, and onyx-colored as it moved in the light."

"Reggie, why are you running from me?" the figure asked. "Your friends and family are here and they have been made whole."

Anderson knew it was Jesus. "His eyes," he said, "shone like the cool waters of the stream between us. His smile was so reassuring, like the one a loving mother gives to her baby."[79]

When it was over, he woke to discover that he had fallen asleep not in his tent but next to the campfire, under a canopy of trees. Trying to recall every detail of the dream, he began to feel the weight of his sin. In the presence of a being so great, his own flaws had become painfully obvious. He thought back to an experience he'd had as a twelve-year-old, when he'd had the conviction to walk to the front of the church so that he could be immersed in the baptismal waters. He wanted to feel that clean again.

Hiking to a nearby pool, Anderson stripped off his clothes and lowered himself into the water. Standing beneath a waterfall, he began to weep, feeling remorse and joy sweep through him. Turning his face sunward as the water cascaded over his body, he felt new, clean, whole.

"I was truly changed," he said.

"Jesus was real.

"God was real.

"And God was good!"[80]

I've Got Joy, Joy, Joy

Blessed are you when people hate you, and when they exclude you, revile you, and defame you on account of the Son of Man. Rejoice in that day and leap for joy, for surely your reward is great in heaven; for that is what their ancestors did to the prophets. Luke 6:22–23 NRSV

My friend Dolores collects joy, which seems ironic in light of the fact that her name means "sorrowful." More specifically, she collects artwork, plaques, bumper stickers, bric-a-brac—anything that features the word "Joy" on it. She isn't looking for pithy statements or elaborations but only the three-letter word itself. She wants to luxuriate in, celebrate, and spread joy wherever she goes.

Dolores's unique collection provides collateral for her life circumstances. She and her husband, who is often unemployed, struggle to make ends meet. Their only son came back from a stint in the army with post-traumatic stress disorder, and his behaviors continue to trouble family and friends. Three winters ago, Dolores fell down a steep concrete stairway and shattered her leg in too many places to count. Before she had the chance to recover, her unmarried sister-in-law moved in, not to help but because she herself required round-the-clock care until she died a year later of Alzheimer's disease.

None of this sounds like a recipe for joy. Fortunately, it's not circumstances that have motivated Dolores's search for joy, but faith in the God who promised it. When Dolores gets to heaven, make no mistake about it, she's going to get that great big reward that Jesus promises.

Highway to Heaven

And a highway shall be there, and it shall be called the Way of Holiness; the unclean shall not pass over it. It shall belong to those who walk on the way. Isaiah 35:8 ESV

One day, Billy Graham's wife, Ruth, spotted a construction sign while she was driving down the highway. It read: "End of construction. Thank you for your patience." Those words now serve as her epitaph, carved into the headstone of her grave at the Billy Graham Library in Charlotte, North Carolina.

Ruth Graham recognized the fact that nobody's highway to heaven is smooth, but that the best way to approach all the bumps and ruts, starts and stops, is to surrender to the restoration process. When it comes to heaven's highway, it helps to realize who the contractors are: God the Father, his Son Jesus, and the Holy Spirit. Not only do they know exactly what they're doing. They have the ability to complete every project right on time.

Regardless of what you might want your epitaph to read, why not thank in advance all those—especially your ever-patient heavenly Father—who are traveling with you right now through all the ins and outs of the construction process.

Rearview Mirror

Where sin increased, grace increased all the more, so that, just as
sin reigned in death, so also grace might reign through righteousness
to bring eternal life through Jesus Christ our Lord. Romans
5:20–21 NIV

Immediately after he wrote the words above, Paul posed an obvious question: "Why not go ahead and sin, then, if every sin falls under heaven's grace?" Since sin seems to attract grace like a magnet, why not indulge your worst inclinations in order to draw more grace your way?

Because, quite simply, sin was part of your old life, and you don't want to go back to that. Even if your old life wasn't all that racy or fascinating compared to your new one, you've learned the difference between "old" and "new," and it happens to look a lot like the difference between hell and heaven.

Sin and death go hand in hand: "the wages of sin is death" (Romans 6:23). And now, because of Jesus, you have died to sin. No longer on a self-directed tour of hell, you have embarked with Christ on the road to heaven.

So put your temptations behind you, keep sin in your rearview mirror, and then hang on tight and enjoy the ride.

Better Off Dead

> *Truly, in our own hearts we believed we would die. But this*
> *happened so we would not trust in ourselves but in God, who raises*
> *people from the dead.* *2 Corinthians 1:9 NCV*

You have prayed and prayed. But your circumstances do not change, except to get worse. It's hopeless. This is worse than death, you think. God must be deaf.

Eventually, of course, you come out the other side, battered perhaps—but, I hope, with a story that verifies Paul's experience. You have discovered that God (the one with a proven history of raising the dead) had something better in mind for you than merely rescuing you from the pain you dread.

It's the same for all of us. Some prayers appear to go unanswered. They are not answered in the way we want. Perhaps one reason for this is that God can't resurrect a person who hasn't yet died. And there are all kinds of deaths.

On the other side of difficulty, you can begin to echo Paul's understanding of how God works, because your renewed life will have turned out better than the one you were afraid of losing. You may need time to grieve, but every loss will bring into better focus his gift to you of heavenly life.

"I Saw the Other Side"

If I go up to the heavens, you are there;
if I make my bed in the depths, you are there.   Psalm 139:8

Laura Schroff, author of *The Invisible Thread*, lost her mother twice.

When Laura was twenty-four, her mother died of uterine cancer. Just after a priest administered the last rites in the emergency room at Memorial Sloan Kettering Hospital in New York, a doctor turned to Laura and her sister and pronounced the words they both feared to hear: "She is gone."

Earlier that day, her mother had seemed frightened, inconsolable. Laura had tried to comfort her, assuring her she would be all right though dreading she might not be.

A few minutes after the physician had pronounced her mother dead, a nurse broke in excitedly: "Oh, my God, your mother is alive! Talk to her; talk to her!" The oncologist seemed as surprised as everyone else to see that her mother was not only alive but perfectly lucid, as she had not been for most of the last few weeks. What's more, she was smiling and seemed perfectly at peace.

"The next six hours," Laura says, "were nothing short of a miracle. My mother's vital signs were inexplicably strong, and she was completely calm and in charge." During that time, she was able to speak lovingly with every member of her family. A few days later she passed away.

What had happened in those few minutes—the time between when the physician examined her and pronounced her dead and when the nurse noticed that her mother had started breathing again? Laura's mother tried to explain by telling her daughters, "I saw the other side. It is far more beautiful and peaceful than we could ever imagine."[81]

Heaven Cannot Contain Him

"But will God indeed dwell on the earth? Even heaven and the highest heaven cannot contain you, much less this house that I have built!" 1 Kings 8:27 NRSV

King Solomon, the world's wisest man, uttered these words as he dedicated a magnificent temple to God in Jerusalem. Stunning as it was, Solomon realized that no temple on earth could ever contain the Almighty God. But God did dwell there in a special way, just as he had promised he would.

Over the centuries humans have continued to build magnificent churches, perhaps hoping to entice God's presence. The Hagia Sophia of Istanbul, built in the fifth century, was known for its immense dome and ornate interior. When it was completed, Emperor Justinian declared, "Solomon, I have surpassed you!"

But no matter how lavish or large, no earthly building can ever contain the majesty and glory of God, whose dwelling is in heaven and, mysteriously, also in the heart of all who love him (1 Corinthians 6:19–20).

Who Is Heaven For?

"I desire mercy, not sacrifice." For I have come to call not the
righteous but sinners. Matthew 9:12–13 NRSV

If you asked a dozen people on the street, "Who is heaven
for?" most would probably say something like "Heaven is for
good people." That might sound reasonable, but it's not completely correct. While it's true that heaven is populated with
good people, no one in heaven fit that description until God
transformed them. That doesn't mean human beings are incapable of doing good. But no one is *good enough* to live in the
presence of a God who is completely good.

So heaven was made for sinners—people like you and me
who fall far short of the mark. Jesus showed his preference
for sinners by hanging around so many of them. Some of his
friends were such lowlifes that his relationship with them
shocked all the "good" people in town.

Unfortunately, many of us have redefined heaven, setting up human standards that involve many "good" things—
things like being good, acting good, looking good, and
thinking good thoughts. But while such behaviors may be
praiseworthy, they can't deliver a ticket into heaven. Only
Christ's death and resurrection can achieve that for us.

Archbishop Desmond Tutu of South Africa says it well:
"We may be surprised at the people we find in heaven. God has
a soft spot for sinners. His standards are quite low."[82]

Who is heaven for? It's for people like you and me who
though we are aware of our failings are even more aware of the
gracious gift of life Christ brings.

This Side of Heaven

If I go up to the heavens, you are there;
*   if I make my bed in Sheol, you are there. . . .*
If I say, "Surely the darkness will hide me
And the light become night around me,"
*   even the darkness will not be dark to you*
*   the night will shine like the day,*
*   for the darkness is as light to you. Psalm 139:8*

The idea that God is everywhere is not new to us. But it would have come as a shock to many ancient peoples, who thought of their gods in territorial terms. Their power and presence was concentrated in a particular geographic region.

By contrast, the Jewish people came to believe in a God who transcended all boundaries. Whether they were in the desert or in the city, in captivity or on the march, they understood that God was right there with them. Realizing that God's power was unbounded and that he was not held captive by geography would have made it easier for many of them to comprehend the truth that death itself could not be a barrier to the God who loved them.

As Christians our view of heaven has developed even further because we worship a man who died and rose again and who has ascended into heaven to sit at the right hand of God. Our faith tells us that we will one day live with him in heaven. On that day there will no longer be shadows or confusion or darkness to trouble us.

The good news is that though we live this side of heaven we belong to a God for whom darkness is never an impediment. Though trials, grief, and confusion may shroud our vision, we are held firmly in the grasp of the One for whom, as the psalmist assures us, even the darkness is not dark. To him the night still shines as bright as day.

A Near-Death Experience
in the New Testament

"I see heaven open and the Son of Man standing at the right hand of God." Acts 7:56

You may wonder whether every account of a near-death experience is reliable. For a Christian, anything that contradicts the truths contained in Scripture is to be rejected. It's important to be careful when evaluating accounts of those who claim to have seen heaven, especially those who say that everyone, regardless of their faith or lack of it, will be welcomed into heaven. Still, the Bible provides ample testimony of the existence of heaven. Consider the story of Stephen, the first Christian martyr, who was granted a vision of heaven just before he was stoned to death.

> When the members of the Sanhedrin heard this, they were furious and gnashed their teeth at him. But Stephen, full of the Holy Spirit, looked up to heaven and saw the glory of God, and Jesus standing at the right hand of God. "Look," he said, "I see heaven open and the Son of Man standing at the right hand of God...."
>
> While they were stoning him, Stephen prayed, "Lord Jesus, receive my spirit." Then he fell on his knees and cried out, "Lord, do not hold this sin against them." When he had said this, he fell asleep. *(Acts 7:54–56, 59–60)*

Paul's Vision of Heaven

I know a man in Christ who fourteen years ago was caught up to the third heaven. 2 Corinthians 12:2

The Apostle Paul also speaks of experiencing heaven. Though Paul doesn't give details, some commentators believe that his experience might have happened at Lystra, located in modern-day Turkey, when he was stoned and left for dead (Acts 14:19–20). Here's how he later describes his vision to believers in Corinth. Note that when Paul says "I know a man" he is speaking of himself.

I know a man in Christ who fourteen years ago was caught up to the third heaven. Whether it was in the body or out of the body I do not know—God knows. And I know that this man—whether in the body or apart from the body I do not know, but God knows—was caught up to paradise and heard inexpressible things, things that no one is permitted to tell. *(2 Corinthians 12:2–4)*

Does Everybody Go to Heaven?

"Between us and you a great chasm has been set in place." Luke 16:26

Considering how many people speak positively of a near-death experience, you may wonder if everyone, regardless of the quality of their life on earth, ends up in heaven. Again, the Bible, especially the words of Christ, should be our guide.

Jesus tells a story that reflects the belief that there are two very different destinations—one for the wicked and another for the righteous.

> "There was a rich man who was dressed in purple and fine linen and lived in luxury every day. At his gate was laid a beggar named Lazarus, covered with sores and longing to eat what fell from the rich man's table. Even the dogs came and licked his sores.
>
> "The time came when the beggar died and the angels carried him to Abraham's side. The rich man also died and was buried. In Hades, where he was in torment, he looked up and saw Abraham far away, with Lazarus by his side. So he called to him, 'Father Abraham, have pity on me and send Lazarus to dip the tip of his finger in water and cool my tongue, because I am in agony in this fire.'
>
> "But Abraham replied, 'Son, remember that in your lifetime you received your good things, while Lazarus received bad things, but now he is comforted here and you are in agony. And besides all this, between us and you a great chasm has been set in place, so that those who want to go from here to you cannot, nor can anyone cross over from there to us.'" *(Luke 16:19–26)*

What's Good About Death?

So the LORD *God banished him.   Genesis 3:23*

Do you remember the story of Adam and Eve and how an angel drove them from paradise after they had disobeyed God and eaten the forbidden fruit? What's all that got to do with heaven?

Genesis 3:22–23 says, "And the LORD God said, 'The man has now become like one of us, knowing good and evil. He must not be allowed to reach out his hand and take also from the tree of life and eat, and live forever.' So the LORD God banished him from the Garden of Eden to work the ground from which he had been taken."

Apparently, eating from the tree of life would have immortalized human beings in their sinful condition. Because sin always alienates us from God, he didn't want us to be forever separated from him. So he allowed death to enter the picture. As one pastor points out, "Thus God prevented Adam and Eve from eternal sinfulness by giving them the gift of death, the ability to exit this life and arrive safely in the wondrous life to come. Death, though it would appear to be man's greatest enemy, would in the end, prove to be his greatest friend. Only through death can we go to God."[83] And only through Christ's death are we given the opportunity.

"It Felt Like Heaven to Me"

Though the mountains be shaken
and the hills be removed,
yet my unfailing love for you will not be shaken.   Isaiah 54:10

Pat Etter blanked out, not once but two different times. The second time, her husband drove her to the hospital. Once there, she discovered she had a cerebral aneurysm. If her brain didn't stop bleeding, she would need surgery that might leave her paralyzed and without the ability to speak.

Though Pat was having a stroke, she wasn't afraid. "Lord, do for me what I can't do for myself," she prayed.

Instead of panicking, she began reviewing her life. All the while she felt enveloped in the presence of a Being who loved her unconditionally. In the light of that loving, powerful presence, hurtful events took on a more positive twist as she felt God's healing flowing through her.

Nothing disturbed her except being woken up every hour by the intensive care nurse, who was concerned that she might slip into a coma. Why, she wondered, would anyone want to pull her away from the intense love she felt?

"Finally the bleeding stopped and I was sent home. My neurologist seemed puzzled each time I saw him. Pulling out my X-rays, he would point out how much blood was in my brain. That kind of damage would usually result in paralysis and the loss of speech. He couldn't understand why I was still walking and talking and not in a nursing home.

"But I know why, God was answering my prayer—doing for me what I couldn't do for myself, healing me inside and out. Though I didn't die, I felt as though I had, because being in the loving presence of God felt like heaven to me."

A Touch from Heaven

If God is for us, who can be against us?   Romans 8:31

Though Pat Etter experienced a touch from heaven during her medical crisis, the next few years presented their share of challenges. It took two years to recover from the stroke. Though she could still speak, she often found herself saying the opposite of what she meant—"no" when she meant "yes" or "black" when she meant "white."

Pat spent six months on the couch, too weak to do much of anything, and a year undergoing physical therapy. Despite her difficulties, there was never a time when she said "poor me." She felt too much joy for that.

Though Pat and her husband were supporting two sons in college, she wasn't strong enough to return to work. Then her husband, Bill, lost his job in the banking industry. Without health insurance, they worried about how to pay for Pat's treatment.

Experiences that would normally have thrown her into a state of high anxiety no longer did. She simply trusted God. What had been mostly head knowledge about God's faithfulness had now become heart knowledge.

Bill changed, too. After losing his job, he transitioned into the housing industry, but it wasn't long before the housing market collapsed. Even when spec homes they owned were threatened with foreclosure, they both knew God would help them, and he did.

The sensation of God's love had been so profound in the hospital and beyond that Pat says she would go through it all again if that's what it took to know God more deeply.

Rest in Peace?

In Christ all will be made alive.   *1 Corinthians 15:22*

Though Jesus and others use the metaphor of sleep to describe death, Scripture seems to indicate that our souls are awake after they are separated from our bodies in death. It would seem, then, that the images of sleep apply to our bodies but not to our souls.

Painful as it is to die, we are promised a new and better body at the end of time. As Paul tells believers in Corinth: "If only for this life we have hope in Christ, we are of all people most to be pitied.

"But Christ has indeed been raised from the dead, the firstfruits of those who have fallen asleep. For since death came through a man, the resurrection of the dead comes also through a man. For as in Adam all die, so in Christ all will be made alive (1 Corinthians 15:19–22).

Take a few moments to think about how it will feel to have a brand-new body. Imagine never catching a cold, spraining a finger, becoming arthritic or overweight. The World Health Organization has 12,420 different codes to designate various diseases and maladies. Because of what Christ has done, you will not suffer from even a single one.

Safe Harbor

We have this hope as an anchor for the soul, firm and secure. Hebrews 6:19

Where water is too shallow, conditions too treacherous, or the harbor too crowded to navigate, passengers on ships have to be ferried to shore in smaller boats. In ancient times, a forerunner was used to ease a ship safely into port. Wading through the water, this man would tie a rope that had been fastened to the ship to a rock close to shore. Then a winch would bring it safely in.

Erwin Lutzer uses this analogy to speak of Christ's role in our own lives. "Our forerunner," he says, "has gone to heaven, where He stands ready to guide us safely into the Holy of Holies. We are fastened to a rock that cannot be moved. Let the storms tear our sails to shreds; let the floors creak; let the gusts of wind attempt to blow us off course; let the tides overwhelm us; we shall arrive safely into the port. Each day we are pulled a notch closer to the harbor by the One who proved He is more powerful than death."[84]

The next time you become painfully aware of the perils of your journey through life, remember that Christ will bring you safely home to the harbor we call heaven.

Big or Small?

And he will send out his angels with a loud trumpet call, and they
will gather his elect from the four winds, from one end of heaven to
the other. Matthew 24:31 ESV

On a beautiful spring evening, burglars smashed one of the
windows in our home and made off with a computer, a television, some video games, jewelry, and a jar of loose change
labeled "Missions." Every member of the family felt violated
and nervous. For weeks after that, the slightest household
noise startled me.

"I guess it shouldn't seem like such a big deal, should it?"
my husband said on the way home from purchasing a new
computer with some of the insurance money. "In a hundred
years, nobody will remember this anymore. It's just a blip on
the screen of eternity."

Have you ever read Richard Carlson's *Don't Sweat the Small
Stuff . . . and It's All Small Stuff*? I haven't, but I confess to loving the title. Traffic accidents, leaky roofs, dog bites, divorce,
and even robberies—from the worst to the least of all that we
suffer—one day will fall away into oblivion at the final trumpet call. Until then, let's hand over whatever distresses us,
asking God to help us approach each new challenge in light
of eternity.

The Father's Welcome

*Let us eat and celebrate; for this son of mine was dead and is alive
again; he was lost and is found! Luke 15:23–24 NRSV*

The story of the prodigal son and the father who forgives him
is everyone's story, a universal story of sin and loss, of love and
forgiveness, and of wholehearted rejoicing. Imagine a broken-
hearted father, concerned for a child who has disappeared,
his whereabouts and status unknown. Now picture that same
father running out to greet his son in amazement and joy.

Maybe the scene doesn't sound far-fetched to you. But in
those days Jewish fathers simply did not lift up their robes,
show their legs, and then run out and greet a wayward son.
It would have lowered their dignity, shaming them. Jesus'
description of the prodigal's father would have shocked his
listeners because that wasn't how a Middle Eastern father was
supposed to behave.

But that's exactly Jesus' point. God doesn't behave as we
expect him to. He doesn't treat us as we deserve to be treated.
If we come to him humbly, repenting of our foolishness, he
will open his arms and throw a party to announce our coming
home to heaven.

Put Your Arms Around Someone

"A new command I give you: Love one another. As I have loved you, so you must love one another." John 13:34

Trudy Harris is a former hospice nurse. After her father died, an investment broker she knew seemed overly curious about the details of his passing. Mary Anne's nonstop questions puzzled her. Then one day she learned the reason for her curiosity. Mary Anne had been diagnosed with inoperable cancer.

Trudy realized that this businesswoman was just doing what came natural, trying to develop a plan that would help her face her own death. The questions kept coming. Mary Anne wanted to know what Trudy thought about the meaning of life. What did she think about God, about Jesus? The two became close over the course of their long conversations.

As the months wore on, Trudy prayed for her friend: "Lord, put Your arms around her, hold her in your tender, loving care, and help her to know she is safe with You."

One day Mary Ann told her about a spiritual encounter she'd had, saying, "I was not asleep. I was awake, and He came to me here in my room. He put His arms around me, and I felt so safe and warm."

"That was Jesus," Trudy told her.

Smiling, Mary Anne said, "No, it wasn't, Trudy, it was you."[85]

The message was clear: Jesus had been in the room that day and Mary Anne knew it. He'd used Trudy to wrap his loving arms around her, helping her to feel safe and warm.

Sometimes, to our surprise, we become the answer to our own prayers. Join me today in asking God to use you to express his love to someone who needs his touch.

Living Under Heaven

Our citizenship is in heaven, from which also we eagerly wait for a Savior, the Lord Jesus Christ.   Philippians 3:20 NASB

Most Americans believe that heaven is a real place, a wonderful continuation of earthly life without its evils and unhappiness.

But most of us make the mistake of thinking of heaven linearly rather than vertically. What do I mean by that? We picture ourselves living first on earth and then, after our death, in heaven. But the Apostle Paul puts it a bit differently. He says we are already citizens of heaven.

Most people fail to realize that earth and heaven exist on a continuum that is vertical rather than linear. They forget that earth is "under heaven." While it's true that we will go to heaven when we die, our citizenship in heaven is what should determine the kind of lives we live right now, shaping our understanding of our purpose on planet earth.

Why not dedicate the next twenty-four hours to focusing on the fact that in Christ your citizenship has already been transferred from earth to heaven. Ask God to help you respond to the events of the day as though you already have one foot in heaven, because you do.

Close to Home

Enoch walked with God; then he was no more, because God took
him away.   Genesis 5:24

Once upon a time there lived a good man by the name of
Enoch. Through some good fortune, God spared Enoch the
indignity of death and took him straight to heaven.

Here's one little girl's take on this Bible story: "One day
Enoch and God took a long walk together until Enoch said it
was getting late. And the Lord said, 'We are now closer to my
home than we are to yours . . . Why don't you just come to my
house tonight.'"

One day, we, too, will be closer to heaven than we are to
earth. On that day, God will say, "Why don't you just come to
my house tonight?"

Dying Grace

"Therefore I tell you, do not worry about your life." Matthew 6:25

You do not want dying grace till dying moments. What would be the good of dying grace while you are yet alive? A boat will only be needful when you reach a river. Ask for living grace, and glorify Christ thereby, and then you shall have dying grace when the time comes.

Your enemy is going to be destroyed but not today.... Leave the final shock of arms till the last adversary advances, and meanwhile hold your place in the conflict. God will in due time help you to overcome your last enemy, but meanwhile see to it that you overcome the world, the flesh and the devil. If you live well, you will die well.

—CHARLES SPURGEON

God's Heavenly Glory

The heavens proclaim his righteousness; and all the peoples behold his glory. Psalm 97:6 NRSV

Contemplation is a lost art. We're too busy multitasking to spend time sitting quietly, thinking deeply about one thing at a time. But if there's anything we should lavish our time on, it's thinking about the glory of "the upper world," as George Whitefield here expresses: "The glories of the upper world crowd in so fast upon my soul, that I am lost in the contemplation of them."

The upper world is where we ultimately belong—in fellowship with God, our Creator. From the first day of creation, he has always intended to be in a close and perfect relationship with us. Human disobedience destroyed that perfection. But it's coming back to stay. In heaven, God will restore his dream of an ideal fellowship with the people he has created.

Seeing God face-to-face will be one of the great glories of heaven. But we don't have to wait until then. Even now, we can contemplate that moment when we will look on his face.

Stop for just a moment today, focusing your thoughts on heaven. Ask God to bring the glory of the upper world into the life you live now.

What About Hell?

> *And if anyone causes one of these little ones who believe in me to*
> *sin, it would be better for him to be thrown into the sea with a large*
> *millstone tied around his neck. If your hand causes you to sin, cut it*
> *off. It is better for you to enter life maimed than with two hands to*
> *go into hell, where the fire never goes out.   Mark 9:42–43*

Imagine that just outside your city is a putrid, burning dump.
Even though you close the windows of your car, you still smell
its acrid smoke every day as you drive to work. At night when
you return home its flames are a noxious reminder that child
sacrifices were once practiced there.

If you had been a first-century resident of Jerusalem, you
wouldn't have been driving a car, of course. But you would
have been acutely aware that this place, known as the valley
of Ben Hinnom, was the very picture of hell. (The Hebrew
word *gehenna*, translated as "hell" in the New Testament, was
derived from the name of this valley.)

In the twenty-first century most of our cities are not
located next to burning garbage dumps. Nor do we think
much about hell. In fact in many circles talk about hell is considered downright rude. But what are we to make of the fact
that Jesus spoke of hell, not once but several times? Can we
afford to ignore what he says?

As a child I was horrified to think there might be a place
that was literally on fire forever. As an adult I've wondered
whether the image of hell has more to do with desires that can
never be fulfilled or a sense of guilt that can never be appeased.
Made for God, we will be forever separated from him.

In hell, there will no longer be words for "remedy," "hope,"
or "healing." Frightening as it is to contemplate such a place,
doing so may increase our longing for heaven, motivating us

to pray and share our faith with others. Thinking of hell can also remind us of the good news—that because of the sacrificial love of Christ there exists an all-powerful remedy for our sins.

What Wondrous Love Is This

Shout for joy, you heavens;
rejoice, you earth;
burst into song, you mountains!
For the LORD *comforts his people*
and will have compassion on his afflicted ones.   Isaiah 49:13

What wondrous love is this,
O my soul! O my soul!
What wondrous love is this!
O my soul!
What wondrous love is this!
That caused the Lord of bliss!
To send this precious peace,
To my soul, to my soul!
To send this precious peace
To my soul!

And when from death I'm free,
I'll sing on, I'll sing on,
And when from death I'm free,
I'll sing on.
and when from death I'm free,
I'll sing and joyful be,
and through eternity
I'll sing on, I'll sing on,
and through eternity
I'll sing on.

Time to Go

All the days ordained for me were written in your book before one of them came to be.   Psalm 139:16

Trudy Harris's grandfather, George, had been diagnosed with pancreatic cancer. The day before he died, he pointed out the window toward the lake and asked who the man was who was standing by the lake.

When Trudy responded that it was only the weeping willow tree, he said, "I see the tree. I mean the man who is standing underneath the tree, by the water. Who is he?"

Trudy looked but could see no one. That night when she was putting her young son to bed, she recounted the incident to him.

"Do you think he saw Jesus?" he asked.

Trudy wasn't sure.

Later that night, while tucking George into bed, she asked him whether the man he had seen might have been Jesus.

"Yes, dear, why?" he replied. She remembers thinking that he was answering her in the same matter-of-fact, confident way that she had witnessed in so many others who were approaching death.

Early the next morning, at three o'clock, George passed away.

When his nurse received the news of his death the next day, the family was surprised to hear her say, "George died at three this morning, didn't he?" She went on to explain how she knew. She had been woken up at three by a voice that said: "I've come for my servant George."[86]

Find the Slipstream

*Therefore, since we are surrounded by such a great cloud of
witnesses, let us throw off everything that hinders and the sin
that so easily entangles. And let us run with perseverance the race
marked out for us. Hebrews 12:1 NIV*

When a flock of geese flies in a V formation, it is taking advantage of a principle of aerodynamics known as "slipstreaming"
or "drafting." Except for the lead bird, the rest of the geese can
fly with less effort because of the extra lift from the air cur-
rents created by the wings of the bird in front. Racers (cyclists,
skaters, automobile drivers) apply the same principle when
they arrange themselves in a neatly staggered procession.
Those who follow closely and carefully can conserve a significant amount of energy.

It's not that the followers get a free ride; they must exert
themselves as much as they can in order to keep up with the
group. But they don't need to worry about choosing the route
or setting the speed; they simply have to maintain their position and keep up the pace. Errant followers soon learn the hard
way that they have only made the journey harder.

Heaven-bound men and women can take advantage of
slipstreaming as they encourage one another, sometimes taking the lead position to make the way easier for others who
are coming along behind and other times slipping smoothly
into the position of a follower. The guiding words of Scripture
make all "slipstreamers" graceful, swift, and vigorous.

I Go to Prepare a Place for You

Trust in the LORD. Psalm 4:5

The Bible does not give explicit details about what we should expect heaven to be like, and some of its information seems almost contradictory. Will heaven be a place of peaceful rest— or a place of unceasing, over-the-top worship? The Book of Hebrews urges everyone to "make every effort to enter that rest" (Hebrews 4:11), and yet the scene before God's throne (see Revelation 4) sounds anything but restful!

None of us will fully know what heaven is like until we get there. Could it be that God only discloses what we need to know—that heaven is wonderful and that he's reserved a place for us there—so that we can focus our energy and attention on living in the here and now? One thing we do know, regardless of whether we're living on earth or in heaven, is that Jesus is always with us.

While we're here on earth, we know that he has our back. And knowing this should give us the confidence to share our faith so that many more may come to know his love.

The Final Performance

For the wages of sin is death, but the free gift of God is eternal life in Christ Jesus our Lord. Romans 6:23 NRSV

Although Zoe took several years of piano lessons in elementary school, she never had a knack for it. Her husband, however, was highly talented, blessed with near-perfect pitch. He played trumpet in a variety of groups that played a repertoire of jazz, classical, and big-band music. You name it, he could play it. He also loved corny jokes. One of his favorites goes like this: "Excuse me, do you know how to get to Carnegie Hall?" The punch line, of course, is "practice, practice, practice."

Some people think that the answer to the question "How do I get to heaven?" is similar—practice, practice, practice. They believe they will make it if only they can rehearse their behavior until it is perfect. So they do their best to edit their actions into perfect alignment with social correctness, and they guard every word out of their mouths in order to adhere to a perceived standard.

But all the practice in the world will never make us perfect enough to enter the gates of heaven, because getting to heaven doesn't depend upon our doing. It depends on what God has already done.

I'm not saying we should give up on becoming more Christlike. I'm only making the point that however good we are, we will never find the way to "Carnegie Hall" on our own.

"I'm Not Afraid to Die"

Where, O death, is your victory?
But thanks be to God! He gives us the victory through our Lord
Jesus Christ. 1 Corinthians 15:55, 57

Pat Etter experienced God's love enveloping her when she suffered a stroke that should have paralyzed her. Because of her medical crisis, she came to know God in a much deeper way.

"I know a lot of people," she says, "who seem devoted to God but who appear hopeless when someone they love dies. I understand that grief takes time to process, but sometimes it's all I can do not to say, 'Where is your faith!! Don't you know how great heaven is?'

"When my mother-in-law died, I remember feeling a little bit jealous because I had an inkling of what she must be experiencing in heaven.

"Her death reminded me of something that happened when her second husband, Mr. M, passed away. The two had met and married in an assisted-living home. Mom was a lovely, faith-filled woman who didn't remarry after her first husband's death until she was ninety. Sadly, her new husband died just six months later.

"When I heard the news, an image suddenly formed in my mind. I could see my father-in-law, her first husband, stepping out from a crowd that had gathered to welcome Mr. M into heaven. I watched as the two men embraced and my father-in-law thanked him for loving his wife so well, for taking such good care of her when he wasn't able to.

"I could see the relief on my mother-in-law's face when I told her about the experience. As it happens, she had felt guilty about remarrying, as though she were betraying her first husband's memory. Now she knew there was no longer any reason for her guilt."

The Fragrance of Heaven

Thanks be to God, who in Christ always leads us in triumphal
procession, and through us spreads in every place the fragrance
that comes from knowing him. For we are the aroma of Christ to
God among those who are being saved and among those who are
perishing; to the one a fragrance from death to death, to the other a
fragrance from life to life. 2 Corinthians 2:14–16 NRSV

What does heaven smell like? Paul's second letter to the Corinthians gives us an idea. Like everything about heaven, the
answer concerns Jesus. Heaven smells like Jesus. If we belong
to Christ, we should carry his fragrance everywhere.

Paul is talking about becoming so much like Christ that
people will see Jesus in us and become attracted to his kingdom by virtue of the way we live. But Paul also indicates that
not everyone will respond the same. The sweet smell of glory
will attract some and repel others. Those who turn their backs
on God will find it repugnant. And if we pursue God's virtue
in our human strength, the fragrance of heaven will come out
smelling like the stench of death. Nobody will be attracted to
God by perfectionism or legalism.

Our heavenly scent comes simply from knowing Christ.
The longer we have known and followed him, the sweeter our
spirits will become, marked by love, wisdom, mercy, kindness, joy, and truth.

Candy Land in the Sky

Eating too much honey can make you sick.   Proverbs 25:16 CEV

When I was a child I had a powerful sweet tooth. The moment I heard about heaven I imagined it as a mixture of *The Sugar Plum Tree,* with its storybook chocolate cats and lollipop sea, and the board game Candy Land. To me, heaven was an Oz-like place where vegetable gardens grew candy canes, and no child was ever forced to eat broccoli.

"Our Father, who art in heaven" became something like King Kandy, who presided over a promised land in the sky, a land of milk (chocolate) and honey.

I'm glad to say that my idea of heaven has matured since then. Heaven won't be a matter of fulfilling all my earthly appetites. It will be something better, far better, because it will be a place in which my appetite for joy will always be satisfied.

2 a.m.

I will fear no evil, for you are with me.   Psalm 23:4

"Yea, though I walk through the valley of the shadow of death, I will fear no evil for thou art with me."

The words lingered in her mind as Faye Field awoke from her dream. It was two o'clock in the morning. In her dream, Faye had been standing alone in a small auditorium. The words had been spoken from backstage. She recognized the voice, which belonged to her nephew, Samuel, who years ago had been one of her students.

Samuel had often stepped out from behind the curtains in stage plays she had directed. Of all the recitations she'd taught him, Psalm 23 had been one of his favorites. Now Samuel was a lonely, middle-aged man, suffering from a terminal illness. She was especially concerned for him because he seemed to have wandered away from God.

Faye had prayed many times for him and tonight was no different. After her dream, she fell asleep with a prayer on her lips: "God, please help Samuel not to be afraid. Let him know that broken people are near to your heart."

Early that morning she awoke to a ringing phone. It was her sister, who told her that Samuel had passed away.

"When?" Faye asked.

"Two o'clock this morning," came the reply.

Then she recalled the last words she'd heard her nephew say in her dream—*for thou art with me*. "I knew," she says, "that Samuel had found his way again."[87]

Visitation

Submit yourselves, then, to God. Resist the devil, and he will flee from you. James 4:7

Elliott was fifty-two and dying. A recovering alcoholic, he had come to know Christ more personally during his struggle.

One day, he confided to his nurse that he was having nighttime visitations. A horrible "creature," ugly and frightening, would lean up against him while he was lying in bed. He thought it was some kind of evil presence.

His nurse agreed that evil is real and told him how easy it is for people who are fatigued or ill to feel as though it might overcome them. Then she encouraged him to pray. He promised that's what he would do the next time the "creature" appeared.

A few nights later, the same thing happened. The creature entered his bedroom, walked over to his bed, and then leaned against him. Overcoming his fear, Elliott demanded, in Jesus' holy name, that it leave him alone. That was all it took, and he was never plagued by that evil visitor again.

When Elliott died, he did so in perfect peace.

If you think that you or someone you love is being harassed by the presence of evil, place your concern before God and ask for his help. Read Scripture passages about God's authority and power (Matthew 8:14–16; Matthew 10:8; Ephesians 1:18–22). Then pray in the name of Christ against any evil that threatens. No matter how powerful Satan may appear, God's power is greater still.[88]

Angel Food from Heaven

The next morning the area around the camp was wet with dew. When the dew evaporated, a flaky substance as fine as frost blanketed the ground. The Israelites were puzzled when they saw it. "What is it?" they asked each other. They had no idea what it was. And Moses told them, "It is the food the Lord has given you to eat." Exodus 16:13–15 NLT

[God] commanded the skies to open; he opened the doors of heaven. He rained down manna for them to eat; he gave them bread from heaven. They ate the food of angels! Psalm 78:23–25 NLT

Birthdays in Lisa's home always centered on cake. Her mother had two special recipes that had become family favorites. Both started with angel food cake and whipping cream. For one, she added a filling of chocolate pudding with chocolate whipped cream on top, and for the other, a filling made of crushed pineapple folded into vanilla pudding with plain whipped cream on top. Each birthday child got to pick his or her favorite.

Why is it called "angel food cake"? The first recipes for angel food cake date back to the late 1870s, because the light and fluffy cake reminded people of clouds in heaven. It seemed the perfect food for angels, just as the manna from heaven was the "food of angels."

A Song of Living

Give thanks to the LORD, for he is good;
his love endures forever.   Psalm 107:1

Because I have loved life, I shall have no sorrow to die.
I have sent up my gladness on wings, to be lost in the blue
of the sky.
I have run and leaped with the rain, I have taken the wind
to my breast.
My cheeks like a drowsy child to the face of the earth I have
pressed.
Because I have loved life, I shall have no sorrow to die.

I have kissed young love on the lips, I have heard his song
to the end,
I have struck my hand like a seal in the loyal hand of a friend.
I have known the peace of heaven, the comfort of work
done well.
I have longed for death in the darkness and risen alive out
of hell.
Because I have loved life, I shall have no sorrow to die.

I gave a share of my soul to the world, when and where my
course is run.
I know that another shall finish the task I surely must leave
undone.
I know that no flower, nor flint was in vain on the path I trod.
As one looks on a face through a window, through life I
have looked on God,
Because I have loved life, I shall have no sorrow to die.
—AMELIA BURR, AMERICAN POET

Don't Give Up

I have fought the good fight, I have finished the race, I have kept the faith. 2 Timothy 4:7 NIV

In the time it takes to read this devotion, 68 people will have died. On average 107 people die every minute, 6,000 die every hour, and about 150,000 die every day of the year. If you succeed in living to the age of seventy, nearly four billion people will have passed away during your lifetime. We all know the mortality rate for human beings is 100 percent. But why dwell on such depressing statistics? Because it's important both to face the facts and know the hope that heaven offers.

In his bestselling book about heaven, Randy Alcorn tells us why having a biblical perspective about heaven is important. He begins by citing the story of Florence Chadwick, a champion swimmer who was the first woman to swim the English Channel, but who failed in her quest to swim from Catalina Island to the California mainland. After Florence was pulled from the water exhausted, she realized she had been only a half mile from her goal when she gave up. "All I could see was the fog," she told reporters. "I think if I could have seen the shore, I would have made it."[9]

As people of faith, we, too, need to see the shore, to envision what awaits us in heaven when we've come to the end of our lives on earth. If we can see the shore, we won't give up.

The Devil You Say!

And he [the devil] spoke terrible words of blasphemy against God,
slandering his name and his dwelling—that is, those who dwell in
heaven.　Revelation 13:6 NLT

I bet the devil is upset about all the books people are reading about near-death experiences. Truth is, he doesn't like it
when we focus on heaven. Why not? Because he'd rather we
think only about this life, not the next. He wants our spiritual
imagination to remain stunted and small so that we develop an
earthly, rather than a heavenly, perspective. People who have
heaven in their sights are dangerous. They're not easy targets
for his lies. They don't believe, for instance, that trouble will
ever swallow them whole. They won't listen to doubts about
God's character that imply he's uncaring or cruel. Nor are
they seduced into thinking that life is all about pleasure and
comfort.

Focusing on heaven can remind us of a singular truth.
Though we don't know every single page of the story God
is writing with our lives, we already know the ending. Our
story will end happily not because we so desperately want it to
but because it's part of God's great story. In God's story, Jesus
has become the protagonist, the hero who saves, loves, and
forgives us. He's the one who was nailed to a cross in order to
rescue us. Having made such a costly investment, why would
he ever give us up?

Remember that, the next time Satan tries to tell you there's
no such place as heaven and even if there is you're not going
there. If your life belongs to Christ, you will one day be with
him in paradise.

The Light of Heaven

This is the message we heard from Jesus and now declare to you:
God is light, and there is no darkness in him at all.   1 John 1:5 NLT

Sixty-mile-per-hour winds shook trees and rattled windows. Tornadoes sprang up as warm air collided with a cold front barreling in from the north. The storms knocked out electrical power and left my home in total darkness, along with thousands of other area residents.

Suddenly, I realized how dark total darkness is. Even the small light from my phone charger and the digits on my clock radio had gone dark. My bedroom was wrapped in impenetrable shadows. I grabbed for the small flashlight in a drawer next to the bed and then found matches with which to light a few candles, enough to find my way around.

Most of us experience only infrequent blackouts. But my experience that morning reminded me that in God's heaven there is no darkness at all, ever. No spiritual darkness, no physical darkness.

I was relieved when the lights finally came on as the power was restored. Today let's rejoice that God himself is not only full of light. He is the light. That's why in heaven there will be no darkness at all.

Blue-Ribbon Citizens

> *"The Lord does not see as man sees; for man looks at the outward*
> *appearance, but the Lord looks at the heart."*   1 Samuel 16:7 NKJV

In his book *Born After Midnight,* A. W. Tozer expressed his opinion of clueless people who believe that basic good citizenship guarantees them a place in a star-spangled heaven: "The man who knows himself least," he says, "is likely to have a cheerful if groundless confidence in his own moral worth. Such a man has less trouble believing that he will inherit an eternity of bliss because his concepts are only quasi-Christian, being influenced strongly by chimney-corner scripture and old wives' tales. He thinks of heaven as being very much like California without the heat and smog, and himself as inhabiting a splendiferous palace with all modern conveniences, and wearing a heavily bejeweled crown. Throw in a few angels and you have the vulgar picture of the future life held by the devotees of popular Christianity."[90]

Tozer believed that since the human heart is "deceitful above all things, and desperately wicked" (Jeremiah 17:9 NKJV), we should reasonably conclude that we are bound for hell and not heaven. Fortunately, if we have trusted Christ to save us, that reasonable conclusion has been overturned, which is what makes the good news so good.

The Painting

*Here I am! I stand at the door and knock. If anyone hears my voice
and opens the door, I will come in and eat with that person, and
they with me. Revelation 3:20*

Trudy Harris tells the story of a dying man who wasn't sure why
smart people would believe in a God they couldn't see. One night
Johnny asked if she would mind taking him to the screened-in
porch of his nursing home so he could have a smoke. As he sat in
his wheelchair, he pointed to a wall on which hung a famous picture of Jesus knocking on a door. "What's that about?" he asked.

Trudy explained that it symbolized Jesus knocking on the
door of a person's heart.

"Why doesn't the door have a nob on it?"

Trudy explained that God would never force himself on anyone. "He wants you to open it from your side and invite Him in,"
she explained. "The door has to be opened from the inside, by
you. He only wants to come into your heart and make Himself
known to you and take you to heaven with Him."[91]

They talked about God for a little while longer and then
she wheeled him to his room and tucked him into bed. Johnny
died peacefully the next morning.

Later that day, Trudy passed through the porch where she
and Johnny had been sitting the previous night. Oddly, she
couldn't spot the painting. When she asked a nurse about it,
she was told there never had been a picture of Jesus on that
wall. Carefully examining the wall where the painting had
hung, she could find no evidence of nails or fading. Yet it
was the only porch in the nursing home.

Though Trudy doesn't know how that picture appeared on
the wall of the porch, she does know that a dying man needed
to hear about God's love before he would be ready to pass
on to the next life.

Better Things to Come

I consider that the sufferings of this present time are not worth comparing with the glory that is to be revealed to us.   Romans 8:18 RSV

After another week of bombings, deaths, deprivations, and a flare-up of a chronic illness, Canon Andrew White, the "Vicar of Baghdad," noted in a blog entry: "My present suffering does not compare with the glory that is to come. The suffering is so *real;* it is not a theoretical suffering for Christ. Our loved ones are murdered and tortured, our nation is broken and in total despair and then one's body breaks down. In all of this our Lord is always near because he who has called us will never fail us."[92]

Iraqi Christians understand what it means to suffer for Jesus. Daily, even hourly, they suffer, sustained by their hope of heaven. Let us pray that they and other persecuted Christians will experience the truth of God's promises in the midst of their challenges: "When you go through deep waters, I will be with you. When you go through rivers of difficulty, you will not drown. When you walk through the fire of oppression, you will not be burned up; the flames will not consume you" (Isaiah 43:2 NLT).

That's a promise. Let's stand with them today in prayer, asking God to manifest his presence in their midst, increasing their hope and strengthening their faith.

Goodbye Nightmares

Instead of shame and dishonor, you will enjoy a double share of honor. You will possess a double portion of prosperity in your land, and everlasting joy will be yours. Isaiah 61:7 NLT

God's people were living a nightmare. They were scattered and broken, their land overrun. Their homes had been ransacked and their capital city burned. And many of them had been led into exile.

Into the midst of this darkness, God spoke through Isaiah, making a promise that must have cheered a desolate nation. Life, he said, won't always be this difficult. Instead of feeling ashamed and depressed, you will be happy again. In fact, you will be twice as prosperous as you were before. Instead of your shame, I will give you a double portion of honor so that nobody will look down on you. Not only that, I will give you everlasting joy.

Sometimes we feel as though we are mired in our own personal nightmare. Life has not turned out as we had hoped. We've lost a job, a marriage, our health. A thousand troubles assail us and we wonder if we will ever be happy again.

If that describes you, even a little bit, take heart today by reading the message God gave Isaiah, because it is a message to you as well. Someday soon, whether on this side of life or the next, the Lord will reverse your fortunes and you will know the meaning of everlasting joy.

I'll Be There

And I saw a great white throne and the one sitting on it. . . . I saw
the dead, both great and small, standing before God's throne. And
the books were opened, including the Book of Life. And the dead
were judged according to what they had done, as recorded in the
books.   Revelation 20:11–12 NLT

The inspiration for James Milton Black's 1893 hymn, "When
the Roll Is Called Up Yonder," came when one of his Sunday
school pupils fell ill with pneumonia. After noting her absence
at the roll call, he decided to visit her at home. Ten days later,
she was dead. The girl's death gives special poignancy to the
lyrics:

> *When the trumpet of the Lord shall sound, and time shall*
> *be no more,*
> *And the morning breaks, eternal, bright and fair;*
> *When the saved of earth shall gather over on the other shore,*
> *And the roll is called up yonder, I'll be there.*
>
> *When the roll is called up yonder,*
> *When the roll is called up yonder, I'll be there.*
>
> *On that bright and cloudless morning when the dead in*
> *Christ shall rise,*
> *And the glory of His resurrection share;*
> *When His chosen ones shall gather to their home beyond*
> *the skies,*
> *And the roll is called up yonder, I'll be there.*

Waiting Patiently

But you must not forget this one thing, dear friends: A day is like a thousand years to the Lord, and a thousand years is like a day. The Lord isn't really being slow about his promise, as some people think. No, he is being patient for your sake. He does not want anyone to be destroyed, but wants everyone to repent. 2 Peter 3:8–9 NLT

Have you ever noticed how stretchy time can be? When I was in elementary school, the time between the last day of school to my midsummer birthday seemed to stretch on endlessly. I couldn't wait for the day to arrive. These days, I would love to slow things down a bit as the birthdays keep zooming by.

Though time seems to warp a bit for us, we always experience it linearly. First one thing happens, then another, and so on. We can neither move forward nor backward in time. But God is not subject to time as we are because he exists in eternity. Want to know what will happen the day after tomorrow? No problem. God has already seen it. Want to look back on the world's beginning? He can see it right now. All times and all seasons are present to him always. He never has to wonder what will happen or untangle what just happened. He simply knows it. And he knows something else—exactly who will be in heaven when the time comes to establish the new heaven and the new earth.

Fortunately, God is patient. He plans to bring as many people as possible into heaven before the world as we know it ends. He's waiting for us and for countless others to enter into the joy that will go on forever.

Imagining Heaven

I saw heaven opened. Revelation 19:11 KJV

One reason heaven sometimes sounds boring is that we lack imagination. Randy Alcorn says that "the best of life on Earth is a glimpse of Heaven; the worst of life is a glimpse of Hell."[93] Randy capitalizes words like "Earth" and "Hell," because he says they are real places, just like Buenos Aires and Liverpool.

So perhaps there are ways to fill in our picture of heaven. In addition to reading what the Bible says about heaven, we can ask God to help us imagine it. Here are some things that come readily to my mind.

In heaven, you will never suffer a single misunderstanding. No one will annoy, cheat, embarrass, or abandon you. There will be no hypocrites because no one will have anything to hide. In heaven dictionaries might be rather small because words like "racism," "poverty," "worry," or "anguish" will cease to exist. Of course medical dictionaries will be unknown because no one will ever get sick or hurt. In heaven there will be no shame.

Whatever is hateful or fearful or hurtful simply will not exist. But what about the positives? In heaven you will love every single person you meet. You will always feel healthy and rested. You will never sin, and you will have perfect clarity about anything you need to know. Neither will you doubt God or his love because you will see him face-to-face. In heaven, as Julian of Norwich so famously said, "All shall be well, and all shall be well and all manner of thing shall be well."

"I'm Ready"

"For I myself am a man under authority, with soldiers under me." Luke 7:8

Alex had spent his career in the navy. His father and grandfather had both been navy men and so were his sons. Now, at the age of sixty-six he was dying of lung cancer.

Each day brought with it additional challenges, which he managed to meet with strength and grace. Eating, bathing, walking—the simplest tasks became difficult, even with help. It wasn't long before Alex began talking about going to heaven. "It will be time to meet my Commander soon," he would say.

One morning, at three o'clock, he told his wife and sons he needed to get cleaned up. Insisting that he couldn't wait until later that day, he convinced his sons to help him shower, shave, and dress up in his navy blues. When Alex emerged from the bathroom, he was beaming. Propped up with pillows that helped him sit straight up in his king-sized bed, he told them, "I am ready to meet my Commander now, whenever He is ready for me."

Alex died a few hours later surrounded by friends and family who were certain he had passed into the presence of the Lord he had loved and worshipped.

Trudy Harris likens Alex to the centurion who asked Jesus to come and heal his servant. While Jesus was still on his way, the man sent a servant to tell Jesus he needn't bother coming all the way to his house. The centurion knew Christ had the power to answer his request from afar. "But say the word," he said, "and my servant will be healed. For I myself am a man under authority, with soldiers under me. I tell this one, 'Go,' and he goes; and that one, 'Come,' and he comes. I say to my servant, 'Do this,' and he does it" (Luke 7:7–8).

Like a good soldier, Alex believed in the faithfulness and power of God, the Commander he loved.[94]

Discouraged?

Stand firm then, with the belt of truth buckled around your
waist.   Ephesians 6:14

Someone once said that discouragement is never from God.
So what should we do when we feel down? First, we should
stop listening to lies from the enemy, especially untruths
about God, ourselves, and others. The ones about God always
impugn his character with the objective of planting doubt in
our minds. The ones about us are often designed to shame,
flatter, or frighten us. The ones about others are meant to
make us fearful or angry.

Of course, lies become more believable the more they
rumble around in our minds, repeating themselves ad nau-
seam. Voicing them to people we trust can also be helpful
because they may be able to provide perspective and remind
us of the truth. Another way to combat deceptions is to do so
proactively. We do this by nourishing our relationship with
God and by arming ourselves with the truth, reading the
Bible regularly and putting ourselves on a steady diet of great
preaching and teaching. If we take every opportunity to fill
ourselves with God and his truth, we will be well armed when
the devil comes whispering.

Banking on Heaven

*"But store up for yourselves treasures in heaven, where moths
and vermin do not destroy, and where thieves do not break in and
steal." Matthew 6:20*

In the early part of the eighteenth century, a young man by the
name of Jonathan Edwards wrote a series of seventy life reso-
lutions, one of which said: "Resolved, to endeavor to obtain
for myself (as much happiness, in the other world,) as I possibly can, with all the power, might, vigor, and vehemence, yea
violence, I am capable of, or can bring myself to exert, in any
way that can be thought of."[95]

Edwards, who would later become one of America's most
famous preachers, was remarkable not for his determination
to become as happy as possible—we all want that—but for his
insight on how to obtain and amass happiness.

Any investor knows the power of delayed gratification—
you delay your desire for what you want today so that you can
avoid debt and save money. The ability to delay gratification is
a mark of maturity that can lead to financial success.

In spiritual terms, delaying gratification means responding to God by conforming your life to his, even and especially
when you are tempted to embrace a worldly lifestyle that
promises happiness now.

Like us, Edwards was hardwired for happiness. He knew
that happiness comes not from amassing the most toys on
earth, but from dedicating your whole being, your talent,
time, and treasure to God. That's a recipe for happiness, not
just in heaven, but here on earth as well.

Aim High

"Set your hearts on things above, where Christ is, seated at the right hand of God. Colossians 3:1

Last night I had to pick my daughter up at a youth group activity. So I hopped in the car and entered the address in my GPS and away I went—only to arrive at the wrong destination. Sometimes GPS systems are like that; they steer you wrong.

When it comes to heaven, many of us are operating with a faulty GPS. Paul tells the Colossians to "set your hearts on things above, where Christ is, seated at the right hand of God." Paul's not urging his listeners simply to think lofty thoughts. No, he's telling them to make heaven their aim, because that's where Christ is.

Randy Alcorn points out that the Greek word translated "set your hearts on" is the same word used in the parable of the woman who searches for a lost coin and the merchant who searches for fine pearls. They have set their hearts on and won't be satisfied until they find the priceless treasure they are seeking.

But why does Paul phrase it as a command? As Alcorn points out, commands are only necessary when there is some kind of resistance that needs to be overcome. Nobody has to tell us, for instance, to avoid jumping off buildings, because most of us have no desire to annihilate ourselves. Paul makes it a command because he knows there will be resistance. In our case, the resistance comes from inside ourselves as well as from the pleasure-seeking culture we live in.[96]

If you are serious about heaven, ask God today for the grace to aim high and aim right—and he will help you set your heart on heaven.

The Gate Was Closed

*"Everyone who calls on the name of the Lord will be
saved." Romans 10:13*

"I had a nightmare last night," Mr. Winters confided to his
nurse, Cookie Schnier. "I dreamed I was in a place that had
two tall iron fences, one in front of the other. Through the
fences, I could clearly see many people on the other side that I
knew had already died." No one spoke to him as he opened the
first gate, which quickly snapped shut behind him. Trapped in
the space between the first and second gate, he kept pleading
for help but to no avail. Suddenly, a man appeared and told
him point-blank: "You need to do your paperwork first."

The dream repeated itself night after night. "Do you think
it means anything?" he asked Cookie.

She told him it seemed like a warning that his time on
earth was nearing its end but that he had work to do before
he was ready to meet God. "You need to get busy and make
certain that everything is right between you and others and
with your Creator.... Whatever is not resolved between you
and your family or friends and whatever is not settled between
you and God, work on that now." Then she assured him that
he had only to ask for God's help in order to receive it.

One morning as Cookie was making her rounds, she
peeked into his room. When Mr. Winters caught sight of her,
he smiled and said, "Last night, the man came to me in my
dream again. He said to me, 'Your paperwork is now finished,
there is nothing left to be done.' "[97]

The night before he was to be released, Mr. Winters died
peacefully in his sleep. Cookie felt confident that this time
he was welcomed home, not with closed gates but with open
arms.

Heaven's Floodgates

Test me in this," says the LORD Almighty, "and see if I will not throw open the floodgates of heaven and pour out so much blessing that there will not be room enough to store it." Malachi 3:10 NIV

The road near Sarah's house winds its way along the banks of a river. Most of the time the river flows gently, contained within its natural boundaries. Thanks to a series of dams, the water level is constant, making the river a lovely place to play. In summer, speedboats, Jet Skis, canoes, and kayaks skim the calm water. In spring and fall, fishermen wade in the placid waters to catch fish.

Only after unusually high spring rains does this river overflow its natural boundaries and threaten the property of homeowners living along the riverbanks. During times of extreme high water levels, county maintenance workers open the floodgates of the dams. The spectacular overflow of water at the dam draws area residents to watch in awe as water cascades over the dam and roars into the river below. The floodgates, open to their fullest, pour out millions of gallons of water without restraint.

Scripture tells us that God opens the floodgates of heaven to pour down blessings upon his people. Ask God today to open your eyes to the blessings you take for granted—the ones he is showering you with right now.

What If We've Got It All Wrong?

If only for this life we have hope in Christ, we are of all people most to be pitied.   1 Corinthians 15:19 NIV

First-century Christians did not have the benefit of leaning into the experience of faithful believers who had gone before them. The New Testament was still being written, and as time went on, fewer and fewer eyewitnesses to the life and ministry of Jesus remained. Yet men and women continued to stake their lives on the truth that Jesus came to open the gates of heaven.

Today, we have the New Testament in countless translations. We have masterpieces such as Milton's *Paradise Lost*, Bach's Mass in B Minor, Michelangelo's *Pietà*, and da Vinci's *The Last Supper*. We have the works of church fathers, reformers, and scholars, artists, musicians, preachers, and miscellaneous saints. And we have the examples of those who have died for their faith.

How could it be that, despite the overwhelming weight of such evidence, some people still consider faith illusory? Could the millions of believers who've gone before us all be wrong? Was their witness worthless? To Harry Blamires, an English professor and student of C. S. Lewis, "The thought that all these [earlier believers] should have been acting under an unspeakably erroneous delusion seems to be staggeringly incredible."[98]

"Incredible." That means "beyond belief." Indeed.

Billboards on the Highway to Heaven

As you go, proclaim this message: "The kingdom of heaven has come near." Matthew 10:7 NIV

All along the way to heaven, the route is lined with signboards on which are posted succinct statements of truth that can help the heaven-bound traveler. Here are a few:

Humble we must be, if to heaven we go; high is the roof there, but the gate is low. —ROBERT HERRICK[99]

Aim at heaven and you will get earth thrown in. Aim at earth and you get neither. —C. S. LEWIS[100]

God's in His heaven—all's right with the world! —ROBERT BROWNING[101]

When you speak of heaven let your face light up. . . . When you speak of hell—well, then your everyday face will do. —CHARLES SPURGEON[102]

We talk about heaven being so far away. It is within speaking distance to those who belong there. —D. L. MOODY[103]

Every path that leads to heaven is trodden by willing feet. No one is ever driven to paradise. —HOWARD CROSBY[104]

Each generation posts a few more signs. Let's pay attention to them and keep our eye on the road.

The Unseen World

For He will command his angels concerning you
To guard you in all your ways.   Psalms 91:11

S. Ralph Harlow, a professor at Smith College, possessed degrees from Harvard, Columbia, and Hartford Theological Seminary. By his own account, he was a scholar who shunned guesswork and admired scientific principles of investigation. But one spring day he and his wife experienced something science could not explain.

As he and Marion were walking in the woods near Ballardvale, Massachusetts, they heard voices behind them. Looking around they saw nothing. Suddenly they realized that the voices were no longer behind but above them.

Harlow felt a surge of exaltation as he looked up. "There were six of them," he explains, "young beautiful women dressed in flowing white garments and engaged in earnest conversation. If they were aware of our existence they gave no indication of it."

Neither he nor his wife understood a word of what was said. But they continued to watch as the group passed overhead and then finally out of sight.

Harlow later said, "I have related this story with the same faithfulness and respect for truth and accuracy as I would tell it on the witness stand. But even as I record it, I know how incredible it sounds."[105]

The experience made a profound impact, helping him to realize that heavenly beings are all around us. Quoting the Episcopal clergyman Phillips Brooks, he said, "This is what you are to hold fast to yourself—the *sympathy and companionship of the unseen worlds*. No doubt it is best for us now that they should be unseen. It cultivates that higher perception that we call 'faith.' But who can say that the time will not come when, even to those who live here upon earth, the unseen worlds shall no longer be unseen."

Banqueting Table

Let us be glad and rejoice and give Him glory, for the marriage
of the Lamb has come, and His wife has made herself ready. . . .
Then he said to me, "Write: 'Blessed are those who are called to the
marriage supper of the Lamb!' " Revelation 19:7, 9 NKJV

Who but an undernourished movie star or an extreme exercise addict wouldn't get excited about a good feast? In heaven we will have the pleasure of eating the best food we have ever tasted in the company of the best people we have ever known. We will all be participating in the greatest of all celebrations, which the Bible calls the Marriage Feast of the Lamb.

What Scripture is talking about will happen when the earth as we know it ends and all who belong to Christ are called into God's presence. At that time we will be perfectly united.

Until that day, let's allow the pleasure of eating here on earth to remind us of the far greater pleasure of sitting down with God in heaven to enjoy a great festive meal. What's your favorite food? Savor it. Share it with friends. Take delight in it, and then thank God that the best is yet to come.

Crossing the Thin Partition

We will all be changed, in a moment, in the twinkling of an eye.
1 Corinthians 15:51 NRSV

In 1884, Charles Spurgeon preached a sermon titled "A Heavenly Pattern for Our Earthly Life." Here's what he said: "Between Earth and Heaven there is but a thin partition. The home country is much nearer than we think. Heaven is by no means the far country, for it is the Father's house. Heaven is . . . so near that in a moment we can speak with him that is King of the place, and he will answer to our call. Before the clock shall tick again you and I may be there. Can that be a far-off country which we can reach so soon? . . . We are within hearing of the shining ones; we are nearly home. A little while and we shall see our Lord. Perhaps another day's march will bring us within the city gate. And even if another fifty years of life on Earth should remain, what is it but the twinkling of an eye?"[106]

From our limited perspective, the distance between earth and heaven seems vast and unbridgeable. Yet the travel time is less than the time it takes to draw a single breath. It has never been far away and it never will be.

Visions of God

On July 31 of my thirtieth year, while I was with the Judean exiles beside the Kebar River in Babylon, the heavens were opened and I saw visions of God. All around him was a glowing halo, like a rainbow shining in the clouds on a rainy day. This is what the glory of the Lord looked like to me.   Ezekiel 1:1, 28 NLT

"What does God look like?" Most children ask the question at some time in their young lives. As we get older, perhaps wiser, we don't ask it as openly and boldly as we did when we were young, but still we wonder.

As if to emphasize the fact that it really happened, the prophet Ezekiel mentions both his location and his age when he saw the heavens open, and before his eyes the glory of God glowing like a rainbow. Though there are many strange things in Ezekiel's vision, all of us can relate to a rainbow: colors vivid as an untouched paint box, the sparkles and prisms of raindrops, the graceful, expansive bow filling the sky.

Ezekiel's vision of God in heaven is awesome. Strange as some of it may sound, we can be grateful that there is at least one familiar image, that of a rainbow, which speaks not only of God's glory but also of his mercy and our hope. But then again, God's mercy is also part of his glory.

On Earth as It Is in Heaven

"Look! God's dwelling place is now among the people, and he will dwell with them" They will be his people, and God himself will be with them and be their God. Revelation 21:3

I remember traveling to Germany just months before the Berlin Wall came crashing down. Constructed in 1961, the wall was a fixture of the Cold War. At that time, people could hardly conceive of a Germany that was not divided into east and west. Then, in 1987 during a speech at the Brandenburg Gate in West Berlin, Ronald Reagan issued a challenge to Mikhail Gorbachev, the general secretary of the Communist Party of the Soviet Union. "Mr. Gorbachev, tear down this wall!"

Reagan went on to say, "I noticed words crudely spray-painted upon the wall, perhaps by a young Berliner, 'This wall will fall. Beliefs become reality.' Yes, across Europe, this wall will fall. For it cannot withstand faith; it cannot withstand truth. The wall cannot withstand freedom."[107] Two years later the wall was torn down and East and West Germany were reunited. The unthinkable had happened.

Someday God is going to do the unthinkable and tear down what seems like an impenetrable wall between heaven and earth. Right now, heaven and earth exist in different spheres, but one day they will be joined together. As Randy Alcorn explains, "Their present incompatibility is due to a temporary aberration—Earth is under sin and the Curse. Once that aberration is corrected, Heaven and Earth will be fully compatible again."[108]

And so we pray for God's kingdom to come and his will to be done, for God to dwell on earth just as he dwells in heaven. Dear God, please tear down this wall!

Are You Afraid?

"Everything is possible for one who believes."
Immediately the boy's father exclaimed, "I do believe; help me
overcome my unbelief!" Mark 9:23–24

Is it wrong to be afraid to die? That's a question you might wonder about, especially after reading the stories of so many who were given the gift of peace at the end of their lives.

I love the story of the father in Scripture who brings his son to Jesus to be healed. The boy has been tormented since childhood, and the father longs to see his son set free. When Jesus challenges the father, asking him if he believes, he responds truthfully: "I do believe; help me to overcome my unbelief." This father acknowledges that though he has faith, he doesn't have as much as he needs. Then Jesus heals his boy.

Likewise, we may possess a mixture of faith that is tinged by doubt.

Here's something else to think about. If it was wrong to experience fear at the prospect of your own death, why would Jesus have been in anguish just prior to his? Matthew's gospel says that "he fell with his face to the ground and prayed, 'My Father, if it is possible, may this cup be taken from me. Yet not as I will, but as you will' " (Matthew 26:39). Clearly, Jesus was afraid of what he would have to suffer. Stronger than his fear, though, was his desire to do what God wanted. As the gospel says, the Father heard his prayers and sent an angel to strengthen him (Luke 22:43).

If you feel afraid when the time comes to face your own death, pray as Jesus did, asking your heavenly Father to strengthen you. And he will.

He Needed Permission

He gives strength to the weary
and increases the power of the weak. Isaiah 40:29

Ten-year-old Luke was dying of leukemia. But he didn't feel ready to let go. Ever since his father and brother had gone to prison, he had done his best to become the man of the house. His mother was isolated and alone.

Whenever Jackie Aquino, Luke's nurse, came to visit, she couldn't help noticing the lack of a phone, furniture, and food in the refrigerator. Though she would frequently drop off groceries, Luke would respond by saying, "That's all right, we have plenty of food, thank you." She knew he was trying to protect his mother from the judgment of others.

One day Luke confided in Jackie, telling her that Jesus would sometimes visit him, inviting him to come with him. But each time he would tell Jesus, "I can't go yet, not yet."

As the boy grew worse, he could be overheard saying, "Oh God, I can't go now, I can't go now."

Jackie explained to Luke's mother that her son needed permission to die. Could she find the strength to reassure him she would be all right?

Frightened to let go of the son she loved, she struggled. But that night she called Jackie to tell her she'd found the strength to tell her son that she would be fine and that he should take Jesus up on his invitation the next time he came.

A few days later, Luke turned to her and said, "Mommy, I see Jesus now and I want to go with Him."[109] Then he closed his eyes and died.

Years later, Jackie heard from Luke's mother again. She had returned to school to finish her GED and then gone on to graduate from college. She felt happy and settled. God had taken care of her, enabling her to let go just when she needed to.

Blotted Out

*The Lord said to Moses, "Whoever has sinned against Me, I will
blot him out of My book." Exodus 32:33 NASB*

This passage seems to infer that everyone has their name
inscribed in God's book of life. If your name is in that book,
you're going to end up in heaven. There's only one problem.
And it's the usual suspect. Sin is like a great big ink blot that
covers over the names of those who depart from God.

The New Testament backs this up, saying that "nothing
dirty or defiled will get into the City [the New Jerusalem],
and no one who defiles or deceives. Only those whose names
are written in the Lamb's Book of Life will get in" (Revelation
21:27).

Since no human being is perfect except Jesus and since
every one of us has sinned, does that mean that every page
of the book of life is covered with billions of dark ink blots,
obscuring every name but his? No, and here's why: Jesus gave
his life in order to deliver us from sin. He erases its stain. Now,
when God looks at us, he sees Jesus, someone who is perfectly
clean and sinless. If we surrender our lives to Christ, one day
God will look into his book and see our names. Now that is
really something to celebrate.

Mercy, Always

"And who is my neighbor?"

". . . Which of these three do you think was a neighbor to the man who fell into the hands of robbers?"

". . . The one who had mercy on him."

Jesus told him, "Go and do likewise."   Luke 10:29, 36–37 NIV

One day, Jesus encountered a lawyer (an expert in the Mosaic Law) who tried to test him by asking how he could inherit eternal life. Instead of answering, Jesus simply asked him what Moses taught on the subject. When the man gave the standard response about loving God first and loving your neighbor as yourself, Jesus nodded as if to say, "Yes, that is correct; so why did you ask?"

Trying to justify himself, the lawyer posed another question: "Who is my neighbor?" That's when Jesus told the story about the merciful Samaritan who was not deterred by protocol when he found a fellow traveler who had been beaten and robbed on the road. The Samaritan, as we know, was the only person who showed compassion and mercy to the injured man. The story is striking because back then Jews looked down on Samaritans. And yet it was he and not the holy people—the priest and the Levite who ignored the man—who helped.

So Jesus is saying that our neighbors are everyone and anyone. They are those who happen to cross our paths at any given moment. To inherit eternal life, then, we need to show active compassion to whoever is "on our screen" today. Think how heavenly life would be if everyone on earth would pay heed to Jesus' words.

Are There Rewards in Heaven?

If the work survives the fire, that builder will receive a
reward. 1 Corinthians 3:14

Scripture makes it clear that none of us will make it into
heaven on the strength of our good deeds. We "make" it to
heaven only because Jesus has made it possible for us to be forgiven so that our relationship with God can be restored.

But the Bible also makes it clear that good deeds do count
and that they will affect the kind of reward we receive in
heaven. Listen to what Paul tells the Corinthians: *"For no one
can lay any other foundation than the one we already have—Jesus
Christ. Now anyone who builds on that foundation may use gold, silver, jewels, wood, hay, or straw. But there is going to come a time of
testing at the judgment day to see what kind of work each builder has
done. Everyone's work will be put through the fire to see whether or not
it keeps its value. If the work survives the fire, that builder will receive
a reward. But if the work is burned up, the builder will suffer great
loss. The builders themselves will be saved, but like someone escaping
through a wall of flames"* (1 Corinthians 3:11–15).

Whether you know it or not, you're a builder. If you are a
follower of Christ you are called to build on the foundation
he has already laid through what he has done. We build up his
kingdom whenever we respond in love to what he asks of us,
whether that means heading a multinational corporation or a
mission organization, or changing a diaper. Because of God's
power at work within us, we have the chance to impact the
world forever.

Do People in Heaven Know What's Happening on Earth?

> *Therefore, since we are surrounded by such a great cloud of witnesses, let us throw off everything that hinders and the sin that so easily entangles. And let us run with perseverance the race marked out for us, fixing our eyes on Jesus, the pioneer and perfecter of faith.* Hebrews 12:1–2

The writer of Hebrews uses the imagery of an athletic contest to describe life on earth. In the Greco-Roman world, an athletic contest would often be staged in front of an eager audience seated high in a stadium.

Similarly, the Bible tells us that we are surrounded by a great cloud of witnesses, by people who are no longer living on earth but with God in heaven. This passage and others would seem to indicate that they have at least some awareness of what is happening on earth and that they are invested in the outcome.

Notice how Scripture encourages us to run the race by "fixing our eyes on Jesus." We're not to look at our feet, fixate on the other runners, or focus on the crowd, except to realize they are cheering us on. If we keep our eyes on the goal—on Jesus—we'll run without stumbling, winning the race that God has marked out for us.

"My Mother Was Here in This Room"

There is a time for everything,
and a season for every activity under the heavens:
a time to be born and a time to die. . . .   *Ecclesiastes 3:1–2 NIV*

Tom Huston's wife, Ede, left him for a short while to run errands. When she returned home, she was surprised to see that her terminally ill husband was crying. Sitting up in bed, he told her what had just happened. "While you were gone, my mother came to visit me. My mother was here in this room, she sat there on the cedar chest at the foot of my bed. She looked really pretty, just like she used to. She held out her hand to me and smiled. She said, 'Come on home with me, Tom, it's all right.'"

When Ede inquired about whether he'd been afraid, he said, "No, it was actually kind of nice, it was pretty much okay."[110] After that, Tom seemed peaceful, happy to think that when the time came for him to die, his mother would be waiting for him.

Do loved ones ever visit us after they've passed away? My own mother died a few months ago, after a lingering illness. Weeks before her death, she spoke about her father, indicating that she had seen him earlier that day. Just the thought of him brought her peace.

Though Scripture forbids any attempt on our part to contact the dead, it may be that God sometimes gives those who are near death an experience like the one Tom and my mother had to help them pass peacefully from earth to heaven.

Transformation

But let me reveal to you a wonderful secret. We will not all die, but we will all be transformed. 1 Corinthians 15:51 NLT

As early as the fourth century, Alexander the Great was searching the Far East for a source of water that could preserve youth. Much later, in 1513, Ponce de León declared he had found the Fountain of Youth in Florida. Though Florida is great, you can tell by all the elderly people who live there that no one has found that fountain yet.

But what if the search for water that will produce eternal youth is more than a crazy pipe dream? What if it's based on some kind of inkling that God has planted in human hearts because he intends to fulfill our dreams? Didn't Jesus say, "He who believes in Me, as the Scripture said, 'From his innermost being will flow rivers of living water'" (John 7:38 NASB)?

Jesus offered the "living water" of the Holy Spirit who dwells within those who belong to him. Because we have God's Spirit within us, we will be transformed from death to life. When the resurrection comes and we receive the new bodies Christ has promised, we will enjoy eternal youth.

Describing Heaven

Then the angel showed me the river of the water of life, as clear as crystal, flowing from the throne of God and of the Lamb down the middle of the great street of the city.   Revelation 22:1–2

Asking the question "What is heaven like?" is similar to asking, "What is the ocean like?" When you're standing in a tide pool with warm salt water lapping at your toes, the ocean is a kiddy pool. When you're on a fishing boat searching for king crab in the Bering Sea, the ocean is an icebox. When you're watching waves whipped to a fury in a vicious nor'easter, the ocean becomes a dangerous monster. When you're on a Caribbean cruise watching the sun set over calm turquoise waters, it looks like the world's largest bathtub. Just as there are different ways to describe the ocean, there are different ways to describe heaven.

The writer of Hebrews calls heaven a country with a city (see Hebrews 11:16). The psalmist mentions the heavens as God's throne and his dwelling place (See Psalm 11:4; 33:14).

Heaven is vaster, more beautiful, and more varied than we can ever imagine.

Positively Beatific

Because I am righteous, I will see you. When I awake, I will see you face to face and be satisfied.   Psalm 17:15 NLT

In traditional church language, the term "beatific vision" means seeing (knowing with your whole being) the actual presence of God, especially in the context of heaven. Although the Bible teaches that God "lives in light so brilliant that no human can approach him. No human eye has ever seen him, nor ever will" (1 Timothy 6:16 NLT), it also teaches that many people will someday see him face-to-face: "Blessed are the pure in heart, for they shall see God" (Matthew 5:8 RSV); "Now we see in a mirror dimly, but then face to face" (1 Corinthians 13:12 KJV).

In the meantime, some of us may very occasionally enjoy a brief glimpse of the beatific vision, usually during prayer or corporate worship or in the presence of overwhelming beauty. Such tastes of God whet our appetites for more, and even the absence of such tastes increases our hunger for a firsthand experience of God's overwhelming love and goodness.

Imagine not only seeing with unimpeded eyes the Lord you love, but also feeling perfect happiness within every cell of your body. Even if your imagination is not up to the task because your everyday experience seems so colorless, allow a smile of gratitude and anticipation to spread across your face.

You have something to look forward to.

A Glimpse of Heaven

Precious in the sight of the LORD
is the death of his faithful servants.   Psalm 116:15

Corrie ten Boom and her family were arrested during World War II for sheltering Jews from the Nazis. Though she survived the death camps, her beloved sister Betsie died at Ravensbrück in 1944. Here's how Corrie describes what she saw as she peered through the hospital window hoping to catch a glimpse of Betsie alive and well. She was looking at a bed with two nurses standing nearby.

"I gazed curiously," Corrie says, "at what lay on it. It was a carving in old yellow ivory. There was no clothing on the figure; I could see each ivory rib, and the outline of the teeth through the parchment cheeks.

"It took me a moment to realize it was Betsie.

"The nurses had each seized two corners of the sheet. They lifted it between them and carried the bundle from the room before my heart had started to beat again in my chest."

Running to the back of the building, Corrie approached the entrance of the latrine, where a makeshift morgue had been set up. What Corrie saw stunned her. "For there lay Betsie, her eyes closed as if in sleep, her face full and young. The care lines, the grief lines, the deep hollows of hunger and disease were simply gone. In front of me was the Betsie of Haarlem, happy and at peace. Stronger! Freer! This was the Betsie of heaven, bursting with joy and health. Even her hair was graciously in place as if an angel had ministered to her."[111]

Amid the horror and suffering of a Nazi death camp, Corrie ten Boom had been given a priceless gift, an unmistakable sign that God was near and that heaven is real.

Praying It Forward

*Whenever you pray, go into your room and shut the door and pray
to your Father who is in secret; and your Father who sees in secret
will reward you. . . .*

> *Pray then in this way: Our Father in heaven, hallowed be
> your name. Your kingdom come. Your will be done, on earth as it
> is in heaven.* Matthew 6:6, 9–10 NRSV

You've heard of "paying it forward"—when the recipient of a
good deed chooses to do a similar good deed to a third person,
thus "paying back" someone besides the original benefactor,
so that the ripple effect spreads kindness far and wide. Some
people have changed it to "play" it forward.

Or you can "pray it forward." When Jesus taught his disciples to pray to their Father in heaven, he was recommending
this view. His model prayer looks up and toward the kingdom of heaven and prays into it. Then it moves into requests
for daily bread (present needs) and forgiveness (past needs),
because those things are part of his will being done on earth
as it is in heaven.

It is not complicated to pray this way: "Your kingdom
come. Your will be done, on earth as it is in heaven." It may
sound too nonspecific or sanguine, perhaps a little naïve. Yet
this is Jesus speaking, and he is asking us to pray heaven down,
to make the coming of the kingdom a reality here on earth, in
essence to "pray it forward."

Satisfied

In generations past He permitted all the nations to walk in their
own ways; yet He did not neglect to leave some witness of Himself,
for He did you good and [showed you] kindness and gave you
rains from heaven and fruitful seasons, satisfying your hearts with
nourishment and happiness. Acts 14:16–17 AMP

What is your favorite appetizer? Good ones whet your appetite rather than filling you up so that you don't have room for the main entrée.

In this passage from the Book of Acts, Paul seems to be saying that the blessings God gives us here on earth are like appetizers that increase our longing for more of God. Through Paul, God had just healed a man crippled from birth. He appears to be saying that this healing, as well as more ordinary blessings like plentiful rain and bountiful crops, was meant to bear witness to the presence of God in the world. They are not the main course but only precursors to it.

That's one reason why we never feel satisfied. While we're here on earth, we're still working on the appetizers. While thanking God for them, we can also let them remind us that complete satisfaction awaits us in heaven.

As long as we're waiting, let's join the psalmist in prayer, saying "Blessed (happy, fortunate, to be envied) is the man whom You choose and cause to come near, that he may dwell in Your courts! We shall be satisfied with the goodness of Your house, Your holy temple" (Psalm 65:4 AMP).

Will You Ever Be Sad in Heaven?

As he [Paul] neared Damascus on his journey, suddenly a light from heaven flashed around him. He fell to the ground and heard a voice say to him, "Saul, Saul, why do you persecute me?" Acts 9:3–4

Most people assume that nothing will make them sad once they get to heaven. But is that true? Randy Alcorn raises this question by reminding us of Paul's (formerly Saul) dramatic conversion. Remember how Paul got knocked off his horse and was blinded by a heavenly light while riding toward Damascus to kill believers? Christ appeared to him, saying, "Saul, Saul, why do you persecute me?" When Paul asked who was speaking to him, the voice said, "I am Jesus whom you are persecuting."

You can hear the pain in Jesus' voice. He speaks in the present tense as though Paul is persecuting him right then. Paul was, in fact, persecuting the early believers. Yet Jesus is speaking to Paul from heaven. If Christ can still feel grieved even though he's living in heaven, why do we assume others in heaven cannot? Perhaps it's grief that fuels their prayers for us.

Randy Alcorn goes on to say that though joy predominates in what he calls the "present Heaven," people may at times feel some sadness. It's only when the new heaven and the new earth are established at the end of time that every tear will be wiped from every eye.

God's Answer to Death

For what I received I [Paul] passed on to you as of first importance: that Christ died for our sins according to the Scriptures, that he was buried, that he was raised on the third day according to the Scriptures. 1 Corinthians 15:3–4

Gary Habermas has made the Resurrection his life's study. In 1995, his wife, Debbie, was dying of stomach cancer. During that agonizing period, several of his students called Gary, hoping to offer consolation. Each one said something like this: "At a time like this, aren't you glad about the Resurrection?"

His students were trying to cheer him up by reminding him of what he had already taught them. Sitting on the porch day after day, while his wife was dying, Habermas would pray and think about the Resurrection.

"I knew if God were to come to me," he explained, "I'd ask only one question; 'Lord, why is Debbie up there in bed?' And I think God would respond by asking gently, 'Gary, did I raise my Son from the dead?'

"I'd say, 'Come on, Lord, I've written seven books on that topic! Of course he was raised from the dead. But I want to know about Debbie!'

"I think he'd keep coming back to the same question— 'Did I raise my Son from the dead?' 'Did I raise my Son from the dead?'—until I got his point: the Resurrection says that if Jesus was raised two thousand years ago, there's an answer to Debbie's death in 1995. And do you know what? It worked for me while I was sitting on the porch, and it still works today....

"Losing my wife was the most painful experience I've ever had to face, but if the Resurrection could get me through that, it can get me through anything. It was good for 30 A.D. It's good for 1995, it's good for 1998, and it's good beyond that."

Gary is right. If Jesus was raised, Debbie will be raised. If Jesus was raised, we will be raised.

Crossing the Jordan

Ye shall let your children know, saying, Israel came over this
Jordan on dry land. Joshua 4:22, KJV

The Jordan River, which runs the length of ancient Israel, is mentioned countless times in the Bible. It is an important river both territorially and symbolically, and many significant events happened at or in it. Think of Joshua leading the people of Israel across the Jordan River and into the Promised Land (Joshua 3). Remember Elijah and Elisha crossing the Jordan, which parted for them, when Elijah was taken up to heaven in a chariot (2 Kings 2:1–18). Recall that Jesus was baptized in the Jordan by John (Matthew 3:13–17).

The Elijah-Elisha story was the inspiration in the 1860s for the old spiritual "Swing Low, Sweet Chariot," which begins:

I looked over Jordan and what did I see, comin' for to carry
me home?
A band of angels, comin' after me; comin' for to carry me home.

Because of these associations, "crossing the Jordan" has come to mean passing from death to eternal life. Other songs and poems pick up the theme: "We Are Crossing River Jordan," "On Jordan's Stormy Banks," and many more. The meaning is rich with somber joy. Our own baptism represents a kind of death and rebirth to new and eternal life. On the other side of death is the Promised Land, heaven.

"If you get there before I do, tell all my friends I'm coming, too. . . ."

Relationships in the New Earth

> *They will neither harm nor destroy*
> *on all my holy mountain,*
> *for the earth will be filled with the knowledge of the LORD*
> *as the waters cover the sea.   Isaiah 11:9*

On earth most of us are both wounded and wounders. We bear scars that testify to the sins of others and guilt that testifies to the sins we've committed. Think back to the last day, the last week, the last month. Were they free from offense? Neither you nor anyone you were in contact with did or said anything the least bit offensive or hurtful? For most of us the answer will be that there were numerous offenses, whether small or large. We are broken people who tend to do and say things that break others.

But in the new earth, nothing will be broken. Everyone will say and do only what blesses others. Every person will be perfectly at peace with every other. What's more, even wild animals will be at peace. There will be no more "dog eat dog," "survival of the fittest," or "nature, red in tooth and claw."

Who knows? We may even be able to pet a bear, cuddle a lion, or hold a red fox on our laps. In the world that God is fashioning, there will be no more harm and no destruction but only peace and joy.

Creation Groans

We know that the whole creation has been groaning as in the pains of childbirth right up to the present time. Romans 8:22

My brother has a pit bull named Romeo. Shorter and stockier than most of his breed, he looks like a miniature Arnold Schwarzenegger, a lean, mean fighting machine. But Romeo is a lover and not a fighter. He's one of the lucky ones, a dog rescued from a man who wanted to train him to fight.

For the last few months, my brother has been working to rehabilitate another pit bull who suffers from extreme anxiety. His previous owners used scissors without anesthesia to cut off part of his ears so that in a fight another dog couldn't clamp on to them with his teeth. Dogs like him are often held in intolerable conditions, kept in cramped, filthy cages, beaten, starved, and antagonized to make them aggressive. No wonder this one has so much fear.

Animal cruelty, whether practiced privately or by corporations trying to gin up profits, is symptomatic of a world broken by sin. Called to be stewards of the earth—to take care of it as God would—we have often ravaged it instead.

But we don't have to wait for heaven to start making things right. Like my brother, and like many others who are trying to help, we can ask God how he wants us to defend the poor and the innocent, even if the victims are animals rather than people.

The Need to Know

Intelligent people are always ready to learn. Their ears are open for knowledge. Proverbs 18:15 NLT

You can't go anywhere without your smartphone these days, at least if you want to stay connected. Whatever you don't know, you can simply google. Instantly, you will have more information than you can handle.

A few years ago I had the opportunity of spending a few days in Paris. It wasn't hard to jump on the computer and find just the right hotel at just the right price, conveniently located at a major subway stop. I knew exactly when the Eiffel Tower was open to visitors and also what exhibits were on at the Louvre. I even mastered a few French phrases to help me avoid sounding like the clueless American I am. Half the pleasure of the trip was in the preparation.

While heaven will be much more pleasant than our preparations for it, preparations are essential. We begin by preparing our hearts, repenting of sin and entrusting ourselves to Christ. We continue by living each day in God's presence aware that even small decisions can bend our hearts either toward or away from heaven. And we ask God to expand our understanding so that we can begin to envision what he has in store for us.

As you go about your day today, try to filter everything—your words, your thoughts, your actions and reactions—through the lens of heaven. Let God make you so heavenly minded that you are no longer afraid or reluctant to prepare now in a way that will increase your joy then.

Ninety Minutes in Heaven

He will take our weak mortal bodies and change them into glorious
bodies like his own.   Philippians 3:21a NLT

Don Piper was cruising along at fifty miles an hour, driving over
a bridge, when he was struck head on by an eighteen-wheeler
traveling at least sixty miles an hour. With a combined impact of
about 110 miles an hour, the truck flew over him, crushing the
roof of his car. With no pulse, numerous broken bones, and blood
seeping from eyes, ears, and nose, emergency personnel simply
covered his body when they arrived. It was only a matter of time
before a hearse would transport the victim to the funeral home.

Unbeknownst to those on the scene, during the ninety minutes following the accident, Don was enjoying an incredible
experience in an entirely different location. Just before clearing
the east end of the bridge he noticed that he was suddenly surrounded by a brilliant light. He was looking at a beautiful and
very ornate gate, in front of which stood a large crowd. At once
everyone began rushing toward him. There was his grandfather
and great-grandfather, a childhood friend who had died in a car
wreck, a high school classmate who had drowned, two teachers
who had often talked with him about Christ. He knew instinctively that they were his heavenly welcoming committee.

Don could recognize everyone he saw because, as he explains,
"Age expresses time passing, and there is no time there. All of the
people I encountered were the same age they had been the last
time I had seen them—except that all the ravages of living on
earth had vanished. Even though some of their features may not
have been considered attractive on earth, in heaven every feature
was perfect, beautiful, and wonderful to gaze at."

The love he felt was intense, emanating from every person
present. Heaven, Don Piper says, was many things, "but without a doubt, it was the greatest family reunion of all."[112]

The Sound of Heaven

Then I heard what sounded like a great multitude, like the roar of
rushing waters and like loud peals of thunder, shouting:
"Hallelujah!
For our Lord God Almighty reigns.
Let us rejoice and be glad
and give him glory!" Revelation 19:6–7

People who claim to have visited heaven often speak of incredible scenery, of beautiful colors and brilliant lights too vivid to describe. Though Don Piper talks about such things, what he remembers most is the sound of heaven, which he describes as a song that goes on forever. "I didn't just hear music," he says. "It seemed as if I were part of the music—and it played in and through my body."

But it wasn't just one song that was being sung. It was a never-ending hymn of praise that was composed of the beating of angels' wings and countless songs of worship all being sung at once. Somehow all the songs and sounds blended into a beautiful hymn of worship.

"As strange as it may seem," he says, "I could clearly distinguish each song. It sounded as if each hymn of praise was meant for me to hear as I moved inside the gates.

"Many of the old hymns and choruses I had sung at various times in my life were part of the music—along with hundreds of songs I had never heard before. Hymns of praise, modern sounding choruses, and ancient chants filled my ears and brought not only a deep peace but the greatest feeling of joy I've ever experienced."[113]

Don's experience makes me wonder. Will the songs we've sung on earth be played back to us in heaven? Will our own voices, blending with countless others across the ages and throughout the world, move our hearts as we become part of the perfect song of praise that is being sung to God in heaven?

Powerful Prayer

"If you abide in me, and my words abide in you, ask for whatever you wish, and it will be done for you." John 15:7

Don Piper was returning home from the Baptist General Convention of Texas when the semi swerved over the center line and killed him. Finding no pulse, paramedics declared him dead at the scene and threw a tarp over his body. While Don was spending time in heaven, a Baptist preacher began to pray for him. By then, Don had been dead for about an hour and a half.

Dick Onerecker had also been at the convention. Stopping his car at the scene of the multi-car accident, he asked a police officer if he could pray for the man in the car that had been so badly crushed. The officer tried to dissuade him saying, "He's dead, and it's really a mess under the tarp."

But Dick persisted, certain that God was telling him to pray for the man in that car. Entering through the trunk of Don's car, Dick tried to find a pulse but couldn't. Then he placed his hand on Don's right shoulder, praying, singing, and crying out to God on the dead man's behalf.

As he prayed and wept for the man in the car, Dick began to sing: "O what peace we often forfeit, O what needless pain we bear, all because we do not carry everything to God in prayer!" As he sang the lyrics to the old hymn "What a Friend We Have in Jesus," something incredible happened. The dead man began to sing with him.

In that first moment of consciousness, Don explains, "I was aware of two things. First, I was singing—a different kind of singing than the tones of heaven—I heard my own voice and then became aware of someone else singing.

"The second thing I was aware of was that someone clutched my hand. It was a strong, powerful touch and the first physical sensation I experienced with my return to earthly life.

"More than a year would lapse before I understood the significance of that hand clasping mine."[114]

Held by His Hand

So do not fear, for I am with you; do not be dismayed, for I am your God. I will strengthen you and help you; I will uphold you with my righteous right hand. Isaiah 41:10

"I'm not certain what the world record is for exiting a wrecked car, but Dick Onerecker must have surely broken it that Wednesday afternoon," says Don Piper.

Racing over to the nearest paramedic, Dick shouted, "The man's alive! He's not dead! He's alive!" But no one would believe him. It wasn't until he threatened to lie down on the bridge and block traffic that someone finally paid attention.

Though Don's recovery would be long and agonizing, he was eventually able to walk on his own. Dick had specifically prayed that God would heal unseen, internal injuries, and it seemed that God had done just that.

A little more than a year after the accident, Don was standing at the pulpit of Dick's church, telling the story of how he had gone to heaven and how Dick had prayed him back to earth. He recounted how he had joined Dick singing "What a Friend We Have in Jesus" and how Dick's hand had gripped his own and held it tight.

At lunch that day, Dick's wife, Anita, thanked Don for telling his story and then shocked him by challenging something he had said. "Don, Dick never held your hand," she told him.

"Think about it," she continued. "Dick leaned over from the rear of the trunk over the backseat and put his hand on your *shoulder* and touched you. You were facing forward and your left arm was barely hanging together....There was no way Dick could have reached your right hand."

"If it wasn't Dick's hand," Don asked, "whose was it?"

Smiling, Anita said, "I think you know."[115]

Homeland Security

This is how God showed his love among us: He sent his one and only Son into the world that we might live through him. 1 John 4:9 NIV

It's one thing to believe heaven is your home, but another to be certain that you are going to get there someday. How can you know? It may sound clichéd, but it really is as simple as A-B-C. Many people explain the plan of salvation this way:

A: Admit that you are a sinner in need of salvation. "For all have sinned and fall short of the glory of God" (Romans 3:23 ESV).

B: Believe that salvation comes through Jesus Christ. Believe that he is the Son of God who lived on earth as a man, was crucified, and rose from the dead.

C: Confess him as your Lord and Savior. "If you confess with your mouth that Jesus is Lord and believe in your heart that God raised him from the dead, you will be saved" (Romans 10:9 ESV).

If you're in doubt of whether you will make it to heaven, take a moment now to speak directly to God, asking him to save you. Here's a prayer to get you started: "Jesus, I want to be saved. I know I have sinned and do not deserve to go to heaven. But I believe that you took upon yourself the punishment for my sins by dying on the cross and rising from the dead. Forgive my sins and save me. Come into my life and be my Lord; take charge of my life. I trust you. I accept your gift of eternal life in heaven. Amen."

A-B-C . . . and continue on to D, for "Do it." Keep talking with God, doing what he tells you. You could call it "homeland security"—without any bureaucracy.

Crowned

Now, a crown is being held for me—a crown for being right with
God. The Lord, the judge who judges rightly, will give the crown
to me on that day—not only to me but to all those who have waited
with love for him to come again.   2 Timothy 4:8 NCV

According to the Bible, you can look forward to receiving a
crown in heaven. You may picture a royal tiara made of gold
and encrusted with jewels. But that kind of crown is nowhere
to be found in Scripture.

Heavenly crowns are even more beautiful than the most
ornate earthly ones, because they represent heavenly qualities.
The "crown for being right with God" is also called the
"crown of righteousness." Such a crown guarantees permanence in heaven. Believers who have shepherded others faith-
fully will earn a "crown of glory": "Then when Christ, the
Chief Shepherd, comes, you will get a glorious crown that
will never lose its beauty" (1 Peter 5:4 NCV).

On the final day of judgment, anyone who is deemed to
be humble and self-denying will receive an "incorruptible"
or "imperishable" crown (see 1 Corinthians 9:25). Psalm 149:4
also refers to this crown: God "crowns the humble with victory" (NIV), or with "salvation" (ESV). According to 1 Thessalonians 2:19, those who have introduced others to Jesus can
look forward to a "crown of rejoicing" (KJV), in the form of the
saved ones themselves.

Last but not least, anyone who perseveres in faith even
under severe hardships can expect to receive the "crown of
life": "God blesses those who patiently endure testing and
temptation. Afterward they will receive the crown of life that
God has promised to those who love him" (James 1:12 NLT).

God Knows Your Name

Do not be afraid, for I have redeemed you. I have called you by name, you are mine.
For I am the Lord your God, the Holy One of Israel, your Savior.   Isaiah 43:1, 3 NRSV

Kristen didn't really know who she was. She had grown up in various foster homes, shuttled from one place to the next, never finding a "forever family."

"With each new home, the people there would change my name," she said. "First I was Samantha, then my name was changed to Jennifer. I always felt lost because no one knew my real name. They just changed it to whatever they preferred, never thinking that it would matter to me. I always wished someone knew my real name and stuck with it."

Our names are precious. They identify us and make us feel secure. Surnames also root us in families and connect us to community.

My wish for Kristen is that she will come to understand that the most important Being in the universe already knows her name. Furthermore, those who know him can be assured that they belong to his family. Hasn't he already said, "I have called you by name, you are mine."

Listen to the words of someone who spent time in heaven and lived to tell the story, a man named Ian McCormack, who said, "There were waves of light of comfort, peace and joy. And God called my name."[116]

Will There Be Work in Heaven?

If we died with him,
we will also live with him;
if we endure,
we will also reign with him. *2 Timothy 2:11–12*

I have a friend who's being eaten up by her work—work she loves. There's just too much of it. She can't get a break. I have another friend who hates his work, but doesn't think he can get a better job. Retirement is a long way off but he hangs on, hoping to survive by sheer willpower until he can afford to resign.

Even in the best of jobs, we can have a love/hate relationship with our work. No wonder many us make the mistake of thinking there will be no work to do in heaven. Heaven will be one big happy retirement, won't it?

That's not what the Bible says.

Though we'll get lots of rest in heaven, we won't be lying around in hammocks all day long. Instead, the Bible says we will be reigning with Christ, and one would have to assume that "reigning" takes work. The Book of Genesis tells us that God placed human beings in the Garden of Eden and then charged them to take care of it. That was their work. Because of the Fall, working the ground (and every other kind of work, by implication) became difficult. But in the new earth the full blessing of work will be restored. Whatever our assignment may be, it will be work we're good at, work we enjoy, and work that will always bear fruit.

God Restores

"Behold, I make all things new." Revelation 21:5 NKJV

If you are ever in New York, don't miss the chance to visit the Brooklyn Tabernacle at 17 Smith Street in downtown Brooklyn. The church is a wonder because of all the work God is doing there, bringing drug addicts, thugs, gang members, and many ordinary people from a variety of cultural and ethnic backgrounds to himself. The building itself is a testament to God's faithfulness.

I remember when the congregation was located in a former theater on Flatbush Avenue. The church was too small to hold all the people who wanted to attend, so people began praying for a larger building. What God gave was a vaudeville theater that had been turned into a four-plex cinema that had become an abandoned wreck. It took enormous faith to look at that disaster of a building and believe it could ever house a church. Though it would have been cheaper by far to tear it down and start over, the church decided to renovate—a multimillion-dollar project and a huge step of faith for a church with little money. But God provided, often miraculously.

It has always seemed to me that this renovated building, which reflects the opulence of the original vaudeville theater, is a symbol of how God has rebuilt the lives of so many who have passed through its doors. He is, after all, in the business of rebuilding lives, of redeeming, restoring, regenerating, and renewing human beings.

One day, he will do the same for the earth, restoring it to the beauty and the majesty he has always intended for it.

Describing Heaven

It [the heavenly Jerusalem] shone with the glory of God, and its brilliance was like that of a very precious jewel, like a jasper, clear as crystal. Revelation 21:11

Why do people who claim to have spent time in heaven describe it in different ways? Marv Besteman has a plausible theory.

Imagine that you live in the Congo, he says. You've never had the chance to travel to America. But one day someone offers to fly you in to Estes Park, Colorado. When you arrive by helicopter you gaze in awe as you watch mule deer, chipmunks, bears, bobcats, coyote, and badgers ranging below in the Rocky Mountains. Then you head straight back to Africa. Though you have only seen a tiny portion of the United States, you might make the mistake of thinking this is exactly what America looks like. It's the same with heaven. God sometimes offers glimpses of heaven but not the whole picture.

Most people find it difficult to put their experience of heaven into words. But Marv doesn't mind trying. "The thing about the colors in heaven," he says, "is that they are all shot through with a brightness, a luster that seems to incorporate the sun's rays, the moon's beams, a fire's flicker, and a star's glitter, stirred together by a master lighting director and splashed out over the canopy we will spend eternity watching."

As he stood outside the gates of heaven, Marv watched as "pyrotechnics boomed and crackled (except they didn't make you want to plug your ears like they do down here), decorating heaven in shapes like cakes, spiders, peonies, and of course shapes and formations not of this world.

"Every color you can think of—purples, reds, blues,

silvers, greens, whites—interwove with each other in shining sequences."[117]

What is heaven like? Just ask Marv or Crystal McVea or Don Piper or Alex Malarkey or Mary Neal or any of the other people whose stories reveal the beauty of heaven.

"Keep Eternity Before the Children"

If a man keeps My word, he will never taste of death into all eternity. John 8:52 AMP

Dallas Willard, the Christian philosopher who wrote *The Divine Conspiracy* and many other books, spoke often of our eternal destiny. After his death, pastor-author John Ortberg honored his friend in an article in *Christianity Today*.[118] He mentioned the fact that Dallas's mother died when he was two years old, and her last words to her husband were these: "Keep eternity before the children." That is what Dallas did for his many philosophy students and readers.

Dallas's "take" on heaven and its entryway, which is, of course, death, was always unusual and insightful. For example, soon after being diagnosed with terminal cancer he said to John, "I think that when I die, it might be some time until I know it." What he meant was that anyone whose life already consists of conscious experiences of the reality of Jesus might not notice the interruption of death, because heaven would be a seamless continuation. Besides, he said, Jesus told his disciples that people who trust him and lean on him will overflow with life—and will not taste death (see John 8:52).

On more than one occasion, his friends also heard Dallas say, "God will certainly let everyone into heaven that can possibly stand it." That one is worth thinking about, long and hard.

You Can't Get to Heaven on Roller Skates

*"The twelve gates were twelve pearls, each gate made of a single
pearl." Revelation 21:21a*

The Book of Revelation describes the heavenly city as having
twelve gates, each one of them a single pearl—thus the "pearly
gates" of popular tradition. In the ever-evolving campfire
song, "You Can't Get to Heaven on Roller Skates (Ain't Gonna
Grieve My Lord No More)" this idea plays into the first verse:

> *Oh, you can't get to heaven*
> *On roller skates*
> *'Cuz you'll roll right by*
> *Those pearly gates.*

Not one of the verses of the song is profound, but the message is nevertheless clear and true, namely that you cannot get
into heaven by means of anything you can try on your own
strength. It just won't work. Perhaps the closest to good advice
comes in this verse:

> *Oh, you can't get to heaven*
> *In a rockin' chair*
> *Git down on your knees*
> *An' say a prayer.*

And then there's the final verse, sung only when the campfire was dying down and the camp counselors needed to round
out the day:

> *There's one more thing*
> *I forgot to tell;*
> *If you don't go to heaven,*
> *You'll go to . . . bed.*

A Martyr's Vision of Heaven

*But Stephen [Christianity's first martyr], full of the Holy Spirit,
looked up to heaven and saw the glory of God, and Jesus standing
at the right hand of God. "Look," he said, "I see heaven open and
the Son of Man standing at the right hand of God." Acts 7:55–56*

Saturus and Perpetua were early Christians, martyred in Carthage on March 7 of the year 203. A twenty-two-year-old married woman, still nursing her infant son, Perpetua kept a journal while in jail. One of the earliest pieces of Christian writing produced by a woman, it tells of a vision in which this young aristocrat saw herself climbing to heaven on a great bronze ladder. At the top was her friend Saturus, urging her on.

Saturus also had a vision of heaven, prior to suffering martyrdom in the arena. Here's what he wrote:

*And we came near to a place of which place the walls were such,
they seemed built of light; and before the door of that place stood
four angels who clothed us when we went in with white raiment. And we went in, and we heard as it were one voice crying
Sanctus, Sanctus, Sanctus, without any end. And we saw sitting in that same place as it were a man, white-headed, having
hair like snow; youthful of countenance; whose feet we saw not.
And on his right hand and on his left, four elders; and behind
them stood many other elders. And we went in with wonder
and stood before the throne; and the four angels raised us up and
we kissed him, and with his hand he passed over our faces. And
the other elders said to us: Stand you. And we stood, and gave
the kiss of peace. And the elders said to us: Go you and play.
And I said to Perpetua: You have that which you desire. And
she said to me: Yes, God be thanked; so that I that was glad in
the flesh am now more glad.*[119]

What gave these early Christians the courage to lay down their lives rather than recant their faith? Only Christ, who loved them, and led them to heaven to behold his face.

"Momma's Kitchen"

Better a dry crust eaten in peace than a house filled with feasting—
and conflict. Proverbs 17:1 NLT

Beautiful houses can be filled with expensive furnishings, lavish tapestries, and imported rugs, but if the home is a place of chaos and conflict, no amount of interior design will fix the problem. What matters in a home is the atmosphere.

A recent story on HGTV (Home & Garden Television) featured a home that was badly in need of remodeling. When asked for their "must-haves," one member of the family got straight to the point. "Everybody gathers in the kitchen. Momma cooks for dozens at a time and the place is packed. We all stand up to eat since there's not enough room for a big table. The linoleum shows the marks of shoe scuffs and worn paths, counter space is limited, and the Formica is wearing thin from use. Only two burners work on the stove. Momma makes do with what she has and cooks up a storm. Everyone is welcome."

Clearly, though the physical accommodations were sparse, what mattered to this family was the spirit of the place.

Perhaps we need to worry less about the physical details of heaven and instead focus more on the atmosphere of heaven. Surely our Father in heaven will welcome us, making us feel even more at home than that family feels in Momma's kitchen.

Clothes in Heaven?

After this I looked, and there was a great multitude that no one could count, from every nation, from all tribes and peoples and languages, standing before the throne and before the Lamb, robed in white, with palm branches in their hands.   Revelation 7:9 NRSV

I never thought much about what we will wear in heaven. It's probably because I always figured we'd leave our old bodies behind, so what would we have left to dress? (That was before I did much thinking about God's promise to give us resurrected bodies.)

It may be a big disappointment to those who have closets full of the latest fashions, but we may not be making a major fashion statement in heaven. Perhaps white robes will be standard.

White, of course, is the symbol of blessedness and purity. And many who have experienced heaven even for a short time and returned to tell us about it, say that they've seen people dressed in white robes.

I have to confess there are also many accounts in which people were dressed just as they were on earth. Perhaps God tailors the vision to the person who is having it. Whether or not we will all be wearing white robes isn't all that important. What is, however, is that we will all be pure.

Commute to Nowhere

Enter by the narrow gate; for wide is the gate and broad is the way that leads to destruction, and there are many who go in by it. Because narrow is the gate and difficult is the way which leads to life, and there are few who find it. Matthew 7:13–14 NKJV

When I carpooled my kids to a distant school, I used to say it was my "commute to nowhere" because I always ended up back where I started. I would get up before dawn, hurry everyone through morning routines, run out the door, cram my offspring and their backpacks into the van, pick up a couple of neighbor children, and head out . . . only to turn around and come right back.

I never want my journey to heaven to become a commute to nowhere. Instead, I want to stay on the straight and narrow way all the way to my destination.

Not only is the road to heaven a narrow one, it also has low clearance. To travel on it, you must value both obedience and humility; you must lower your head and lose your pride on a regular basis. Remember Paul's advice to Timothy: "But you, the man of God . . . Set your heart not on riches, but on goodness, Christ-likeness, faith, love, patience and humility. Fight the worthwhile battle of the faith, keep your grip on that life eternal to which you have been called, and to which you boldly professed your loyalty before many witnesses" (1 Timothy 6:11–12 PHILLIPS).

Unless you're intentional about reaching your destination, you'll end up back where you started, facing something much worse than unmade beds and a sink full of dirty dishes.

"I Went to the Gate of Heaven"

"I will deliver this people from the power of the grave;
I will redeem them from death.
Where, O death, are your plagues?
Where, O grave, is your destruction?" Hosea 13:14

Eight months after losing his grandson Dwight, D. L. Moody lost his young granddaughter Irene, who succumbed to tuberculosis.

Shortly after that, Moody declared, "Some day you will read in the papers that Moody is dead. Don't you believe a word of it. At that moment I shall be more alive than I am now."

Just four months after his granddaughter's death, Moody himself lay dying. For a time he lost consciousness. Then suddenly he opened his eyes and exclaimed, "I went to the gate of heaven. Why, it was so wonderful, and I saw the children! I saw Irene and Dwight."[120]

A short time later, D. L. Moody was dead. Or rather, he was more alive than he had ever been.

Shadows?

The city does not need the sun or the moon to shine on it, for the glory of God gives it light, and the Lamb is its lamp.   Revelation 21:23 NIV

Just as fifteenth-century people were eager to hear the tales of explorers returning from far-off lands, many of us like to hear from people who testify that "heaven is for real." We are especially intrigued when their retelling duplicates what we read in the Bible. Although we know that God's word is true, we relish hearing the firsthand accounts of others.

Several people who claim to have visited, speak of walking in heaven without casting a shadow. Could it be because only their souls and not their bodies visited heaven? Or maybe they didn't see a shadow because God's light is so bright that it absorbs even the slightest of shadows.

They also noticed that the quality of the light in heaven was soft and restful; it didn't come glaring down from one direction or location—it was just everywhere—engulfing everything so there were no dark corners, no darkness at all.

No shadows, only light. That's one of the delightful things that these contemporary explorers tell us about the far-off land of heaven.

Jerusalem the Golden

And he carried me away in the Spirit to a mountain great and high, and showed me the Holy City, Jerusalem, coming down out of heaven from God. Revelation 21:10

Jerusalem the golden,
with milk and honey blest,
beneath thy contemplation
sink heart and voice oppressed:
I know not, oh, I know not,
what joys await us there;
what radiancy of glory,
what bliss beyond compare!

They stand, those halls of Zion,
all jubilant with song,
and bright with many an angel,
and all the martyr throng:
the Prince is ever in them,
the daylight is serene;
the pastures of the blessed
are decked in glorious sheen.

There is the throne of David;
and there, from care released,
the shout of them that triumph,
the song of them that feast;
and they who with their Leader
have conquered in the fight,
for ever and for ever
are clad in robes of white.

Oh, sweet and blessed country,
the home of God's elect!

Oh, sweet and blessed country,
that eager hearts expect!
Jesus, in mercy bring us
to that dear land of rest,
who art, with God the Father,
and the Spirit, ever blest.

—Bernard of Cluny, circa 1125

Small World?

For my thoughts are not your thoughts, neither are your ways my ways, saith the Lord. For as the heavens are higher than the earth, so are my ways higher than your ways, and my thoughts than your thoughts. Isaiah 55:8–9 KJV

We find it easy to turn to idols, don't we? Having a great education, a promising job, lots of money, a good marriage. Even the church can become an idol. Our idols may not be made of "wood and stone," but they represent power, security, wealth, and advantage. Somehow, we expect them to give us a leg up on salvation.

M. Craig Barnes, president of Princeton Theological Seminary, advises us to give idol worship a rest, saying, "Any time we think we can find salvation from our hard work, we are in grave danger. If our hard work fails, or worse yet if it succeeds, then we are stuck with ourselves for a god. That means we have destined ourselves to journeying through life's wilderness assuming that the solution to every problem is to try harder.

"People who live life without a Savior do not have any sense of awe or wonder. Nothing amazes or astonishes or overwhelms them because their world is too small for God to fit into. That is an awfully sad world that, unfortunately, has become quite crowded today. Yet I have discovered over and over again that God loves us too much to abandon us to that. He will come looking for us, as he did the Hebrews in slavery, and when he finds us, he will free us from anything that has bound us—even our success."[121]

Tell God today that you don't want to make your world small by trusting in idols. Instead, make it as big as it can be by trusting in him.

A Guessing Game?

Beloved we are God's children now; what we will be has not yet been revealed. What we do know is this: when he is revealed, we will be like him, for we will see him as he is. 1 John 3:2 NRSV

C. S. Lewis, in his book *Letters to Malcolm*, made this comment about heaven: "Guesses, of course, only guesses. If they are not true, something better will be. For 'we know we shall be like him, for we shall see him as he is.' "[122]

But are we really guessing? Do we know that little about heaven, the place we will go after we die? Not really. God has provided information about heaven in the Bible. He's revealed truths we can trust.

But whenever we go beyond what's in Scripture, we are merely guessing. More likely we are just repeating age-old traditions that have become "common knowledge." Our explanations are usually attempts to be helpful or to provide comfort. Sometimes we try to fill in information that's not there simply because we're curious.

Occasionally our curiosity may lead us to accounts about heaven that contradict Scripture. When that happens, it's best to look elsewhere for the information we're seeking. By majoring on the majors—focusing on the foundational truths revealed in Scripture—we won't get into trouble. With a solid foundation beneath us, engaging in a little guesswork about heaven should be fine—and, who knows, it might even be fun.

Dead on Arrival

And the LORD God formed man of the dust of the ground, and breathed into his nostrils the breath of life; and man became a living soul.   Genesis 2:7 KJV

Dr. Reggie Anderson's patient, a twenty-four-year-old male with a stab wound to the chest, had been dead on arrival—with no pulse and no blood pressure. With a second downward thrust, Anderson stabbed the patient's heart to draw out blood that might have pooled in the sac surrounding it. He watched as red liquid began filling the syringe. Then he felt a breeze and a sensation of warmth brush past his cheek.

"Doctor, we have a pulse!" Thanks to Anderson's quick action, DeWayne's blood pressure and breathing had been restored.

Later, DeWayne described everything that happened to him in the emergency room, including the two times the doctor had stabbed him with a syringe. He also described the nurse and respiratory assistant who had been assisting. Then he said he had seen his grandmother. While Anderson was working on him, she had walked over, held his hand, and then calmly assured him he would be all right. And sure enough he was.

Anderson had seen no one. Later he learned that DeWayne's grandmother had passed away four years earlier.

How could DeWayne have seen everything that was happening to him in the emergency room that day? Anderson had heard reports of people having out-of-body experiences as they hovered between life and death. Perhaps that was what had happened to his patient. As for the breeze and the warmth he had felt brushing his cheek just before DeWayne started breathing on his own? Anderson was sure it was evidence of heaven breaking through as DeWayne's heart began beating on its own and he came back to life.[123]

Home in Paradise

[Jesus] replied, "Truly I tell you, today you will be with me in Paradise." Luke 23:43 NRSV

What do you think of when you hear the word "paradise"? Tropical islands, turquoise waters, lush vegetation, year-round sunshine, white coral beaches? Or maybe you think of places like Paradise Island, Paradise Key, Paradise Cove, or Paradise Beach, all of which can be found in the Caribbean.

When Scripture speaks of paradise it's not talking about lying around all day in a hammock in some sunny spot in the Caribbean but about heaven itself.

Do you remember the scene in which Jesus was hanging between two criminals on a Roman cross? Even there, in the midst of that hell on earth, Jesus was welcoming sinners into paradise. All it took was for the thief to affirm that he believed in Christ. And so the man made a remarkable statement of faith, affirming his belief in the man who was dying on a cross beside him.

Do you believe in the cross of Jesus, that by his death you are made whole? If so, you have nothing to fear when the time comes for you to die because Jesus will be right there beside you, saying, "Today you will be with me in Paradise."

God's Royal People

But you are a chosen race, a royal priesthood, a holy nation, God's own people, in order that you may proclaim the mighty acts of him who called you out of darkness into his marvelous light.   1 Peter 2:9 NRSV

Years ago, I met a real princess. She was blond and beautiful, maybe fifty years old, and she wore the most gorgeous mink coat I'd ever seen. She was visiting a home I happened to be staying in. As soon as she sat down on the couch, she was joined by the five-year-old daughter of the friends who lived there. I don't remember much of the conversation because I was busy watching Mo Mo (short for Maureen) pet the princess's coat while the princess was still wearing it. I do remember thinking that being petted as though she were a beloved domestic animal must have been a particularly unusual experience for a princess.

We Americans—even the adults among us—hardly know how to behave around royalty. All that business about kings and queens, princes and princesses—it's just not in our DNA.

Or is it?

Peter says that we have become part of a royal priesthood. We've been set apart in a special way, called to play a particular role in the world, just as earthly queens and king have been set apart for a special purpose. Our purpose is not to govern nations here on earth but to proclaim the truth about the One who called us out of darkness and into his marvelous light.

Next time you start to feel ordinary (perhaps right now), remind yourself that you're the son or daughter of a king—and not just any king. If you heed the call God has placed on your life, one day soon you will receive a royal welcome into heaven's throne room.

Heaven Came Down

". . . your young men will see visions. . . ." Acts 2:17

H. A. Baker and his wife, Josephine, were Pentecostal missionaries working in Tibet from 1911 to 1919 and then in China until 1950. In Yunnan Province, in southwestern China, they founded a rescue mission to provide a home for impoverished Chinese boys. There were forty boys, ranging in age from six to eighteen, at the orphanage when the boys began to have visions of the afterlife.

At the time, many of the boys had little familiarity with the Bible. They were runaways, prodigals, and orphans who had only recently come to Christ. Several of the boys had visions of heaven in which they encountered two boys from their orphanage who had died the previous year. They saw Djany Hsing and His Dien Fu, who would greet them joyfully, lead them to the throne of Jesus, and then take them on a tour of heaven.

H. A. Baker reported, "These boys who had died were so constantly seen in heaven and their names were so frequently shouted in our midst with ecstasy and joy that they did not seem far away—just out of sight. Heaven was so real, so near, so wonderful, so certain, that if one of our children had died in those days, the others would have envied him his privilege."[124]

With that kind of certainty, it's not hard to understand why the boys felt compelled to share their faith, preaching the gospel in the streets to anyone who would listen.

Paradise

The LORD God took the man and put him in the Garden of Eden to work it and take care of it.   Genesis 2:15

If you're an avid gardener, you might enjoy knowing that the word "paradise" comes from the Persian word *pairidaeza*, which means an "enclosed garden" or "walled park." Instead of nature in the raw, what is pictured is nature that is under the care of human beings. This is the word used to describe the Garden of Eden in the oldest known Greek translation of the Hebrew Scriptures.

The New Testament also speaks of paradise. Listen to this passage from Revelation 2:7: "*To the one who is victorious, I will give the right to eat from the tree of life, which is in the paradise of God.*"

According to the Bible, the first human beings were created in a garden and then expelled from it for their sin. But God's plan is to bring his people back into the garden.

Remember the lyrics to the old Joni Mitchell song, made famous by Crosby, Stills, Nash & Young—*Yes, we've got to get ourselves back to the garden?*[125] The problem is that no matter how hard we try, we will never get *ourselves* back to the garden. Only God can do that.

Glimpsing Paradise

For the earth will be filled with the knowledge of the glory of the LORD *as the waters cover the sea.   Habakkuk 2:14*

H. A. Baker, who founded an orphanage for boys in China, says that he never taught the children in his care about paradise. In fact, he said, some of the smallest children, who were the most ignorant about such matters, became his best teachers regarding paradise.

"In paradise," he says, "they saw trees bearing the most delicious fruit, and vistas of the most beautiful flowers of every color, sending forth an aroma of heavenly fragrance. There were birds of glorious plumage singing their carols of joy and praise. In this park were also animals of every size and description: large deer, small deer, large lions, great elephants, lovely rabbits, and all sorts of little friendly pets such as they had never seen before.

"The children held the little pets in their arms and passed them from one to another. They found the lion peacefully lying beneath a tree and climbed on his back, ran their fingers through his shaggy mane, brushed his face, and put their hands in his mouth. . . .

"When hungry, the children ate of the wonderful fruit or gathered the sweet tasting, refreshing manna that was scattered all about. Were they thirsty? Here and there trickled little brooks of the stimulating and refreshing water of life."[126]

If you'd like to catch a glimpse of paradise, why not think for a moment of the most beautiful park you've ever seen—Yellowstone, Yosemite, the Grand Canyon, Banff, the Serengeti, or maybe something closer to home. Now imagine somewhere more vivid, glorious, lush, and teeming with life. It still won't compare to the splendid place God has prepared for those who love him.

Final Judgment

But when the Son of Man comes in His glory, and all the angels with Him, then He will sit on His glorious throne. All the nations will be gathered before Him; and He will separate them from one another, as the shepherd separates the sheep from the goats; and He will put the sheep on His right, and the goats on the left. Matthew 25:31–33 NASB

Jesus must not have gotten the message about political correctness. He speaks straightforwardly about a topic most of us would rather ignore, namely that not all of us will make it into heaven. Theologian Sinclair Ferguson says, "The whole point of Jesus' story of the sheep and the goats is that he *does* have a left hand. The minor motif of the Book of Revelation is that there is, permanently, an *outside*. That's why Jesus says, 'They will go away to eternal punishment, while the righteous go to eternal life' "[127] (verse 46).

Whereas heaven is known to be a place of eternal light, hell is simply *dark*. Have you ever experienced absolute darkness, in a cave, perhaps, or on an overcast night in the woods? If you have, you know the sense of disorientation, even panic, when you can't see your hand in front of your face. You are lost. That's a tiny taste of hell.

Forget about devils with pitchforks. To be "cast into the outer darkness" (verse 30) involves being cast away from God's presence, hopelessly separated from his light and love. After all he has done to make it feasible for us to enter heaven, how can we accuse him of being unloving or insensitive by warning us about the perils of not living for him?

Citizens of Heaven

But as it is, they desire a better country, that is, a heavenly one. Hebrews 11:16 NRSV

"Where's my passport?" I went looking. Sure enough, it wasn't where it should have been (in the lockbox with other valuable papers). Instead it was in a decorative, bright yellow file box on a shelf in my office. A document as important as that should have been in a safer place.

I need that little passport urgently when I travel outside of the United States, whether I jet halfway around the world or drive across the nearest border. And for passage into heaven, I know that another kind of passport—a spiritual one—is required. That one will take me on a one-way voyage beyond the confines of this physical universe.

Passports indicate citizenship. Like my earthly passport, my heavenly passport is issued by a higher authority, the highest in the universe. Though my pocket-sized passport carries many stamps to show the places I have visited, my heavenly passport allows but one destination—the kingdom of heaven. And while my earthly passport cost me dearly and must be safeguarded, my heavenly passport was given to me for free, and God will keep it secure until the day I need it.

I know that the United States of America is only my temporary home; I'm just passing through on my way to heaven. Until then, though, I need to be better at keeping it safe until I don't need it anymore.

Are There Walls Around Heaven?

*It [the heavenly Jerusalem] had a great, high wall with twelve gates,
and with twelve angels at the gates. On the gates were written the
names of the twelve tribes of Israel. There were three gates on the
east, three on the north, three on the south and three on the west.
The wall of the city had twelve foundations, and on them were the
names of the twelve apostles of the Lamb. Revelation 21:12–14*

If you fly to London, Paris, Shanghai, or Mexico City, you won't
see walls encircling the city as you make your descent. But if you
travel to Jerusalem, you will have the chance not only to see the
walls of the Old City but to climb up and walk around on them.

In biblical times, cities were built with fortified walls that
would protect the inhabitants from intruders. Guards were
stationed on the ramparts. So when heaven is described in the
Book of Revelation, it's hardly surprising that it is pictured as
a great walled city with angels to guard the gates.

It's interesting that some of those who have claimed to
have visited heaven have also seen walls. Here's how Marv
Besteman describes them: "Immediately, I saw an enormous
door, several stories tall, attached to the gate, and a wall that
wrapped around the kingdom in either direction with no end
in sight. It was the biggest door I had ever seen, not to mention
the biggest wall and the biggest gate, and so forth."[128]

Here's what Don Piper saw: "I stared, but I couldn't see
the end of the walls in either direction. As I gazed upward, I
couldn't see the top either."[129]

Somehow I find these descriptions reassuring. They suggest that inside these enormous gates is a very big city, capable
of harboring millions upon millions of people. They also suggest that evil will never be capable of breaching the walls of
our heavenly home. For God has built it to be both beautiful
and safe, a place where we will dwell with him forever.

The Way Up Is Down

If you try to hang on to your life, you will lose it. But if you give up your life for my sake and for the sake of the Good News, you will save it. Mark 8:35 NLT

Do you want to go to heaven? I'll tell you one sure way. Be willing to die.

I'm not talking about committing suicide, but about something much harder. Die to yourself daily. "Not my will be done, but yours, Lord." Instead of telling God what to do, obey what you know he wants you to do, regardless of the personal cost. "For you have died, and your life is hidden with Christ in God" (Colossians 3:3 ESV).

God always draws closest to those who continually abandon their right to be their own gods. He loves humility.

Strange as it seems, we find joy when we die to ourselves, accepting the extra work, the inconveniences, the detours, the sacrifices. As A. W. Tozer said: "It is an interesting thing that when he wants to get up, the Christian always starts down, for God's way up is always down. Even though that is contrary to common sense. It is also contrary to the finest wisdom on the earth, because the foolish things of God are wiser than anything on this earth."[130]

Looking Back

*Whom have I in heaven but you? And there is nothing on earth
that I desire other than you.* Psalm 73:25 NRSV

Once you get to heaven, will you want to reach back for your
past life? Will you yearn for the things you loved—chocolate,
snowflakes, red sunsets, apple blossoms, a kiss? Will you be
able to "check in" on others who've been left behind?

Scripture doesn't really tell us clearly. I wonder if perhaps
we will perceive our lives as a dream. When you're just waking up from sleep, still able to recall a dream, you may feel
delighted (or disappointed) to find out that the dream isn't real.
Perhaps you'll feel the same about your past life when you get
to heaven. Maybe some faded images or feelings will linger,
but you won't quite recall the exact details.

I think of the chorus of the hymn "Turn Your Eyes Upon
Jesus":

> *Turn your eyes upon Jesus,*
> *look full in his wonderful face,*
> *And the things of earth will go strangely dim*
> *in the light of his glory and grace.*[131]

Both the sorrows and the sweet things of life may or may
not be erased from your memory once you get to heaven.
We don't know. But what we do know is that whatever we
remember will be seen "in the light of his glory and grace."

Clarity

Then I saw heaven opened. . . . Revelation 19:11 NLT

Dr. Reggie Anderson has practiced family medicine for more than twenty-five years and is medical director of three nursing homes. During that time, he's had many opportunities to be with patients as they have passed from this life to the next. Many times he's noticed something different about a patient's gaze as they near death.

"The signs of this gaze," he says, "are so distinctive and recognizable that they could easily be confused with mental illness. During my early years, if the patients who exhibited this gaze were young and healthy, I'd have probably said they were schizophrenic, because they didn't look at me—they looked *through* me. But with time and experience, I've come to realize that this is just one more sign that heaven is near."[132]

Anderson goes on to say that he believes these patients may be able to sense an unseen presence, someone who gives them great peace. In such cases, he believes God is present in a special way in order to ease people's fears as they make the journey from earth to heaven.

The next time you are with someone who seems close to death, don't be too quick to write off whatever visions they may have. Especially if they produce peace, such visions may indicate, not mental instability, but a heavenly clarity about what is really going on.

New Heaven and New Earth

"Look, I am making everything new!" Revelation 21:5 NLT

While going to heaven when we die is part of the good news, even better news comes from realizing that we will one day live on the new earth that God has promised for all who love him.

Theologian Wayne Grudem explains it this way: "Christians often talk about living with God 'in heaven' forever. But in fact the biblical teaching is richer than that: it tells us that there will be new heavens *and a new earth*—an entirely renewed creation—and we will live with God there."[133]

Truly we will go to heaven to live in Jesus' presence when we die. But heaven as it is now is not our ultimate landing place. In heaven, we will await the final judgment, Christ's return to earth, our bodily resurrection, and the creation of a brand-new heaven and earth. When that happens, we will experience all the joys of heaven that God has stored up for us.

All Creatures Great and Small

*And I heard every creature in heaven, on earth, in the world
below, and in the sea—all living beings in the universe—and they
were singing:*

   *"To him who sits on the throne and to the Lamb, be praise and
honor, glory and might, forever and ever!"   Revelation 5:13 NLT*

Many people wonder whether there will be animals in heaven.
It's interesting to note that the Bible uses the Greek word *zoon*
to mean not only "creatures" but also "animals." According
to Randy Alcorn, "In virtually every case inside and outside
of Scripture, this word means not a person, not angels, but an
animal."[134]

   Why should we be surprised to find animals praising God
in heaven? Like human beings, they tell us something about
God because they are part of his creation. Also, like Adam,
they were created out of the soil: "From the ground God
formed every wild animal and every bird in the sky" (Genesis
2:19 NCV). And "since the creation of the world God's invisible
qualities—his eternal power and divine nature—have been
clearly seen, being understood from what has been made"
(Romans 1:20 NIV).

   Today, let's join the psalmist as he proclaims the greatness
of the God who made us all: "Praise the Lord, all living creatures! Praise the Lord!" (Psalm 150:6 GNT).

It's Not Too Late

For I know the plans I have for you," declares the LORD, *"plans to prosper you and not to harm you, plans to give you hope and a future. Jeremiah 29:11*

I like what philosopher Dallas Willard has to say to those of us who feel disappointed by how their lives have turned out.

"I meet many faithful Christians who, in spite of their faith, are deeply disappointed in how their lives have turned out. Sometimes it is simply a matter of how they experience aging, which they take to mean they no longer have a future. But often, due to circumstances or wrongful decisions and actions by others, what they had hoped to accomplish in their life they did not. They painfully puzzle over what they may have done wrong, or over whether God has really been with them.

"Much of the distress of these good people comes from a failure to realize that their life lies before them. That they are coming to the end of their present life, life 'in the flesh,' is of little significance. What is of significance is the kind of person they have become. Circumstances and other people are not in control of an individual's character or of the life that lies end-lessly before us in the kingdom of God."[135]

So, dear reader, if you feel disappointed, cheer up. For God has promised to prosper you and not to harm you, to give you a future full of hope.

Soon We Will Understand

Think over what I say, for the Lord will give you understanding in all things. 2 Timothy 2:7 NRSV

During the Age of Exploration (the early fifteenth to early seventeenth centuries), adventurous Europeans sailed across oceans into the unknown. Imagine embarking from your native land, as Columbus did, with the knowledge that you might never return. He must have had incredible curiosity coupled with a powerful desire to discover the riches of a whole new world to take the risks he did.

It seems that God has made people curious for a reason. He wants us to discover the secrets of the created world, with each generation building on the knowledge of the last. Rather than leading to pride, such discoveries ought to humble us, because they reveal, not how smart we are, but how great God is.

Though no one is looking for new continents these days, there is still much to discover about the place we call heaven. Fortunately, through Scripture, we do know some things about it. For one thing, God has assured us that heaven is as real a place as China, America, or India was in the Age of Exploration. Just because we haven't yet reached it, doesn't mean it doesn't exist.

Eagles and Palm Trees

Let us go to the sanctuary of the Lord;
let us worship at the footstool of his throne.
Arise, O Lord, and enter your resting place,
along with the Ark, the symbol of your power. Psalm 132:7–8 NLT

Our world is shot through with images of heaven, though we may not recognize them. One way to heighten our awareness of heaven is to let the created world remind us of it.

Think about the history of Western art. Many of the classical paintings on view in our museums were created during a time in which all art was essentially religious. Even works that didn't seem overtly religious would often contain spiritually symbolic images. A painter, for instance, might include an eagle in a landscape to symbolize the resurrection or a peacock to indicate immortality. Or he might indicate "heaven" by portraying peaceful outdoor scenes, banks of clouds, blue sky, or palm trees and vines in a bountiful garden. Artists drew inspiration from the created world to point toward heaven.

Why not consider visiting a museum or pulling up images of classical art on the Internet to see if you can spot symbols of heaven in them. See, too, if you can find ways to look for signs of heaven in your own life, as you take a walk outdoors, gaze up at the night sky, or simply look out the window. If you let them, every leaf and pebble will remind you of the wonders in store for those who love God.

Heaven's Waiting Room

There will be great joy for those who are ready and waiting for his return. Luke 12:37 TLB

What comes to mind when you think of Florida? Beaches, Key lime pie, theme parks, Cape Canaveral? Some people call the Sunshine State "heaven's waiting room" because of the large number of retirees who live there. Of course, it's all relative. From an eternal perspective, the whole planet is heaven's waiting room.

But our life on earth is meant to consist of far more than just passively waiting around for heaven. Jesus tells us we're to use our time here to complete his work. Just what does that work consist of? Our mission is to go out into the world and preach the gospel (Mark 16:15). Spreading the Good News can take many forms, including the work involved in raising children, earning a living, and, yes, even caring for the sick and dying. Wherever we are and whatever we're doing, we're called to tell others about Jesus.

So earth is the busiest waiting room you could ever imagine, with each one of us sharing the Good News so that as many people as possible will come into the kingdom of heaven.

You Can't Take It with You

What good is it for someone to gain the whole world, yet forfeit their soul? Mark 8:36 NIV

Have you heard the joke about why you never see a hearse with a trailer hitch on it?...Because when you die, it's impossible to take any possessions with you. But do we really believe that? If so, why do we work so hard to amass goods and properties that we'll have to leave behind when we die?

Jesus told a parable about a man who tried to store his goods against the future:

There was a rich man who had some land, which grew a good crop. He thought to himself, "What will I do? I have no place to keep all my crops." Then he said, "This is what I will do: I will tear down my barns and build bigger ones, and there I will store all my grain and other goods. Then I can say to myself, 'I have enough good things stored to last for many years. Rest, eat, drink, and enjoy life!'" But God said to him, "Foolish man! Tonight your life will be taken from you. So who will get those things you have prepared for yourself?"

This is how it will be for those who store up things for themselves and are not rich toward God. (Luke 12:16–21 NCV)

Let's not let our need for security distract us from the thing that matters most—being rich toward God by investing ourselves in his work.

We Belong to Each Other

The LORD blessed the latter part of Job's life more than the former
part. He had fourteen thousand sheep, six thousand camels, a
thousand yoke of oxen and a thousand donkeys. And he also had
seven sons and three daughters. Job 42:12

One of the most painful aspects of death is its finality. No chance to touch, see, or talk to the those we love, not ever again. Or so it would seem. But listen to what Charles Spurgeon has to say, speaking about the biblical character Job, who lost everything in the space of a single day. Spurgeon comments on how God eventually rewarded Job in the face of his overwhelming loss.

"Did you ever notice, concerning Job's children, that when God gave him twice as much substance as he had before, he gave him only the same number of children as he formerly had? The Lord gave him twice as much gold, and twice as much of all sorts of property, but he only gave him the exact number of children that he had before. Why did he not give the patriarch double the number of children as well as twice the number of cattle? Why, because God reckoned the first ones as being his still. They were dead to Job's eyes, but they were visible to Job's faith! God still numbered them as part of Job's family—and if you carefully count up how many children Job had, you will find that he had twice as many in the end as he had in the beginning! In the same way, consider your friends who are asleep in Christ as still yours—not a single one lost."[136]

Not a single soul is lost of those who love Christ. They are not lost to God and they are not lost to you. You will see them, talk with them, and embrace them again one day.

Not My Time!

An angel of the Lord appeared to them, and the glory of the Lord shone around them, and they were terrified. But the angel said to them, "Do not be afraid." Luke 2:9–10

"It's not my time, it's not my time!" Dr. Reggie Anderson could hear his patient's loud lament as he walked toward her room. What she said next surprised him. "Keep them away....Their colors are so bright. They're hurting my eyes!" That Lois claimed to have seen anything was amazing, since she had been born blind. Now she seemed to be shooing away invisible beings.

Concluding that she must be hallucinating, Anderson decided to prescribe a sedative to calm her. Just as he got to the nurses' station to pull her chart, he heard a Code 10 alert. Someone needed CPR. The code was for Lois's room.

Racing down the hallway, he asked himself what he had missed. Why hadn't he realized she'd been in danger? But when he got to her room, he realized the person needing CPR was not Lois but her roommate Sissy. Anderson quickly began to administer CPR. But it was too late. Sissy was gone.

Fearing Lois would be even more agitated by now, he pulled back the curtain that separated her from Sissy's bed to inquire how she was. To his surprise her vitals checked out perfectly and she seemed calm. Then she explained why she'd been so upset. It was all those angels that had been flying over her bed prior to Sissy's passing. Their lights were simply too bright for her eyes to handle.

As Anderson left Lois's room that day, he couldn't help but smile. She had been right all along. It wasn't her time to go. The angels had come not to escort her, but Sissy to heaven. For some reason, God had allowed a blind woman to witness another person's passing into heaven. As to the sedative he was going to prescribe? Well, it no longer seemed necessary.

"You Have a Friend in Heaven"

Greater love has no one than this: to lay down one's life for one's friends. John 15:3 NIV

A troop of British soldiers was about to embark for the Crimean War. Knowing they would be fearful, their chaplain invited Charles Kingsley (Anglican priest and well-known writer) to come and encourage them. He spoke to them about how nothing could separate them from Jesus, not even the harsh conditions of war: "You have a Friend in heaven," he said, "who feels for every trouble of yours, better than your own mothers can feel for you, because He has been through it already. You have a Friend in heaven who is praying for you day and night, more earnestly, lovingly, wisely, than your own wives and children are praying for you. But that is not all.

"You have a Friend in heaven for whose sake God will forgive you all your sins and weaknesses, as often as you heartily confess them to Him. . . . You have a Friend in heaven who will help you day by day, where you most need help, in your hearts and spirits; who will give you, if you ask Him, His Spirit, the same spirit of duty, courage, endurance, love, self-sacrifice, which made Him brave to endure ten thousand times more than any soldier can endure."[147]

Like the young soldiers Kingsley was addressing, you and I have a Friend in heaven who will help us day by day where we most need his help.

Valley of the Shadow of Death

Yea, though I walk through the valley of the shadow of death, I will fear no evil: for thou art with me; thy rod and thy staff they comfort me. Psalm 23:4 KJV

Psalm 23 may be the most frequently memorized chapter of the Bible. When we come to the words "the valley of the shadow of death," most of us think of the valley as the approach to death itself, the ultimate horror.

The famous preacher Charles Spurgeon thought otherwise, and here is what he said about it: "'The valley of the shadow of death,' of which David spoke, I do not think was ever meant to be applied to dying. For it is a valley that he walks through, and he comes out again at the other side. It is not the valley of death, but only of the shadow of death.

"I have walked through that valley many times—right through from one end of it to the other—and yet I have not died. The grim shadow of something worse than death has fallen over my spirit, but God has been with me...and his rod and his staff have comforted me....I believe that, often, those who feel great gloom in going through 'the valley of the shadow of death' feel no gloom at all when they come to the valley of death itself."[138]

Whether they are traveling through difficulties here on earth or crossing the dividing line into heaven itself, the Lord is the shepherd of those who follow him closely.

There Are No Ordinary People

> *"For a time is coming when all who are in their graves will hear his voice and come out—those who have done what is good will rise to live, and those who have done what is evil will rise to be condemned." John 5:28*

Why do we insist on talking about "ordinary people," as though there is any such thing? True, most of us will never become superstars, nor even hometown heroes, but none of us are ordinary.

C. S. Lewis reminds us of the truth about ourselves and others by saying, "It is a serious thing to live in a society of possible gods and goddesses, to remember that the dullest and most uninteresting person you can talk to may one day be a creature which, if you saw it now, you would be strongly tempted to worship, or else a horror and a corruption such as you now meet, if at all, only in a nightmare. All day long we are, in some degree, helping each other to one or the other of these destinations. It is in the light of these overwhelming possibilities, it is with the awe and the circumspection proper to them, that we should conduct all our dealings with one another, all friendships, all loves, all play, all politics. There are no *ordinary* people. You have never talked to a mere mortal. Nations, cultures, arts, civilizations—these are mortal, and their life is to ours as the life of a gnat. But it is immortals whom we joke with, work with, marry, snub, and exploit—immortal horrors or everlasting splendours."[139]

Who are you helping today toward one or the other of these destinations?

RSVP

There was once a man who was giving a great feast to which he
invited many people. When it was time for the feast, he sent his
servant to tell his guests, "Come, everything is ready!" But they
all began, one after another, to make excuses. Luke 14:15–18 GNT

In Jesus' parable of the banquet, each prospective guest declines
the invitation. They seem to have watertight excuses for why
they can't be there. But Jesus seems to think that for a feast this
important, no excuse is acceptable. He is really talking about
the great Messianic feast to come, the feast that will take place
in heaven and that will mark the beginning of the new heaven
and the new earth.

Notice that none of those who were invited have the nerve
to refuse the invitation outright. Instead they hem and haw:
"You know I would really love to come, but I have more
pressing things to attend to." Like the people in Jesus' parable,
many people who have heard the gospel have plausible excuses
for not responding. They may politely reject the faith or post-
pone thinking about it, thinking they will get serious about it
later. But "later" is just another word for "no."

If you know someone like that, pray for them because it is
not too late for them to realize their mistake. While they're
here on earth there is still time for them to change their no
to yes.

A Chilling Vision?

Today I have given you the choice between life and death, between blessings and curses. Now I call on heaven and earth to witness the choice you make. Oh, that you would choose life, so that you and your descendants might live! Deuteronomy 30:19 NLT

Eddie hadn't much time left. Dr. Reggie Anderson had been praying for him when he noticed that his patient had begun to stare off into the distance. But the look on Eddie's face was different than what he had previously witnessed as people drew near to death. A man who appeared to be both friendless and without faith, Eddie "seemed to be staring off into a great chasm. His eyes grew wide, he was restless, maybe even anxious, and I detected a look of fear on his face," Anderson recalls.

As Eddie's breath grew ragged, he seemed to cling desperately to each inhalation as though it was going to be his last. When the end finally came, the atmosphere of the room changed abruptly.

"Suddenly," says Anderson, "I felt some type of dark cloud present in the room. The light grew dimmer, and the temperature plummeted. The room was freezing cold as though the temperature had instantly dropped 100 degrees. The warmth I'd come to expect when heaven's door opened seemed to have been replaced by the opening of a liquid nitrogen canister. The room appeared dark and shadowy, as if it were being swallowed by a black abyss. . . . I wanted to get out as fast as I could. Evil had entered the room."[140]

Anderson was terrified by the experience. Reflecting on it, he believes that Eddie probably didn't like what he saw as he crossed to the other side. But he also believes that up to the moment of his death Eddie was free to make a very different choice had he wanted to.

Since that terrible experience in Eddie's room, where the darkness seemed to linger long after his passing, Reggie Anderson has been determined to tell as many people as possible about the reality of heaven and the saving power of Jesus.

He Ascended into Heaven

While he blessed them, he parted from them and was carried up into heaven. Luke 24:51 ESV

After his resurrection, Jesus ascended into heaven in full view of his disciples, who had accompanied him on foot from Jerusalem to the village of Bethany. None of the disciples had seen him rise from the tomb, but all of them had seen him alive, and now they watched, astonished, as his nail-scarred feet lifted off the soil and he disappeared under his own power into a cloud in the sky.

Bethany was the hometown of some of Jesus' favorite people, such as Mary and Martha and their brother Lazarus, whom he had raised from the dead. It was a place of blessing for him. Perhaps that is why he chose to take his disciples there one last time before departing to his Father.

Jesus departed with his hands raised in the act of blessing them. Soon he would send them his Spirit to be with them always. The disciples had been on an emotional roller coaster, but now they could return to Jerusalem filled with joyous anticipation. Now they knew that, like their Master, they too would someday go to their Father in heaven.

Second Shift

"But many who are first will be last; and the last, first. . . ."
" '[Friend,] take what is yours and go, but I wish to give to this last man the same as to you. Is it not lawful for me to do what I wish with what is my own? Or is your eye envious because I am generous?' " Matthew 19:30; 20:14–15 NASB

Jesus wanted to counter the false assumption that people could buy their way into God's favor, so he told a parable. He had just finished explaining to his disciples how difficult it is for a rich man to enter heaven, and his disciples, although none were wealthy men, remained a little dubious. They had always believed that heavenly merit could be acquired through self-sacrifice.

The parable tracks a landowner who was hiring temporary laborers to bring in his harvest. He went several times to the local marketplace to hire available men. Then at the end of the day, he paid the same wage to each laborer, regardless of how many hours each had worked. When the ones who had toiled longest complained, he explained that their relative seniority could not command higher pay from him, since as the boss he could pay people as he wished, and that they should not be rankled about his seeming unfairness because it sprang from his benevolence and generosity.

You and I can take both reassurance and caution from this parable. While we must heed God's initial summons and follow him closely into the "fields," our actual accomplishments do not stack up in our favor, and he does not grade on a curve. We cannot get into heaven by our good works. Only our faithfulness counts.

Heaven Street

I am the way, and the truth, and the life; no one comes to the Father but through Me.   John 14:6 NASB

Just north of the little town of Norlina, North Carolina, a road threads through the rolling countryside. It is called Heaven Street, and it is the only road that goes straight up out of Norlina. (The town name combines "North" and "Carolina.")

In the same way, there is only one way that leads to heaven. Jesus made it very clear when he told his disciples, "I am the way, and the truth, and the life," stating that he himself was the only possible way to approach the Father in heaven.

Sometimes people say, "We're all going to heaven. We are just taking different roads." That's not true for the simple reason that there are no different roads—none that go all the way to heaven, anyway. There's only one Heaven Street; only one Way gets you there.

Work in Heaven?

Let the favor of the Lord our God be upon us, and prosper for us the work of our hands—O prosper the work of our hands! Psalm 90:17 NRSV

Nathan loved his work as a lawyer. He was diligent and conscientious and he loved helping people. Sometimes it concerned him to think that when he got to heaven, he would have to give it up. It didn't really appeal to him to think of himself sitting around on a cloud, plucking a harp, polishing a halo, and attending praise fests. *Why can't we* work *in heaven?* he thought. *After all, God created work as a good thing. Aren't all good things in heaven?*

Good point. God created both work and rest in those first days of creation when he declared everything "very good" (Genesis 1:31). He handed over to Adam the responsibilities of maintaining and caring for the Garden and he gave him specific tasks such as naming the animals (see Genesis 2:19).

God has given talents and abilities to each of us. Some of us find the perfect matchup between our talents and our work here on earth, but all of us will find that combination in heaven. According to David Gregg, "It is work according to one's tastes and delight and ability. If tastes vary there [in heaven], if abilities vary there, then occupations will vary there."[141]

God will use every gift and talent in heaven and in the new heaven and new earth. Our work will be the best ever, whatever it is, and we will do it without frustration, conflict, or weariness.

Throne and Footstool

This is what the Lord says, "Heaven is my throne and the earth is my footstool. Could you build me a temple as good as that? Could you build me such a resting place? My hands have made both heaven and earth; they and everything in them are mine. I, the Lord, have spoken!" Isaiah 66:1–2 NLT

How grand and unfathomable God is! The vast and endless heavens are his throne. But wait . . . you mean this little speck called earth is merely the place where God rests his feet? The world we think is so impressive is only God's footstool? Who am I, then, that God should even care about me?

The incredible truth, as confirmed by Scripture, is that God does care for each one of us (see 1 Peter 5:7). The God whose throne is the vast expanse of heaven calls us his children (see 1 John 3:1). He calls me by my name and says, "You are mine" (Isaiah 43:1 NLT) and he has written my name on the palm of his hand (see Isaiah 49:16). He is simultaneously both the most magnificent and the most personal God.

Heaven is the location of his throne, but it is also his home. When he invites us to join him there, what better place to start from than his very own footstool?

Eternity Is Now

You have been allowed to approach the true Mount Zion, the city
of the living God, the heavenly Jerusalem. You have drawn near
to the countless angelic army, the great assembly of Heaven and
the Church of the first-born whose names are written above. You
have drawn near to God, the judge of all, to the souls of good men
made perfect, and to Jesus, mediator of a new agreement. Hebrews
12:22–24 PHILLIPS

This passage speaks not only about our future reality; it is as
present-tense as what you are doing right now—reading this
page. Those who belong to Christ already have access to eternal life. And that life comes with countless benefits.

As Paul says, "You can be sure that God will take care of
everything you need, his generosity exceeding even yours in
the glory that pours from Jesus. Our God and Father abounds
in glory that just pours out into eternity" (Philippians 4:19
MSG).

I like that word "abounds" and the phrase "everything you
need," which does not imply only the bare necessities. God's
generosity is limitless. Paul's Greek word means "to make
replete, i.e., to cram, to satisfy, to fill up." Heavenly abundance? We have access right now!

The God of All Comfort

Now may our Lord Jesus Christ Himself and God our Father,
who has loved us and given us eternal comfort and good hope by
grace, comfort and strengthen your hearts in every good work and
word. 2 Thessalonians 2:16–17 NASB

Every year as the leaves turn color and the air grows cold, those who live in northern climates start thinking about comfort food: bubbling vegetable soup, creamy mashed potatoes, meat loaf, and chicken pot pies. A friend's recent Facebook post put a lovely twist to the food idea. She shared her status this way: "Pot roast and veggies are in the slow cooker. Banana muffins in the oven. Wonderful aromas waft through the apartment on this cold, grey rainy afternoon. If God is indeed my only comfort, then these heavenly smells must be one of God's sweet ways of providing."

God provides us with the hope and comfort we need. His comfort often comes to us in simple pleasures—like the heavenly smell of pot roast, vegetables, and muffins. His comfort also comes through answered prayers and good friends. Through just the right word spoken at just the right time. Let's be open today to every simple blessing God wants to give, letting each serve as evidence of the overwhelming blessings that we will one day receive when we see him face-to-face.

Early Adopter

We ourselves, who have the first fruits of the Spirit, groan inwardly while we wait for adoption, the redemption of our bodies. For in hope we were saved. Romans 8:23–24 NRSV

The term "early adopter" became popular in the 1960s to describe a person who embraces new technology more readily than other people. Early adopters are the first on their block to purchase the latest and smartest new phone, energy-saving device, or gadget.

Everett M. Rogers, the sociologist who originated the term in his book *Diffusion of Innovations*, wrote that early adopters are not necessarily looking for excitement and risks. They take the plunge because they see no value in waiting until something has proven its reliability and value. Once others see the benefits that are showcased by the early adopters they tend to adopt the technology, too. Eventually the majority of people, even the "laggards," have a chance to taste and see that the new thing is a good thing.

As it turns out, God is both the great innovator and the original early adopter. He created everything. He adopted us early. He waits with urgent patience for each one of us to pay attention to the obvious benefits of his kingdom as we see them manifested in the believers around us. He seems willing to keep the door to heaven propped open until even the most laggardly ones can troop in.

The Kingdom of Heaven Is Like...

[Jesus told his disciples:] You are permitted to understand the secrets of the Kingdom of Heaven, but others are not. To those who listen to my teaching, more understanding will be given, and they will have an abundance of knowledge. Matthew 13:11–12 NLT

Jesus knows heaven better than anyone. To try to describe it to people who had never been there, he used several different metaphors. He said:

Of its worth—"The kingdom of heaven is like treasure hidden in a field, which someone found and hid; then in his joy he goes and sells all that he has and buys that field." (Matthew 13:44 NRSV)

Of its pervasiveness—"The Kingdom of Heaven is like the yeast a woman used in making bread. Even though she put only a little yeast in three measures of flour, it permeated every part of the dough." (Matthew 13:33 NLT)

Of its exclusivity—"Again, the kingdom of heaven is like a net that was thrown into the sea and caught fish of every kind; when it was full, they drew it ashore, sat down, and put the good into baskets but threw out the bad." (Matthew 13:47–48 NRSV)

Of its vastness—"The Kingdom of Heaven is like a mustard seed planted in a field. It is the smallest of all seeds, but it becomes the largest of garden plants; it grows into a tree." (Matthew 13:31–32 NLT)

Heaven is like (but unlike) anything you can see or imagine. Good thing we will have eternity to explore its marvels!

Ours Forever

> *"Son, you are always with me, and all that is mine is
> yours."* Luke 15:31 ESV

Amy Carmichael left Ireland when she was in her early twenties to live out her life in India, sacrificing the comforts of marriage and family for the sake of the outcast Indian children she served. By the time she died, she had published a number of books of prose and poetry.

In her book *Kohila: The Shaping of an Indian Nurse*, she published a short poem called "Ours Forever."[142] The first line reads like this: "All that was ever ours is ours forever."

What *is* "ever ours"? Only the things that count—everything that God has given or has promised to give us—life, grace, mercy, goodness, kindness, rescue, and eternal happiness. He has given us these and more. He has poured out countless blessings for today and even greater promises for tomorrow.

Do You Believe?

> *O send out your light and your truth;*
> *let them lead me;*
> *let them bring me to your holy hill*
> *and to your dwelling. Psalm 43:3 NRSV*

By the age of eighteen, Ben Breedlove had already cheated death many times. When he was only four, he had a seizure that nearly killed him. Suffering since birth from a dangerous heart condition called hypertrophic cardiomyopathy, Ben was being wheeled down a dimly lit corridor to a room in the intensive care unit when it happened. Fixing his eyes on a point right above him, he asked, "Look at the bright light! Do you see that, Mama?"

"Ben, I don't see a light,"[143] his mother responded. In fact, the corridor was exceptionally dark that day because the electricity had been turned off due to construction. Only a little bit of light from the overcast day seeped in through windows that lined one side of the hallway.

Years later, Ben explained his experience. "I got a feeling that I didn't have to care about anything that was happening in the world at that moment. I couldn't see anything else around me, not even in my peripheral vision, just this bright white light above me. Nothing could be heard; everything was calm....

"I know God wanted me to be calm during the situation and have a sense of peace, and not worry about anything that was going on during those moments....

"I know an angel was watching over me, literally."[144]

On Christmas day of 2011, eighteen-year-old Ben Breedlove finally went to heaven, but not before sharing his story with the world. Six days prior to his passing, he uploaded a video on YouTube titled "This Is My Story." Since then, Ben's story has gone viral. In it he asks a simple question: "Do you believe in Angels or God?" Then he follows with his own simple response:

"*I Do.*"[45]

Pie in the Sky

If a brother or sister is poorly clothed and lacking in daily food, and one of you says to them, "Go in peace, be warmed and filled," without giving them the things needed for the body, what good is that? So also faith by itself, if it does not have works, is dead.   James 2:15–17 ESV

"Forget it! You Christians! You are always so 'pie-in-the-sky-bye-and-bye.' Give me something *real*, now." The criticism stings, especially when you thought you *did* offer something very real. What should you think?

A radical labor organizer first used the expression "pie in the sky" in a parody of a Salvation Army hymn called "In the Sweet Bye and Bye." He didn't have much use for people who pointed to a future heavenly reward instead of putting food on a plate right now.

Writer Kathleen Norris neatly captured the argument when she wrote: "Christians have been much castigated over the centuries for having…a 'pie-in-the-sky' mentality. Otherworldliness can be a real temptation in the religion, but the Incarnation itself is a corrective. Down to earth, real flesh and blood."[146]

Yes. Jesus left heaven and came to earth specifically to bridge the yawning chasm between the two. His followers—with a few exceptions—give evidence of his incarnation as they reach out in love to the people around them. True faith brings heaven to earth on a daily basis. What good is a polished facsimile of faith that merely nods sweetly and gazes vaguely toward the sky?

Fearlessness

If God is for us, who is against us? . . . Who will separate us from the love of Christ? Will hardship, or distress, or persecution, or famine, or nakedness, or peril, or sword? . . . No, in all these things we are more than conquerors through him who loved us. For I am convinced that neither death, nor life, nor angels, nor rulers, nor things present, nor things to come, nor powers, nor height, nor depth, nor anything else in all creation, will be able to separate us from the love of God in Christ Jesus our Lord. Romans 8:31, 35, 37–39 NRSV

Most of our fears boil down to the fear of death. Some of us fear dying while others fear only the pain that accompanies death. Yet God has given us a gift that can conquer even that worst of all fears.

I like what philosopher Peter Kreeft says about the invincible protection we have been given. "The theological consequence of believing what we have been told is utter fearlessness. Nothing in the universe can separate us from our joy, from our God. Nothing can harm us. We are impervious. We are redeemed, indestructible souls guaranteed new, indestructible bodies. We can even rejoice in all the sufferings of our earthly bodies (that's what it says, not 'endure' but 'rejoice in'; don't argue with me, argue with the Bible) because they are 'working out an eternal weight of glory' (2 Corinthians 4:17)."[147]

The next time you feel a pang of fear tear through your chest, try blasting it, not with the power of positive thinking, but with the faith God has given you, trusting that he is both strong enough and good enough to allow nothing in the universe to separate you from his love.

Tears That Lead to Heaven

Let us examine and see what we have done and then return to the Lord. Let us lift up our hands and pray from our hearts to God in heaven:

"We have sinned and turned against you, and you have not forgiven us. . . ."

My tears flow continually, without stopping, until the Lord looks down and sees from heaven. Lamentations 3:40–42, 49–50 NCV

The Book of Lamentations is exactly what you might think—one lamentation after another, a funeral dirge for the city of Jerusalem and its inhabitants. Sorrowful as it is, it strikes a clear note of hope throughout.

Jeremiah, the writer of Lamentations, isn't just detailing the woes of God's people for the sake of raising his voice in complaint. He is saying that God allows troubles because he intends them to lead us back to him. Although Jeremiah is known as "the weeping prophet," his faith echoes that of the psalmist who said this about God:

For his anger lasts only a moment,
but his favor lasts a lifetime!
Weeping may last through the night,
but joy comes with the morning. (Psalm 30:5 NLT)

Troubles of our own making will not always lead us straight to heaven, but if we repent of what we've done wrong, they will surely lead us one step closer.

Jesus and Joy

Leap for joy: for, behold, your reward is great in heaven. Luke
6:23 KJV

Billy Graham turned ninety-five last year. Because of his
advanced age, there is concern about when the world might
lose him. Can you imagine the throng of people who will greet
him in heaven, people who gave their lives to God as a result of
hearing him preach the gospel? What a party that will be!

Over the years, Graham has done his own kind of wondering about heaven. Here's what he said:

> *What is heaven going to be like? Just as there is a mystery to
> hell, so there is a mystery to heaven. Yet, I believe the Bible
> teaches that heaven is a literal place. Is it one of the stars? I don't
> know. I can't even speculate. The Bible doesn't inform us. I
> believe that out there in space where there are one thousand mil-
> lion galaxies, each a hundred thousand light-years or more in
> diameter, God can find some place to put us in heaven. I'm not
> worried about where it is. I know it is going to be where Jesus is.
> Christians don't have to go around discouraged and despondent
> with their shoulders bent. Think of it—the joy, the peace, the
> sense of forgiveness that He gives you, and then heaven too.[148]*

Jesus and Joy—these are synonymous.

Perfect Praise

Praise the Lord!
Praise the Lord from the heavens;
　praise him in the heights!
Praise him, all his angels; praise him, all his host! . . .
Let them praise the name of the Lord,
　for his name alone is exalted;
　his glory is above earth and heaven. Psalm 148:1–2, 13 NRSV

Last Sunday I found it hard to concentrate. I was singing, praying, listening to Scripture being read in church, but not feeling much of anything. In fact my mind was wandering, going a thousand miles an hour in a million different directions.

Does that ever happen to you? You want to worship God, but find it difficult because you are so distracted?

Here on earth, it's easy for thoughts about upcoming tasks, vexing decisions, and personal worries to intrude on our worship. Fortunately, God is still being worshipped perfectly by at least one segment of his creation—the heavenly choir of angels. Right now they are focused on one thing only—on God and his greatness, giving him the worship he is due. Unlike us, angels are single-minded. They are never distracted.

Someday our praises will be that way, too. When we get to heaven we will praise God completely and purely. Nothing will tempt or divert us; nothing will tarnish our understanding. Instead, our voices will blend with the choir of heavenly angels in perfect praise to our perfect God.

Until then, God wants us to continue to come to him in worship. But why, if our efforts are so imperfect? Perhaps because he knows that he can make something beautiful from even our feeblest attempts.

The Finest Woman in the World

Let your light shine before others, so that they may see your good works and give glory to your Father who is in heaven. Matthew 5:16 ESV

For we are his workmanship, created in Christ Jesus for good works, which God prepared beforehand, that we should walk in them. Ephesians 2:10 ESV

"I conducted a funeral," writes Benedict Groeschel in his book *Arise from Darkness*, "for an elderly lady named Vivian. She was a devout, kindly, gentle woman and belonged to some little storefront church. In her old age she was really too ill to go out. Her family was on our list for food baskets, and so they asked me to do the funeral service. I walked up to the funeral parlor with her husband, a dignified and friendly gentleman.... 'She was the finest woman in the world...the finest woman in the world.' He kept saying that.... [He] came up to the casket before we left. So simply and directly he stood there with his hands on the casket and said over and over again, 'I love you.' It was beautiful and solemn."[149]

"Heaven" was never mentioned during the funeral. Everyone simply assumed, based on her good life, that Vivian had been short-listed for the ultimate prize.

Quite likely that was true. But not because of her fine character and her good works themselves. More than likely, her character matured and her good works spread themselves over decades because they sprang from a solid foundation of faith in the Savior she knew as "Jesus."

Angelic Escort

Do not forget to show hospitality to strangers, for by so doing
some people have shown hospitality to angels without knowing
it. Hebrews 13:2 NIV

"When death is near, angels appear."

Dan never believed that. A rugged man of the earth, he had built a beautiful log home in the woods for himself and his wife, Bev. Over time, their land had become a bird sanctuary. Bev shared Dan's enthusiasm for the outdoors and for their feathered visitors, but with one important difference—she always kept her eye on a place beyond the birds that she called heaven. Dan wouldn't buy it.

"Fairy tales. Don't expect me to believe—or discuss—it."

Then came the cancer. When the doctors sent Dan home to die, Bev was afraid Dan's hard-line approach to heaven would prevent him from going there.

Then one night, he received some unexpected visitors.

It was near the end. Bev decided to let the dog out before going to bed. She could hear the hooting of a barred owl when she opened the door.

When she returned, she found Dan sitting on the end of his bed with a pleased smile on his face. "Weren't those the nicest folks!" he exclaimed in a raspy whisper.

"Who?"

"Those visitors. You know them! They said they will be back for me soon." He settled back into his pillow and then dozed off. At first Bev didn't know what to think. Could Dan's unexpected visitors have been angels? From the smile on his face, she concluded that he must have changed his mind about the "fairy tale" he called heaven.

Dan breathed his last only a couple of nights later. Outside, the owls shared the news.

By the Power of the Holy Spirit
Sent from Heaven

*Keep alert and set your hope completely on the blessing which will
be given you when Jesus Christ is revealed.* 1 Peter 1:13 GNT

If the Apostle Peter could be a guest speaker in your church on
Sunday, he would preach the same message he preached right
after Jesus' death and resurrection. He would say something
like this:

"Listen, everybody, you've got to keep your attention
focused on the truth, and the only way you can do that is with
the help of Jesus' Spirit.

"The same Spirit has been at work each day of each week
of each month of each year over all the centuries and millennia
since the creation of the earth. He didn't remain hidden away
in heaven. The Holy Spirit is right here, right now. He is still
working, still explaining things to people, still motivating
and helping them concentrate on the things of heaven. You
don't have to be like one of the prophets of old to understand
what God is saying. What God revealed to the prophets was
for your benefit. But now you have heard it more clearly as the
Good News announced by messengers through the power of
the Holy Spirit sent from heaven."

Come, Holy Spirit!

The Second Coming

For as the lightning comes from the east and shines as far as the
west, so will be the coming of the Son of Man.   Matthew 24:27 ESV

Despite varying biblical interpretations about precisely *when*
and *how* it will happen, most Christians have at least a vague
notion of the *who*, *what*, *where*, and *why* of the "Second Coming."

Who is coming? Jesus.

What is the event? Jesus' return to the earth and to the people who call him "Savior."

Where will he come from? Heaven.

Why will he come? Jesus will come to claim his own and
to take his rightful place as ruler and king, quelling all the
competition.

According to Jesus' own words, he will come suddenly.
The timing of the event is impossible for us to know, but when
it happens at long last, it will happen fast—too fast to "make
good" at the last moment.

That is why, instead of quibbling about future details, we
must focus on our present state of readiness. If he came back
this afternoon, would I be ready for him? Would you?

Will We Know Each Other in Heaven?

Precious in the sight of the Lord is the death of his faithful ones.   Psalm 116:15 NRSV

When we get to heaven, will we recognize our friends? Will we know the Apostle Paul when we see him? Will we rub shoulders with illustrious saints who died centuries ago? The English Puritan theologian Richard Baxter tackled this question in 1651, in his book called *The Saints' Everlasting Rest*:

> *It is a question with some whether or not we shall know each other in heaven. . . . Indeed, we shall not know each other after the flesh, not by stature, voice, color, complexion, visage, or outward shape, . . . but by the image of Christ and spiritual relation and former faithfulness in improving our talents, beyond doubt, we shall know and be known.*
>
> *Nor is it only our old acquaintance, but all the saints of all the ages, whose faces in the flesh we never say, whom we shall there both know and comfortably enjoy. Those who now are willingly ministering spirits for our good will willingly then be our companions in joy for the perfecting of our good; and they who had such joy in heaven for our conversion will gladly rejoice with us in our glorification. I think, Christian, this will be a more honorable assembly than ever you beheld and a more happy society than you were ever in before.*
>
> *What a day will it be when we shall join with them in praises to our Lord in and for that kingdom!*[150]

The Last Awakening

There will be no more night. They will not need the light of a lamp or the light of the sun, for the Lord God will give them light.   Revelation 22:5

When Britain's Queen Mother Elizabeth died in 2002, every mourner, whether royal or commoner, could see, even in the midst of the pomp and circumstance of the funeral, that God's grace provides the only admittance to heaven.

The Dean of Westminster commended the deceased queen to God in prayer, incorporating a well-known prayer written by seventeenth-century poet John Donne:

O Eternal God, our Heavenly Father, we bless thy holy name for all that thou has given us in and through the life of thy daughter Elizabeth. . . . We offer thee our heartfelt thanks for the deep affection she drew out of everyone she met, and we pray that thou wilt grant her peace; let light perpetual shine upon her; and in thy loving wisdom and almighty power work in her the good purpose of thy perfect will. . . . "Bring us, O Lord God, at our last awakening into the house and gate of heaven, to enter into that gate and dwell in that house, where there shall be no darkness nor dazzling, but one equal light; no noise nor silence, but one equal music; no fears nor hopes, but one equal possession; no ends nor beginnings, but one equal eternity; in the habitations of thy glory and dominion world without end." Through Jesus Christ our Lord. Amen.

Queen or commoner? It doesn't matter. What does matter is that at the moment of our last awakening God will let the perpetual light of his presence shine upon us.

I Want to Go Home

So we fix our eyes not on what is seen, but on what is unseen. 2 Corinthians 4:18 NIV

"Oh, Ruthie, I'm ready to go Home. I wish God would just take me." Ninety-five-year-old Julianna had lived a long and fruitful life, and now she was bedridden. She knew she had become a burden to her elderly daughter, Ruthie. Not only did she want to leave it all behind, but she found herself yearning for the wonderful place called heaven, where she would be able once again to walk without her bent and frail body getting in the way.

"Mom, it's okay to long for heaven. Sometimes I long for it, too. It will be such a relief. But for now we need to be satisfied with what we have—our time together. I just love you."

Julianna's frustration reminds me of something Billy Graham once said: "I often wonder if God, in His sovereignty, allows our eyesight to cast a dim view of the here and now so that we may focus our spiritual eyes on the ever-after.... Don't let the burdens and hardships of this life distract you or discourage you. Keep your eyes firmly fixed on what God has promised at the end of the journey: Heaven itself."[151]

The Bridge

*Who hath ascended up into heaven, or descended? who hath
gathered the wind in his fists? who hath bound the waters in a
garment? who hath established all the ends of the earth? what is
his name, and what is his son's name, if thou canst tell? Proverbs
30:4 KJV*

Good questions. Nobody quite knew the answer until a long
time after the proverb writer asked. Then a baby was born
in a town called Bethlehem. When he grew up, he said this:
"No one has ever gone up to heaven except the Son of Man,
who came down from heaven" (John 3:13 GNT). He was talking
about himself, of course.

Jesus' comments came just after he had finished telling the
incredulous Nicodemus that he must be born again in order
to enter the kingdom of God. He was explaining how such a
thing was possible. A person could be born all over again if
he was connected to the one who came down from heaven.
Through his death and resurrection, the one who came down
from heaven became the bridge between earth and heaven.

Only those who trust him are able to cross that bridge.
Let's trust him.

"Did You Learn to Love?"

LORD, the God of Israel, there is no God like you in heaven above or on earth below—you who keep your covenant of love with your servants who continue wholeheartedly in your way. 1 Kings 8:23 NIV

True story: Thirty-eight-year-old Bob suffered a ruptured artery and soon hemorrhaged to death. He reports that he saw his own body on the bed and then he entered a tunnel of light, accompanied by an angel. He ascended to a sort of a check-point, where Jesus himself stood. Three other people were also there.

Jesus asked the first one, a young girl who had died of a terminal disease, "Did you learn to love?" She found it easy to answer the question, "Yes!"

He queried the next person, a black woman who had been an evangelist, the same way. She too answered with a big "Yes!" and was admitted to her reward.

Next he asked the question of a bent-over, elderly woman. Life's hardships had embittered her, and although she had kept on loving God, she had not expressed his love to others. When Jesus asked, "Did you learn to love?" she (because nobody can tell a lie in his presence) had to answer accordingly. She was allowed to enter her eternal reward, but without the same level of honor as the others.

Before being asked the question himself, Bob was further surprised when Jesus sent him back to earth to complete his assigned life span. He found himself back on the bed, resuscitated. Needless to say, for the rest of his life he has paid a great deal of attention to growing in love—and he has always urged others to do the same!

Sweet Parting

Death gets its power to hurt from sin, and sin gets its power from the Law. But thanks be to God who gives us the victory through our Lord Jesus Christ! 1 Corinthians 15:16–17 GNT

I grew up in a good family, but my parents did not follow any particular faith. They had seen too many religious abuses, and they wanted to steer clear of such things. When I was little, I remember once asking my mother, "What happens after you die?"

"Nothing. It's just blackness."

I believed that for a while. But when I was a young teen, I discovered the reality of Jesus. Much to my parents' dismay, I even joined a church. Later, during college, I met and married a Christian man. We prayed for my parents, but never could persuade them to change their minds about God.

Years passed. My mother fell ill, and the diagnosis was dire: terminal cancer. Hers was not a quick and easy death. Between surgeries and chemotherapy, we spent much time together. As my mother suffered, she realized she had lost her ability to control her own future and she became open to God. Eventually it appeared that she had become a believer.

A conversation about heaven clinched it for me. Once a week, I would drive across the state to visit her. After one visit, I phoned her. "It was good to see you today. I never know if I'll see you again."

"Well, honey, even if I die tomorrow, you will see me again in heaven. I understand that it will seem like a long time to you—although it won't to me."

Heaven! She understood! Death would no longer bring blackness.

Dissed or Blissed?

Again, the Kingdom of Heaven is like a fishing net that was thrown into the water and caught fish of every kind. When the net was full, they dragged it up onto the shore, sat down, and sorted the good fish into crates, but threw the bad ones away. That is the way it will be at the end of the world. The angels will come and separate the wicked people from the righteous, throwing the wicked into the fiery furnace, where there will be weeping and gnashing of teeth. Matthew 13:47–50 NLT

Jesus had come to achieve what had before been impossible— to open the door to the kingdom of heaven—but he had not come to demolish heaven's alternative. In this story he points out that it's not enough to be swept up into God's net because in the last days angels will sort the good fish from the bad ones, throwing the wicked into a place of torment.

As if to underline the point, the next stop on Jesus' itinerant ministry was his native village: "When Jesus had finished telling these stories and illustrations, he left that part of the country. He returned to Nazareth, his hometown." Unfortunately, the people there seemed incredulous. How could this man, whose family they knew, be anything special? They scoffed at him, refusing to believe (Matthew 13:53–54, 57).

Sadly, tragically, they rejected the only man who could save them. The Good News is only good if you accept it.

Kingdom of Heaven?

The kingdom of heaven is near. Matthew 10:7 NCV

What exactly is the "kingdom of heaven," which Jesus speaks of? This phrase appears numerous times and only in the Gospel of Matthew. The other three gospel writers prefer the "kingdom of God," which is also found elsewhere in the New Testament.

Why is this? Do they mean the same thing? Bible scholars have split a few hairs about it.

One persuasive explanation for Matthew's usage is a simple one: Matthew avoided using the name of God because his gospel was written for Jews, who, out of reverence, avoid pronouncing the name of God. Instead they use "the Name" and other substitutes, of which "Heaven" is one.

The non-Jew Luke felt no such constraint on his use of the term "kingdom of God," because he wrote for other non-Jews (Gentiles). Throughout the gospels, parallel passages use the terms interchangeably. Each time, the thrust of the message remains unchanged. The kingdom of heaven = the kingdom of God.

For example, Jesus is quoted as saying, "Let the children come to me, and do not hinder them; for to such belongs the kingdom of heaven" (Matthew 19:14 RSV) and "Let the children come to me, do not hinder them; for to such belongs the kingdom of God" (Mark 10:14 RSV).

When Do We Get New Bodies?

". . . and at the last day I will raise them up." John 6:44 NLT

This winter broke records for snowfall, power outages, ice storms, and polar vortexes. But when spring finally arrived, it was a whole different story. With rising temperatures, flowers in bloom, and a steady supply of sunshine, everybody was so happy that you wondered if people were going to burst into song, as though they were characters in some kind of crazy musical. No wonder we cherish spring and wait for it with longing.

Will there be seasons in heaven? I don't know. But I'm pretty sure we won't be spending a lot of time waiting for spring because we're sick and tired of the season we're in. Waiting, though, will still be part of heaven, at least in one respect. Why? Because we will still be waiting for God to wrap things up, to complete his plan, to bring the new heaven and the new earth together.

We will also be waiting to be made whole again. After all, human beings are meant to be creatures with both a body and a soul. Death separates these parts of our being, but only temporarily.

What will these bodies be like? "I think," says Peter Kreeft, "our new resurrection body will be related to the body we have now in the same way that our current body is related to the body we had in our mothers' wombs. If a fetus saw a picture of itself at the age of twenty, it would at first not recognize itself, so unforeseen and surprisingly new would it be. Yet it is the same self, even the same body, now grown radically more mature."[152]

When God gathers all people together and sits on his judgment throne, that's when we'll get the kind of bodies we were always meant to have.

The River of Life

Then the angel showed me the river of the water of life,
bright as crystal, flowing from the throne of God and of the
Lamb.   Revelation 22:1 NRSV

In Brooklyn on a hot July day in 1864, Baptist pastor Robert Lowry was in a mental haze from the heat. With the long Civil War raging and a deadly epidemic in the city, his thoughts turned to funerals and death. He is reported to have said, "I began to wonder why the hymn writers had said so much about the 'river of death' and so little about the 'pure water of life, clear as crystal, proceeding out of the throne of God and the Lamb.'"

He turned in his Bible to the passage above and penned the now-famous hymn, "Shall We Gather at the River?" Part of it goes like this:

> *Shall we gather at the river,*
> *Where bright angel feet have trod,*
> *With its crystal tide forever*
> *Flowing by the throne of God?*
>
> *On the bosom of the river,*
> *Where the Savior-King we own,*
> *We shall meet and sorrow never*
> *'Neath the glory of the throne.*
>
> *Yes, we'll gather at the river,*
> *The beautiful, the beautiful river,*
> *Gather with the saints at the river*
> *That flows by the throne of God.*[153]

God Speaks in Many Different Ways

"To the one who conquers I will grant to eat of the tree of life, which is in the paradise of God." Revelation 2:7 ESV

Mary Neal's stepfather, George, had planted a Bradford pear tree in his yard several years earlier, eager for the day when he and his wife could enjoy looking out at its large, pink blossoms from their breakfast table. But though the tree grew taller over a period of years, it never produced a single blossom. Disheartened, he decided to cut it down in order to plant a new one.

Before he had the chance, he became ill with pneumonia and was taken to the local hospital. Despite the fact that George's physician seemed confident of his recovery, Mary decided to fly from her home in Jackson Hole, Wyoming, to be at her stepfather's side. Her first visit seemed to confirm the physician's prognosis. George appeared to be making good progress. The next morning as she and her mother sat together at the breakfast table looking out at the barren pear tree, her mother told her about George's plans to replace the tree.

Later that day, when they arrived at the hospital, both were shocked to see that George's condition had deteriorated. In only a matter of hours, he was dead.

The following morning, she and her mother were sitting at the breakfast table once again. As Mary Neal tells the story, they gasped when they looked out the window and saw that the "once forlorn Bradford pear tree was bursting with color." "The tree," she continued, "which had been barren just twenty-four hours earlier, was now filled beyond capacity with large, beautiful, perfect pink blossoms."[154]

What was going on? While Bradford pear trees can take years to produce their first blossoms, was it just a coincidence that this one burst into bloom the moment her stepfather passed from this life to the next? She didn't think so and neither do I.

To Heaven and Back

The LORD will keep you from all harm—
he will watch over your life;
the LORD will watch over your coming and going
both now and forevermore. Psalm 121:7–8

Mary Neal and her husband traveled to Pucón, Chile, in January 1999. An orthopedic surgeon and an experienced kayaker, she was looking forward to her run down a section of river known for its challenging waterfalls.

When it came time for the first drop, her boat rocketed down the falls, but then became trapped beneath them. With water thundering down, forcing her torso over the front deck of the boat, her arms reaching out in front of her, she tried in vain to raise her head above water. Unable to loosen the skirt of the kayak to free herself, she prayed, "Please, God, help me!" Though Neal knew she was drowning, she suddenly felt an overwhelming sense of peace and absolute calm, certain she would be all right even if the worst happened.

With no way to reach her, her companions watched helplessly as the water sucked her body out of the kayak and into the current, breaking her knees and ripping off her life jacket and helmet. Certain he was too late to save her, one of the men reached for her empty life jacket, thinking he could retrieve at least that much for her family. Suddenly he felt her body bump against his legs. Reaching into the water, he grabbed her wrist and swam her "purple, bloated, oxygen-starved body to the shore." It had been at least eleven and possibly fifteen minutes since she was first missed. And longer than that since she had been trapped facedown beneath the falls.

Meanwhile, something altogether different was taking place in Mary's mind. When her body was sucked out of her kayak and into the current, she felt a pop. "It felt," she said, "as if I had finally shaken off my heavy outer layer, freeing my soul. I rose up and out of the river...." At once she found herself in a different world, one she describes as "exponentially more colorful and intense. It was as though I was experiencing an explosion of love and joy in their absolute, unadulterated essence."

Mary felt herself being drawn toward a brilliant, light-filled hall, a place in which she believed "each of us is given the opportunity to review our lives and our choices, and where we are each given a final opportunity to choose God or to turn away—for eternity." As she approached, she sensed pure love radiating from the entryway. But before she could pass through, she was given disappointing news: her time had not yet arrived. There remained more for her to do on earth.

The rest of her story and how she was miraculously revived is told in dramatic detail in her book *To Heaven and Back*. Little wonder that Mary Neal's daily creed incorporates this statement: *I believe heaven is real*. How different our own lives would be if, like Mary, we embraced the reality of heaven in the midst of every trial.[155]

Minimizing Our Suffering?

For our light affliction, which is but for a moment, worketh for us
a far more exceeding and eternal weight of glory.   2 Corinthians
4:17 KJV

"Light affliction"? Doesn't it minimize life-shattering trag-
edies to call them "light"?

One November day when he was at the height of his football career, New York Jets defensive end Dennis Byrd crashed
headfirst into one of his teammates—and never got up from
the field. He was paralyzed from the waist down. Even after
months of surgeries and physical therapy his condition seemed
to be permanent.[156]

Author Mike Bickle picks up the "glory" part of his story:
"A reporter interviewed him for a prime-time special. After
telling the story of Dennis' career with interviews and video
clips, the reporter commented that the football player must
have a very strong faith. Dennis said quietly, 'Yes, I am a
believer in Jesus Christ.' When the reporter asked how Dennis' faith could be reconciled with having endured such a horrible accident, he probably wasn't expecting the answer he
received. With the conviction of a man who had thought this
through a thousand times, Dennis leveled his steely gaze at the
camera and said: 'For I consider that the sufferings of this present time are not worthy to be compared with the glory that
shall be revealed in us' (Romans 8:18)....

"Dennis was not minimizing his misfortune. He was placing
it in the context of eternity. He knew that this was not the first
time God had overlooked his broken humanity. In his physical
and emotional brokenness, Dennis was being beautified."[157]

Whether or not it feels like it in the present moment, nothing we suffer will go wasted. God will use every last drop of it
to reveal his glory in us.

Shine Forth as the Sun

Beloved, now we are children of God; and it has not yet been revealed what we shall be, but we know that when He is revealed, we shall be like Him, for we shall see Him as He is. 1 John 3:2 NKJV

One of my favorite Bible verses comes from the Book of Daniel. Jesus must have liked it, too, because he quotes it after telling several parables about the kingdom of heaven: "Then the righteous will shine forth as the sun in the kingdom of their Father. He who has ears to hear, let him hear!" (Matthew 13:43 NKJV).

As translated in the New American Standard Bible, the original line from Daniel reads: "Many of those who sleep in the dust of the ground will awake, these to everlasting life.... Those who have insight will shine brightly like the brightness of the expanse of heaven, and those who lead the many to righteousness, like the stars forever and ever" (Daniel 12:2–3 NASB).

Jesus did not need to exaggerate in order to impress people. These words express a true picture of the staggering beauty of ordinary people, once they have been transformed in heaven.

Think about it! Even the least attractive person you have ever seen will be beautiful beyond belief in the place we call heaven.

The Water of Life

> *Then the angel showed me a river with the water of life, clear as crystal, flowing from the throne of God and of the Lamb. It flowed down the center of the main street. Revelation 22:1–2 NLT*

Scripture refers often to living water and water that gives life. The prophet Zechariah prophesied, "On that day life-giving waters will flow out from Jerusalem" (Zechariah 14:8 NLT). The psalmist wrote: "There is a river whose streams make glad the city of God, the holy habitation of the Most High" (Psalm 46:4 ESV). And the prophet Jeremiah called the Lord "the fountain of living water" (Jeremiah 17:13 NLT).

Jesus once spoke to a woman at a well about living water: "If you only knew the gift God has for you and who you are speaking to, you would ask me, and I would give you living water.... Those who drink the water I give will never be thirsty again. It becomes a fresh bubbling spring with them, giving them eternal life" (John 4:10, 13–14 NLT). On a second occasion, Jesus shouted to the people, "Anyone who believes in me may come and drink! For the Scriptures declare, 'Rivers of living water will flow from his heart'" (John 7:38 NLT).

The water of life is heavenly, both in its origin and in its effect. Have you tasted it today?

Blessed Assurance

Anyone who loves is a child of God and knows God. But anyone who does not love does not know God, for God is love. God showed how much he loved us by sending his one and only Son into the world so that we might have eternal life through him. This is real love—not that we loved God, but that he loved us and sent his Son as a sacrifice to take away our sins. 1 John 4:1–10 NLT

No one can deny it: the mortality rate for human beings is 100 percent. Though many of us are good at pretending we'll live forever, the evidence to the contrary is all around us. We lose loved ones, neighbors, acquaintances. Every day we hear of tragic stories in the news. No one is invincible.

But fortunately we also have the evidence of Scripture and the experiences of credible people who tell of dying and then returning to life after spending time in heaven. The most credible of these is of course Jesus Christ, who died and was resurrected.

Still, science can't prove that heaven exists. It's simply not built for the task. Only faith can bridge "the gap between the death that no one denies and the life to come that Christians proclaim."[158]

Ask for the faith you need. The God of love will supply it.

Heavenly Clothes

Here indeed we groan, and long to put on our heavenly dwelling,
so that by putting it on we may not be found naked. For while we
are still in this tent, we sigh with anxiety; not that we would be
unclothed, but that we would be further clothed, so that what is
mortal may be swallowed up by life.   2 Corinthians 5:2–4 RSV

Fashion Week never dreamed of such perfectly fitted and impeccably designed garments. One and all, we will emerge from the heavenly dressing room looking every bit as good as the Chief Designer intended.

Modesty will not be an issue, but neither will nakedness. Yours will not be one of countless, identical, unisex garments turned out en masse in some airy factory planted in a cloud. In fact, your immortal soul will have started to acquire its newness while you were still on earth, as you experience heaven's new life. "I will greatly rejoice in the Lord, my soul shall be joyful in my God; for He has clothed me with the garments of salvation, He has covered me with the robe of righteousness, as a bridegroom decks himself with ornaments, and as a bride adorns herself with her jewels" (Isaiah 61:10 NKJV).

C. S. Lewis wrote: "Women sometimes have the problem of trying to judge by artificial light how a dress will look by daylight. That is very like the problem for all of us: to dress our souls not for the electric lights of the present world but for the daylight of the next. The good dress is the one that will face that light. For that light will last longer."[159]

Slip of the Knife

There are those—how lofty are their eyes, how high their eyelids lift!
There are those whose teeth are swords, whose teeth are knives. Proverbs 30:13–14 RSV

We women are much better at some things than men are. I hate to say it but one of them is cattiness. Purring prettily, some of us have the instinctive ability to know just where to slip a word-knife into someone we want to put down.

Not that men don't throw their own set of word bombs. The truth is that tongue problems and heart problems have plagued the human race ever since Adam and Eve first tried to deceive God. Because of his role as instigator of that first human sin, Satan has been thrown out of heaven, kicked out of paradise. Now he wants to take everyone down with him.

For my part, I'm not going. I have decided to rebel against that rebellion. Through God's grace, I'm on a lifelong campaign to get back on track, heading straight to heaven. That's why, in every circumstance, I am determined to use the power of my tongue not for evil but for good.

Homesick for Heaven

For we know that if the tent that is our earthly home is destroyed,
we have a building from God, a house not made with hands,
eternal in the heavens. For in this tent we groan, longing to put on
our heavenly dwelling. 2 Corinthians 5:1–2 ESV

Except for her daughter Susan, Margaret had outlived all of her family and friends. She was ninety when she suffered a mild heart attack, living alone in the home she had shared with her husband, who had passed away a year earlier.

Now she was about to be discharged from the hospital. But before that happened her daughter Susan received a call from the nurse. "I am so sorry," she said. "Just now I was with your mother, helping her get dressed. Suddenly, she sat down on the edge of the bed and died. Right before that, she was telling me how she dreaded going back to her empty house. She said she was just homesick for heaven."

Later that week, the pastor who performed the funeral read a passage from 2 Corinthians that Margaret had bookmarked in her Bible: "Now He who has prepared us for this very thing is God, who also has given us the Spirit as a guarantee. So we are always confident, knowing that while we are at home in the body we are absent from the Lord. For we walk by faith, not by sight" (5:5–7 NKJV).

It seemed that ninety-year-old Margaret had walked by faith right on into heaven.

Dressed Alike?

Put on the Lord Jesus Christ, and make no provision for the flesh, to gratify its desires.   Romans 13:14 RSV

A few years ago, George W. and Laura Bush hosted a holiday reception at the White House. Laura wore a stunning long-sleeved gown in a flattering shade of red. The $8,500 dress had been designed by the famous designer Oscar de la Renta, and it suited the occasion perfectly.

Too perfectly, in fact, because three of her guests showed up in the identical gown. "They all should have congratulated one another on their good taste and the fact that they could afford the dress," chuckled Letitia Baldrige (former White House social secretary under the always-fashionable Jacqueline Kennedy).[160]

According to Baldrige, the ever-gracious Mrs. Bush simply "went upstairs and changed. Very easy for her to do. The right thing to do. Take the heat off the other three women."

Though you and I will probably never need to worry about wearing the same outfit as a famous host or hostess, did you know that in heaven it's not a faux pas to show up dressed like your host? In fact, the reverse is true. Only those wearing the identical Designer garment will be given entry.

Make it your goal, then, to "put on Jesus Christ," so that you will be ready to walk through heaven's gates when the time comes. Then you will be dressed just right for the party that will never end.

All the Rest

He has set another time for coming in, and that time is now. . . .
This new place of rest he is talking about does not mean the land
of Israel that Joshua led them into. If that were what God meant,
he would not have spoken long afterwards about "today" being the
time to get in. So there is a full complete rest still waiting for the
people of God. Christ has already entered there. He is resting from
his work, just as God did after the creation. Hebrews 4:7–9 TLB

Built into any well-orchestrated life are times of regular rest
and refreshment. We Christians have inherited from our Jewish forebears the idea of keeping a "Sabbath rest," and although
many of us don't, we recognize that doing so would bring a
wholesome balance back into lives that are frequently stressed
and frayed.

But is a typical Sunday a good picture of heavenly rest?
Will your life in heaven be like a super-Sabbath, going to
worship and then lounging around afterward? For the over-
worked, that may seem like a welcome prospect right now.
But surely we won't be eternally loitering on streets of gold
with throngs of other equally redeemed-but-idle people, or
taking one afternoon nap after another.

More likely, our heavenly rest will resemble life in the Garden of Eden before the Fall, with satisfying work in a beautiful environment, enjoyable companionship, fresh food, happy
and pervasive worship, and an atmosphere of eager discovery.

"Do Let Me Go!"

> *"What have you lacked here that you want to go back to your own country?" Pharaoh asked.*
>
> *"Nothing," Hadad replied, "but do let me go!"* 1 Kings 11:22 NIV

Hadad was an Edomite prince. When the king of Edom fought against King David and lost, Hadad sought refuge in Egypt. Years later, when he received the news of David's death, he asked Pharaoh for liberty to return home. Perplexed, Pharaoh asked why he would want to leave his comfortable, safe new home.

Because he was living in exile; that's why. Refugees and expatriates always prefer their homelands. It's in their blood. Hadad had been only a child when he left Edom. His sharpest memories would have been formed in the land of Egypt. Still, he wanted to go home as soon as possible.

Whether or not we realize it, we're all a little like Hadad, desiring to go home to heaven. Even though we may be afraid to die, we long for the safety, peace, and delight that heaven will bring. Let's allow ourselves to feel that longing today as we recall the words of the psalmist who lamented his exile in Babylon: "By the rivers of Babylon we sat and wept when we remembered Zion" (Psalm 137:1 NIV). Let us remember our heavenly homeland.

"I'm Going"

I heard a voice from heaven saying, "Write this down: Blessed are those who die in the Lord from now on. Yes, says the Spirit, they are blessed indeed, for they will rest from their hard work; for their good deeds follow them!"   Revelation 14:13 NLT

Despite the deformities and indignities of advanced age, Marguerite's mind was sharp and her spirit strong.

Her family had gathered to celebrate Thanksgiving on the family homestead, where Marguerite lived with her daughter and son-in-law. Though the turkey was roasting and the table was set, everyone stayed in the bedroom with Grandma/Auntie/Great-Gramma, who seemed to be fading. Someone recited the Lord's Prayer and Psalm 23, and Marguerite joined in, feebly but without hesitation.

Suddenly she put both hands on top of the covers and said, "I think you'd better go now, because I'm going." Then she sank back into the pillows. Marguerite died on Thanksgiving Day, in the bedroom where she had been born 103 years earlier.

The next day, the family gathered for a reheated Thanksgiving dinner, keeping open her place at the head of the table. As they ate, it wasn't hard to imagine Marguerite sitting down to a heavenly banquet that was so much better than their best home cooking.

Ancient of Days

*In my vision at night I looked, and there before me was one like
a son of man, coming with the clouds of heaven. He approached
the Ancient of Days and was led into his presence. He was given
authority, glory and sovereign power; all nations and peoples of
every language worshiped him. His dominion is an everlasting
dominion that will not pass away, and his kingdom is one that will
never be destroyed. Daniel 7:13–14 NIV*

Daniel calls God the "Ancient of Days" because he has always
existed. The "one like a son of man" in Daniel's vision is, of
course, the Messiah. Six hundred years later, Jesus fulfilled the
vision described here. When he ascended into heaven, he was
given authority, glory, and sovereign power over every nation
and person in the universe.

Fortunately, Jesus cannot be dislodged from his position.
His dominion will last forever. Eventually the world as we
know it will crumble. Only God's kingdom will last. And we
will last, too, because we are part of his perpetual kingdom.

In the meantime we wait in faith, trusting God's promises
even though the waiting may seem long. As Peter says, "The
Lord is not slow about His promise, as some count slowness,
but is patient toward you, not wishing for any to perish but for
all to come to repentance" (2 Peter 3:9 NASB). Remember that
you and I are among those who have come into his kingdom
only because of God's great patience.

The Door of Heaven

Then as I looked, I saw a door standing open in heaven. Revelation 4:1 TLB

A lovely poster in my friend's dining room pictures nothing but doors. Now that might not sound like a stunning piece of décor, but it is. The doors on the poster are not just any old doors; all of them can be found right in the neighborhood on homes that were built in the 1940s and '50s. The only other thing they have in common is that they are closed. Other than that, they vary in color, in architectural style, in adornment. One displays an autumn wreath; another is draped with ever-green swags and Christmas lights. Each is a piece of art in its own right.

John's vision in Revelation describes another very special door—the door of heaven. However, John cannot tell us anything about its color, design, or embellishments—because it is standing wide open. How the door looks is much less important than its position.

An open door is always an open invitation to enter.

All Cleaned Up for Heaven

*We are citizens of Heaven; our outlook goes beyond this world to
the hopeful expectation of the saviour who will come from Heaven,
the Lord Jesus Christ. He will re-make these wretched bodies of
ours to resemble his own glorious body, by that power of his which
makes him the master of everything that is.   Philippians 3:20–21*
PHILLIPS

Encouraged by the moderate temperatures one winter day,
a succession of car owners brought their vehicles to the local
car wash. The vehicles inched forward, each one covered with
dirt and icy salt stains. Trying to be patient as she waited her
turn, Lynn analyzed the cars in front of her. They looked
pretty much like hers with their mud-spattered rear windows,
encrusted wheel rims, and caustic road spray. Then she caught
sight of an old SUV exiting the car wash tunnel. The road
grime was gone and it looked shiny new.

Isn't this a little bit like entering heaven? she wondered. We
leave earth covered with the dirt and sin of the miles we have
traveled. But we will enter into the joy of heaven sparkling
and clean, ready to make our appearance before God. Jesus
Christ will "re-make these wretched bodies of ours to resemble his own glorious body." The same "model and make" as
before, we will be altogether new creatures!

Heaven's Glory

The heavens proclaim the glory of God. The skies display his craftsmanship. Day after day they continue to speak; night after night they make him known. Psalm 19:1–2 NLT

Scripture talks a lot about "God's glory" or the "glory of God." The night sky displays his glory and the heavens are filled with it (see Habakkuk 3:3 and Psalm 8:1), his glory filled the temple in Jerusalem (see 2 Chronicles 5:14), and it surrounded the shepherds on the night of Christ's birth (see Luke 2:9). What is this glory?

In his book *Beyond Words,* Frederick Buechner gives his definition of glory. Explaining that the work of a master artist, writer, or composer shows its creator's glory, and that appreciating their work introduces us to them although we cannot meet them face-to-face, Buechner writes, "To behold God's glory, to sense God's style, is the closest you can get to God this side of paradise. . . . Glory is what God looks like when for the time being all you have to look at him with is a pair of eyes."[161]

God's glory is on display all around. In preparation for the great glory of heaven, look for it.

Clear and Bright

And then they will see the Son of Man coming in clouds with great
power and glory. And then he will send out the angels and gather
his elect from the four winds, from the ends of the earth to the ends
of heaven. Mark 13:26–27 ESV

Like devout Jews, who still await the first coming of the Messiah, Christians are supposed to wait for his Second Coming with faith-filled expectation.

But how many of us do? Some of us are so enamored with life on earth that we don't think much about it. Others think it's such a long way off, why bother? And still others, troubled by all the disputes about the exact manner and timing of his coming, try not to think about it.

Near the end of his life, Martin Luther showed that he was awaiting the Second Coming with faith-filled expectation. He wrote this prayer: "Ah! Loving God, defer not thy coming. I await impatiently the day when the spring shall return, when day and night shall be of equal length, and when Aurora shall be clear and bright. One day will come a thick black cloud out of which will issue three flashes of lightning, and a clap of thunder will be heard, and in a moment, heaven and earth will be covered with confusion. The Lord be praised, who has taught us to sigh and yearn after that day."[162]

Lord, teach us right now to sigh and yearn for that day.

Heavenly Beings

Our God is merciful and tender. He will cause the bright dawn of salvation to rise on us and to shine from heaven on all those who live in the dark shadow of death, to guide our steps into the path of peace. Luke 1:78–79 GNT

Joni Eareckson Tada, who has been confined to a wheelchair since 1967, has had plenty of time to think about heaven. In 1995, she wrote a book about it, *Heaven: Your Real Home.*

In it, she tells about the time she saw an angel when her young niece died: "I actually saw an angel once. It was 2:00 a.m. on a pitch-black night. I was wide awake, propped up in bed, and straining my ears to hear the muffled voices of my family in the bedroom directly above me. They were surrounding the bed of my five-year-old niece, Kelly, who was dying of cancer. We knew her passing into heaven could happen at any moment, but I was unable to get up the narrow stairs to say goodbye with the others. Suddenly, a brilliant golden shape that glowed whisked by the large bay window I was facing—it didn't move from left to right, but from bottom to top. I screamed....In the next second, my sister Jay called down the steps, 'Kelly's gone!'

"A few of the family came downstairs to find out why I screamed. I told them exactly what I saw. My sisters sank on the edge of my bed in amazement. We knew I had seen a large spiritual being, probably sent from heaven to escort Kelly's soul into eternity."[163]

Point of View

> [May] the Father of glory . . . give you the Spirit of wisdom and of
> revelation in the knowledge of him . . . that you may know what
> is the hope to which he has called you, what are the riches of his
> glorious inheritance in the saints . . . according to the working
> of his great might that he worked in Christ when he raised him
> from the dead and seated him at his right hand in the heavenly
> places. *Ephesians 1:17–20 ESV*

Ever wish to be a fly on the wall at your own funeral? Looking on from heaven, what would you think of the ritual conducted in honor of your dear departed self?

Scottish novelist George MacDonald wondered about that, and framed his thoughts in his novel *Donal Grant*: "One cannot help reflecting what an indifferent trifle the funeral, whether plain to bareness, as in Scotland, or lovely with meaning as so often in England, is to the spirit who has but dropt his hurting shoes on the weary road, dropt all the dust and heat, dropt the road itself, yea the world of his pilgrimage—which never was, never could be, never was meant to be his country, only the place of his sojourning—in which the stateliest house of marble can be but a tent—cannot be a house, yet less a home. Man could never be made at home here, save by a mutilation, a depression, a lessening of his being; those who fancy it their home, will come, by growth, one day to feel that it is no more their home than its mother's egg is the home of the lark."[164]

I don't know about you, but if I could attend my own funeral, I would cheer everybody up by telling them the good news—that here in heaven I have simply "dropped my hurting shoes" and traded them in for dancing shoes.

Making Preparations

We will be with the Lord forever. 1 Thessalonians 3:14

Making preparations for the holidays adds work to already busy schedules. But somehow we find the time. We often spend hours in the kitchen, preparing favorite foods and then setting the table with our best dishes. Perhaps we spruce up the guest room, putting fresh sheets on the bed and plumping up the pillows. We clean the house thoroughly and then decorate it to the hilt. We want our guests to feel warm and welcome in our homes as we celebrate a special time together.

Would you be surprised to learn that Jesus is doing something similar in heaven? He's making room for us, preparing a place for us, maybe even getting a mansion ready for us to live in so that at just the right time, a time that only God knows, he can take us to himself and welcome us to heaven.

God's Plan A

All things were made by him; and without him was not any thing made that was made. John 1:3 KJV

People sometimes talk as though Jesus is God's Plan B for saving us, because Plan A (for people to get to heaven by obeying the Law) didn't work. Of course, that view makes God look like a bit of a plodder, as though he unwittingly developed a flawed plan and then course-corrected when it wasn't working. But the truth is that Jesus has always been God's Plan A. He alone is the only ladder by which anyone can ascend to heaven.

If you doubt me, try climbing that ladder called the Law. No matter how hard you work at it, you will never be good enough to make it into heaven because of your virtue. The Law is there to show us the goal of perfection God desires. But it's a goal we cannot possibly reach without Christ.

Does that mean that we are supposed to live passively while Christ does all the work? Of course not, but it does mean that God is the one who has taken the initiative to save and sustain us. Our job is simply to respond with faith and obedience.

God Knows

If our hearts condemn us, we know that God is greater than our hearts, and he knows everything.   1 John 3:20 NIV

In his book *Listening to Your Life*, Frederick Buechner writes, "I know no more now than I ever did about the far side of death as the last letting-go of all, but I begin to know that I do not need to know and that I do not need to be afraid of not knowing. God knows. That is all that matters."[165]

Too often we fret about heaven. We want to know what it will be like. Who will I see? How will I know my way around? What will I wear? Will there be food, pets, play, work? Buechner, however, says we don't have to sweat the details, because God knows. He is the God of all knowledge and just as he has provided everything for us on earth, he will provide for us in heaven as well.

We can still try to imagine heaven. We can read stories of those who have visited and returned to earth to tell about it. These things will fuel our hope. But in the long run we can rest easy in the fact that our knowing doesn't matter. All that matters is that God knows.

Death Stinks

Jesus, once more deeply moved, came to the tomb. It was a cave with a stone laid across the entrance. "Take away the stone," he said.

"But, Lord," said Martha, the sister of the dead man, "by this time there is a bad odor, for he has been there four days."

Then Jesus said, "Did I not tell you that if you believe, you will see the glory of God?" John 38–40 NIV

If you want to get an idea of what Jesus thinks about death, you have only to read the story of his good friend Lazarus. One of the most stunning scenes in all of Scripture occurs when Jesus arrives at the tomb. By now Lazarus has been dead four days. Encountering Mary and Martha along the way, Jesus weeps. Then the Bible says he is "deeply troubled."

Immediately following, Jesus orders the stone covering Lazarus' tomb to be rolled away. But the ever practical Martha objects, saying, "What are you thinking? He'll stink by now!" But Jesus goes ahead and, just as the story says, Lazarus comes out.

Okay, it's a familiar story. We've heard it before. But let's back up a minute for an instant replay. At first take, I see a bunch of sad people, including Jesus. Everyone is grieving. But a closer examination of the Greek word that is translated "deeply troubled" indicates that something more is going on. In Greek, it means "to snort like a horse." So Jesus is not just feeling sad. He's feeling good and angry, too. He's like a horse going into battle or a wrestler facing off with an opponent. He's had enough. He's not going to take it anymore. So he shouts into the open tomb—into the face of death—and commands: "Lazarus, come out!" And Lazarus does just that. With one simple command Jesus unwinds death, reversing the curse that fell on the first humans and all of their descendants. And Lazarus comes walking out.

One day, you too will die. Like Lazarus, you will hear the voice of the one who loves you shouting your name and saying, "Come out!" And just like that, you will come out.

Do-It-Yourselfism

But by the grace of God I am what I am. . . . 1 Corinthians 15:10

Television shows like *This Old House* testify to the strong interest in do-it-yourself approaches to everything from kitchen renovations to man caves. It's amazing what human beings can do once we put our minds to it.

But what about do-it-yourself religion? Does it work? I guess it depends on what you mean by work. Perhaps anyone who rolls up their sleeves and tries hard to make themselves a better, happier person might be able to achieve some measurable results. But if by "does it work?" you mean will it get you to heaven, then the answer is no.

Of course your neighborhood Hindu might beg to differ. According to Hinduism, we get endless chances to perfect ourselves. If you're a criminal type in this life, you'll get a chance to reform the next go-round. Who knows, maybe you'll come back as a social worker, helping to undo the hurt you created in your past life.

Of course, you don't need to embrace Hinduism to fall prey to do-it-yourselfism. This attitude pervades the church because it pervades the culture. If you find yourself feeling anxious, stressed, guilt-ridden, and frustrated, maybe you should check your spiritual vital signs to make sure you haven't come down with a bad case of do-it-yourselfism.

So Satisfied!

So whether you eat or drink or whatever you do, do it all for the glory of God. 1 Corinthians 10:31

Ronald Reagan loved jelly beans. So three and a half tons were shipped to the White House for the 1981 inaugural festivities. In order to be politically correct, the company that sent them created a special blueberry-flavored bean so that guests could celebrate with fistfuls of red, white, and blue jelly beans. Today, visitors who tour the Reagan Presidential Library in California can view a portrait of him made from ten thousand Jelly Belly beans. It makes me wonder. Might the illustrious Ronald Reagan be sitting on a cloud in heaven enjoying a handful of his favorite, licorice-flavored Jelly Belly beans?

What is it that you would love to have in heaven? The best artisanal coffee in the world, perhaps? That would be my request. But wait a minute. Coffee is addictive. How could there be anything addictive in heaven? Well, I don't know. God could rejigger our bodies so that we never succumb to addictions. Also we won't have to worry about coffee keeping us up all night because in heaven there will be no night.

Okay, we really don't know whether there will be coffee beans or jelly beans or even lima beans in heaven. And maybe we shouldn't care. What we do know is that whatever will be there will be enough and more than enough to satisfy us, world without end, amen.

Heaven's Antechamber

Are not all angels ministering spirits sent to serve those who will inherit salvation? Hebrews 1:14 NIV

Irene had to take a leave of absence from her job in order to take care of her mother, who was dying of cancer. A hospital bed was moved into a ground-floor room of the family home, and hospice caregivers came every day. At night, Irene slept next to the bed on a sofa.

Before long, as expected, her mother lapsed into a coma. Days and nights blended together into a gray fog as the end drew near. Irene phoned her brother, Chad, who lived two thousand miles away, to let him know it was time to say goodbye.

On the morning of his expected arrival, Irene was shifting her mother's inert body to straighten the bedcovers when her mother's eyes suddenly opened. So shocked she almost dropped her, Irene exclaimed, "Mom! You've been in a coma; I never expected to see your eyes open again. Chad is coming today."

With a faint smile and a sigh, her mother simply said, "Maybe that's why they sent me back...."

Apparently, no gray fog had been enveloping *her* as she lingered in heaven's antechamber with her angelic caregivers. She remained conscious until shortly after Chad's tender goodbye.

A Warehouse Full of Blessings

I will send down the showers in their season; they shall be showers of blessing.   Ezekiel 34:26 NRSV

A favorite hymn talks about "showers of blessing" coming from heaven above. It pictures heaven as a great storehouse, overflowing with good gifts.

I wonder how many of God's gifts we take for granted every day. The waning moon and the rising sun. The kiss of dew and the spring rains. Every breath we take and every move we make—all are made possible because of God's generous provision.

Even though his blessings are too numerous to count, we are good at taking them for granted. Ignoring the evidence around us, we focus instead on what we do not have.

Let's counter that tendency by imagining heaven as a great warehouse bursting at the seams with all God's blessings. As the seams burst open and the blessings flow out, imagine yourself standing under a great shower of God's goodness, raining down from heaven above.

Living in a Tent

Now we know that if the earthly tent we live in is destroyed, we have a building from God, an eternal house in heaven, not built by human hands. 2 Corinthians 5:1 NIV

Living in a tent can be fun, as long as it's only temporary. Birdsong wakes you in the morning and tree frogs sing you to sleep at night. The smell of a campfire may bring back great childhood memories. But too many days spent close to nature may make you long for the comfort and shelter of home.

The Bible compares our bodies to "tents." As temporary housing they're pretty marvelous. But even the best body eventually breaks down, wears out, and has to be replaced. Thank God that Scripture speaks of resurrection. One day, all those who love God will receive brand-new bodies. Unlike our current bodies, which provide only temporary shelter for our souls, our new bodies will never wear out. In God's perfect time he will take away our temporary tent and replace it with one that will last.

Hold My Hand

For I hold you by your right hand—I, the Lord your God.
And I say to you, "Don't be afraid. I am here to help you." Isaiah
41:13 NLT

My uncle loved to sing. As a youth leader in his church many years ago, his tenor voice often carried the congregation through favorite choruses. So it seemed only right to mark his passing by singing some of his favorites. He loved so many that the funeral service turned into an extended hymn sing. At the end, we sang a song by Thomas A. Dorsey called "Precious Lord, Take My Hand."

The words of the song are sung as a prayerful request to God, "take my hand and lead me home, Lord."

I imagined God the Father, taking my uncle's withered hand into his own all-powerful hand and gently leading him into heaven. The hand that had sustained him through so many years was now the hand that welcomed him home.

Why not take a moment today to think about how God's strong hand has already guided you. Thank him for never letting go and then praise him because someday that same hand will lead you safely home.

Formula for Heaven?

No one has ever seen this, and no one has ever heard about it. No one has ever imagined what God has prepared for those who love him. Isaiah 64:4 NCV

Collect everything good from the world around you.

Subtract whatever is evil and ugly. Add in friends, family, and favorite people, plus an enormous dose of God's glory and goodness.

Combine the sound of thousands upon thousands of singing angels.

Multiply by a thousand times the brightness of the sun.

And maybe, just maybe, it will all add up to heaven.

Then again, there may be so much more.

On Heaven's Doorstep

Don't be afraid, for I am with you. Don't be discouraged, for I am your God. I will strengthen you and help you. I will hold you up with my victorious right hand. Isaiah 41:10 NLT

Talking about heaven is one thing. But facing it is another. I have a friend who is dying of cancer. In less than a year, perhaps within just a few months, her life will end. Amazingly, she has faced this reality proactively. No longer afraid of death and dying, she has been given the grace to know that God will be with her through it all. So for the time she has left, she is determined to fully *live* every day she has left—living well while facing the inevitable head-on.

Nearly every day she visits a local convent, where she attends Mass. The nuns there have learned of her diagnosis and are praying for her. She also attends classes at a local seminary, listening to lectures and confiding in two professors, who have taken the time to share their knowledge of what heaven is like.

During the course of her illness, her perspective has matured. Instead of worrying or bemoaning her fate she has concluded, "I win no matter what. If God answers my prayers for healing, I win. But I win even bigger if I die because I'll receive the ultimate peace we're all waiting for."

Most of us haven't a clue when life will end. But whether we have nine or ninety years left, we can decide now to focus on Jesus—the one who'll go the distance with us.

Face-to-Face

> *"So all of us who have had that veil removed can see and reflect the glory of the Lord. And the Lord—who is the Spirit—makes us more and more like him as we are changed into his glorious image."* 2 Corinthians 3:18 NLT

A small museum in the middle of the ruins of ancient Corinth contains a mirror from the first century. Looking into that ancient mirror is like looking at your reflection in a mirror in a darkened room.

When Paul wrote his letter to the people in Corinth, he was referring to such a mirror. Here on earth, we have only a vague image of God even as we grow to know him better.

But when we get to heaven, clarity will be ours! We will see God and experience him with our eyes wide open. His glory will fill the heavens, so that even the light of a thousand supernovas will appear dim in comparison to his radiance.

Open 24/7

Its gates will never be shut by day—and there is no night there. Revelation 21:25 NRSV

The sign was located in a prominent place: "This park closes at dusk." Two swinging gates enforced the rule at sunset and prevented cars from entering the parking lot. Some well-to-do communities have similar gates that close at the end of the day.

Most cities in the ancient world were protected by high walls and sturdy gates, and so were the forts of the Wild West. The goal in every case? Keeping out unwelcome intruders.

Closed gates clearly state: "Keep Out" or "Open only to select individuals" or "Open between the hours of…" On the other hand, gates left wide open almost seem to have a "Welcome" sign hanging permanently outside.

We can take comfort in knowing that heaven's welcome sign is always out, and the gates are always open. There is no need to close them for protection from the darkness of night or thieves or enemies—none of which exist in heaven. Heaven is safe. Heaven is open to those who love God.

The Thrones of the Innocent

*God is mighty, but he does not despise anyone! He is mighty in
both power and understanding. He never takes his eyes off the
innocent, but he sets them on thrones with kings and exalts them
forever.   Job 36:5, 7 NLT*

Nothing prepares us for the death of an infant.

Baby Lily was born on a sunny morning in fall. A beautiful
child, she had reddish blond hair, blue eyes, ten fingers, and
ten toes. She seemed perfect. But as Lily drew her first breath,
it became apparent that something was badly wrong. The
delivery room grew silent. The physician who'd delivered her
seemed subdued as he handed the baby girl to her parents. "I'm
so sorry," he said. "Your daughter has a rare birth defect. Her
brain did not develop normally in the early weeks of the preg-
nancy. It's not your fault and we are unsure why this happens.
She may have only hours to live."

Nine months of joyful anticipation had suddenly been
shattered. The baby that Mike and Dee had expected to welcome into their home, the one on whom they were prepared
to lavish their love, would linger only hours. Overwhelming
grief crowded out the momentary joy they had felt. Now, as
they cradled their beloved Lily, they struggled with *why*. Why
would God take an innocent child from them? Why would her
life be so short? No answers were given.

But Lily's parents are people of faith. In time they found
comfort in the psalm that affirms a wonderful truth—God
never takes his eyes off the innocent. They realized that
instead of their arms cradling her, baby Lily would be held
safe in God's arms. When she was ready, he would set her on a
throne with kings and treasure her forever.

Glory Land

And the city has no need of sun or moon to shine on it, for the glory of God is its light, and its lamp is the Lamb. Revelation 21:23 NRSV

> *I've got a home in glory land that outshines the sun, . . .*
> *I've got a home in glory land that outshines the sun, way beyond the blue.*
> *Do Lord oh do Lord, oh do remember me, . . .*
> *Do Lord, oh do Lord, oh do remember me, way beyond the blue.*[166]

My father wasn't much for singing—even in the shower. But I know someone's father who was. I'll let her tell the story.

"When I was little, my father sang about having a home in glory land to my sisters and me as he tucked us into bed. Sitting on the edge of our double bed, Dad would sing at the top of his tenor voice. After we learned the words, we would all sing along before settling down for the night.

"Many years later, he sang that old favorite to my two young sons as they snuggled up on Grandpa's lap in his favorite chair. When Grandpa wasn't around, my boys and I would sing the song together before bedtime, just as Dad had done with me.

"When he passed away at the age of eighty-four, I found peace knowing that he was in heaven with his Lord, singing with a choir of angels in glory land—his final home 'way beyond the blue.'"

"Glory land"—I like the sound of that. It's an old-fashioned image that captures something of the joy we'll feel when we reach the place that "outshines the sun."

Face-to-Face

Thus the Lord used to speak to Moses face to face, as one speaks to a friend. Exodus 33:11 NRSV

In the Old Testament, a face-to-face encounter with another person was serious business, and a face-to-face encounter with God was exceptional. It was general knowledge among God's people that seeing God's face incurred instant death. Gideon was afraid of death when he saw an angel of God (see Judges 6:22). In panic, Samson's parents said, "We shall surely die, for we have seen God" (Judges 13:22 NRSV). Even Moses was afraid to look directly into the burning bush (see Exodus 3:6). There was something about the holiness of God's face that was dangerous to sinful human beings.

Now, because of what Jesus has done for us, the thought of seeing God face-to-face inspires awe and longing. In heaven, seeing God will be our greatest happiness, our deepest joy.

A Christmas Dream

Now I know in part; then I shall know fully, even as I am fully known. 1 Corinthians 13:12b

Eileen Kindig's sister-in-law Carol died suddenly of a heart attack when she was forty-five. When her husband, Dan, decided to remarry within a year of his wife's death, Eileen was delighted, though his family and friends thought he was rushing things.

Just before the wedding, Eileen had a vivid dream. She and Carol were cooking in the kitchen on Christmas Eve when they heard a knock at the door. When Eileen went to answer it, she was surprised to find Carol standing on the other side. "Come out and close the door and don't let anyone know I'm here," Carol said in hushed tones. Holding Eileen's arm, she led her out into a snow-covered world.

"All of a sudden," Eileen says, "she opened an umbrella and we went soaring through the starry expanse of sky, just like Mary Poppins. I felt as though I were flying through a Van Gogh painting.

"As we floated over forests and homes and the white world below, she said, 'See what's here.' I looked down and felt an incredible sense of peace. Though she didn't say it, Carol seemed to be sharing her perspective on everything that was happening down below. She was telling me she was happy and at peace and that she was glad Dan was planning to remarry."

Another dream a week later conveyed the same message.

Despite the Mary Poppins imagery in her dream, Eileen was sure it carried a deeply spiritual message. But she waited to tell Dan about it. Four years later, when she and her husband were having Christmas dinner with Dan and his wife, she decided to tell the story.

"I am certain," she says, "that Christmas Eve dream became a Christmas gift to all of us. It spoke about a life beyond this world, about the happiness and safety of someone we had loved and lost, and about the longing we all have to know there is more to life than we sometimes realize."[167]

"Like a Thousand Christmas Mornings"

All who were sitting in the Sanhedrin looked intently at Stephen, and they saw that his face was like the face of an angel.   Acts 6:15

You may wonder whether people still have visions like the ones recounted in the Bible. Alex Malarkey tells of being visited by angels not once but several times.

"People have told me that after I am with the angels my face is glowing—like a thousand Christmas mornings. It's funny that [after my accident] I could usually only smile with just one corner of my mouth, but that my smiles after the angels' visits were huge. I've heard about Stephen's face in the Bible when he looked up to Heaven. Maybe my face looks like that?"[168]

Alex's story would seem to indicate that God sometimes allows human beings to catch a glimpse of the glory and splendor of heaven, even before it's time for them to move there.

God's Letter Carriers

Suddenly a great company of the heavenly host appeared with the angel, praising God and saying,
   "Glory to God in the highest heaven,
   and on earth peace to those on whom his favor rests."   Luke 2:13–14

Larry Libby calls angels God's letter carriers, because their job is to convey messages from heaven to earth. "Do you remember hearing about the night long ago when Jesus was born?" he asks. "Beneath a star-sprinkled sky, the shepherds were quietly watching over their flocks of sleepy sheep. All at once—

> An angel of the Lord suddenly stood before them, and the glory of the Lord shone around them, and they were terribly frightened. But the angel said to them, "Do not be afraid.... I bring you good news of great joy.... Today in the city of David there has been born for you a Savior who is Christ the Lord." *(Luke 2:9–11 NASB)*

"That angel had the happy job of bringing absolutely wonderful news. And then it was as if Heaven's door suddenly flew wide open and a million other angels said, 'Oh, this is *too much* good news for one angel! We want to deliver the message, too! Let us say the good news too!' And then all of God's letter carriers seemed to come tumbling out of Heaven in a great excited rush—singing and shouting and praising God and chasing away the darkness of night."[169]

What a wonderful picture of that first Christmas night.

The Third Heaven?

I know a man in Christ who was caught up to the third heaven fourteen years ago. Whether I was in my body or out of my body I don't know—only God knows. Yes, only God knows whether I was in my body or outside my body. But I do know that I was caught up to paradise and heard things so astounding that they cannot be expressed in words, things no human is allowed to tell.   2 Corinthians 12:2–4 NLT

Unlike some folks who've written bestselling books about heaven, Paul seems reticent to speak about his own experience. In fact he tries to hide by saying, "I know a man in Christ who..." even though most readers realize that he is speaking about himself.

In case you're wondering, let me explain what the phrase "third heaven" means. In Paul's time people spoke of the first heaven as the sky, the second heaven as farther out in space, and the third heaven as the ultimate location of God's presence.

Paul's experience took place in paradise—where believers who have died are "at home with the Lord" (2 Corinthians 5:8). To him, it is less important to understand whether or not his body went up to heaven than the fact that God knows how it happened.

In heaven, God revealed secrets to Paul that none of us know. Perhaps it was so that he could find the courage and the hope he needed to complete his mission—to spread the gospel to the gentiles so that they, too, might have the hope of heaven. Maybe we should ask not only "What is heaven like?" but "What is heaven for?"

Heaven's Guest Book

All who are victorious will be clothed in white. I will never erase
their names from the Book of Life, but I will announce before my
Father and his angels that they are mine.   Revelation 3:5 NLT

A guest book graces the tea cart in the corner of my friend
Amy's dining room. For the past twenty years she has welcomed a wide variety of people into her home. They have
come for a meal, to find safe haven and a listening ear, to sleep
in the guest room, to conduct a meeting around the dining
room table, or to stay for a few days while searching for an
apartment. She has welcomed missionaries, seminary students, high school friends, business associates, family members, and even a monk. As each person was about to leave,
Amy would ask him or her to sign her guest book.

In heaven, God has a guest book of sorts. It's called the
Book of Life. But his is a guest book in reverse, because it lists
the names of all the righteous "guests" who will one day show
up on his threshold. Unlike Amy's guests, those listed in God's
guest book will stay forever.

If you belong to God, you can rest in the knowledge that
your name has already been inscribed into the Book of Life.

Last Breath

The Spirit of God has made me; the breath of the Almighty gives me life. Job 33:4 NIV

Mike's family gathered in the intensive care unit around the bed of the husband and father they loved. His lungs had been ravaged by cancer and emphysema. Prior to being hospitalized, every breath he had taken was labored and difficult. On life support for over a week, he hadn't shown signs of recovery. The family agonized over whether to wait a little longer or allow for Mike to be taken off the ventilator. Finally they decided to remove him from the ventilator and wait for the inevitable.

Carefully the nurse removed the tubes. A moment passed in the quiet room. Then the unexpected happened—Mike gasped and started breathing once again on his own. The family was amazed! God *was* in control of Mike's every breath. This was not the time for his last.

After that Mike made steady progress and was allowed to return home. For several months he continued breathing on his own. But then he began to decline again. God was doing something in Mike's heart, stirring up a memory of the catechism he had learned as a child. He wanted to hear someone say the words he had learned long ago: "What is your only comfort in life and in death?" Mike's answer? "That I am not my own, but belong body and soul, in life and in death to my faithful Savior Jesus Christ."

After six months of hospice, Mike took his last breath, trusting that in both life and in death he belonged to his faithful Savior Jesus Christ.

The Father Calling

There is no fear in love, but perfect love casts out fear. 1 John 4:18
NRSV

In the middle of the night a powerful storm rattled the windows of the house and snapped the power lines. Pitch darkness descended. A little boy who had been fast asleep suddenly awoke, too frightened to leave his bed. He couldn't see anything. It was so dark and loud! What was out there?

Suddenly he heard a voice that calmed his fears. The voice was strong, and reassuring, and he knew who it belonged to. It was his father calling from the bottom of the stairs. Following the sound of the voice, the trembling boy pushed off the covers and crept through the dark hallway, down the stairs one at a time, and into his father's arms. By listening to the voice he trusted, the boy had overcome his fear and reached a place of safety.

One day, you and I will be suddenly thrown into the darkness of death. But we do not need to be afraid. We do not have to worry about finding our way. Our loving Father will be calling us; his voice will lead us through the gates of heaven and into his loving arms.

The View from a Distance

On that very day the Lord addressed Moses as follows: "Ascend this mountain of the Abarim, Mount Nebo, which is in the land of Moab, across from Jericho, and view the land of Canaan, which I am giving to the Israelites for a possession." Deuteronomy 32:48–49 NRSV

After forty long years of traveling in the wilderness of Sinai, God's people were on the brink of entering the land of Canaan—the Promised Land. God told Moses, the great leader of the Israelites, to hike to the summit of Mount Nebo to preview the land. From there Moses saw the glory and splendor of a land that was "flowing with milk and honey."

We have a promised land, too—it's called heaven. What we know of it, however, is limited. It's only a glimpse, like Moses' view of Canaan. All the books that have ever been written about heaven cannot possibly prepare us for the spectacular surprises awaiting us.

Like the Israelites, we know that the only way to get to the Promised Land is by believing in what we cannot fully see, trusting that God will show us the way.

Notes

1. Richard John Neuhaus, "Born Toward Dying," *First Things*, January 8, 2009 (first published in 2000 in *First Things*), http://www.firstthings.com/onthesquare/2009/01/born-toward-dying.

2. Captain Dale Black with Ken Gire, *Flight to Heaven* (Minneapolis: Bethany House, 2010), 31–32.

3. Ibid., 99–100.

4. The identities of the nurse practitioner and the woman I've call Li Na have been disguised because it is still not safe to be a Christian in China.

5. C. S. Lewis, *The Great Divorce* (San Francisco, CA: HarperOne, 1946, 1973), 21.

6. Randy Alcorn, *Heaven* (Carol Stream, IL: Tyndale House, 2004), 394–95.

7. Black, *Flight to Heaven*, 108–109.

8. See Alcorn, *Heaven*, 78–79.

9. Story retold from Ann Spangler, *When You Need a Miracle* (Grand Rapids, MI: Zondervan, 2009), 158–60.

10. Joni Eareckson Tada, *Heaven: Your Real Home* (Grand Rapids, MI: Zondervan, 1995), 177.

11. Neuhaus, "Born Toward Dying."

12. James Garlow and Keith Wall, *Encountering Heaven and the Afterlife* (Bloomington, MN: Bethany House, 2010), 13.

13. Trudy Harris, *Glimpses of Heaven* (Grand Rapids, MI: Revell, 2008), 17.

14. Marvin J. Besteman with Lorilee Craker, *My Journey to Heaven: What I Saw and How It Changed My Life* (Grand Rapids, MI: Revell, 2012), 14.

15. Anthony DeStefano, *A Travel Guide to Heaven* (New York: Doubleday, 2003), 79.

16. Mary C. Neal, MD, *To Heaven and Back* (Colorado Springs, CO: Waterbrook Press, 2011, 2012), 73.

17. Charles Haddon Spurgeon, "Heavenly Worship," a sermon (number 110), December 28, 1856, posted at http://www.spurgeon.org/sermons/0110.htm.

18. R. C. Sproul, *Surprised by Suffering* (Wheaton, IL: Tyndale, 1988), 120.

19. Retold from Ann Spangler, *Dreams: True Stories of Remarkable Encounters with God* (Grand Rapids, MI: Zondervan, 1997), 38–40.

20. C. S. Lewis, *George MacDonald: An Anthology* (New York: Macmillan, 1978), no. 15, p. 8, as quoted in Peter Kreeft, *Heaven: The Heart's Deepest Longing* (San Francisco: Ignatius, 1989), 67.

21. Kreeft, *Heaven*, 67.

22. Retold from Spangler, *Dreams,* 119–22.

23. Calvin Miller, Lil Copan, and Anna Trimiew, *Images of Heaven* (Wheaton, IL: Harold Shaw Publishers, 1996), 140.

24. Kreeft, *Heaven,* 135.

25. Retold from Spangler, *Dreams,* 123–127.

26. Ronald Reagan quoted in Maurice Rawlings, *To Hell and Back*, TBN Films, posted at http://www.divinerevelations.info/documents/rawlings/to_hell_and_back_english.doc.

27. Ann Spangler, *The Tender Words of God* (Grand Rapids, MI: Zondervan, 2008), 218.

28. Kay Warren, "The Loudest Cheers in Heaven," in *Glimpses of Heaven* [multiple authors: *Christianity Today*] (Eugene, OR: Harvest House, 2013), 27–28.

29. Justin Martyr, quoted in DeStefano, *A Travel Guide to Heaven*, 22.

30. Ibid., 16–17.

31. Quoted in Alan F. Segal, *Life after Death: A History of the Afterlife in Western Religion* (New York: Doubleday, 2004), 620.

32. Lewis, *The Great Divorce*, 75.

33. The story is retold from material in James L. Garlow's *Heaven and the Afterlife* (Minneapolis: Bethany House, 2009), 44, and *To Hell and Back*.

34. Ann Voskamp, *The Greatest Gift* (Carol Stream, IL: Tyndale House, 2013), 68.

35. Retold from Ann Spangler, *Dreams: True Stories of Remarkable Encounters with God* (Grand Rapids, MI: Zondervan, 1997), 139–141.

36. J. Vernon McGee, *Death of a Little Child* (Pasadena, CA: Thru the Bible Radio, July 1970), 20, quoted in Randy Alcorn, *Eternal Perspectives* (Carol Stream, IL: Tyndale House, 2012), 68.

37. D. L. Moody as quoted in William Revell Moody, *The Life of Dwight L. Moody* (New York: Revell, 1900), 537.

38. Besteman, *My Journey to Heaven*, 123–24, 136.

39. Ibid., 129.

40. Joni Eareckson Tada and Steven Estes, *When God Weeps* (Grand Rapids, MI: Zondervan, 1997), 210–11.

41. From many sources, including Robert Philip, *The Life, Times, and Characteristics of John Bunyan, Author of the Pilgrim's Progress* (London: Thomas Ward, 1839), 569.

42. Alcorn, *Heaven*, 305.

43. C. S. Lewis, *Mere Christianity* (San Francisco: HarperSanFrancisco, 2001), 134.

44. Tada, *Heaven: Your Real Home*, 5.

45. Ann Spangler, *A Miracle a Day* (Grand Rapids, MI: Zondervan, 1996), 181–82.

46. Retold from Ann Spangler, *When You Need a Miracle* (Grand Rapids, MI: Zondervan, 2009), 161–62.

47. Augustine, *Confessions*, Book I, chapter 1.

48. C. S. Lewis, *The Problem of Pain* (New York: Macmillan, 1962), 145.

49. Lewis, *Mere Christianity*, 137.

50. Retold from Ann Spangler, *Dreams and Miracles* (Carmel, NY: Guideposts, 1997, 2000), 194–97.

51. This quote is attributed either to Henry Scott Holland or Henry Van Dyke. Quoted in Randy Alcorn, *Eternal Perspectives* (Carol Stream, IL: Tyndale House, 2012), 131–32.

52. Kevin and Alex Malarkey, *The Boy Who Came Back from Heaven* (Carol Stream, IL: Tyndale House, 2010, 2011), 9, 14.

53. Ibid., 26–27.

54. Ibid., 29–30.

55. See Ashley Pescoe, "Authorities still unsure if abused puppy, Heaven, will survive," NJ.com, Nov. 18, 2013, http://www.nj.com/monmouth/index.ssf/2013/11/authorities_still_unsure_if_severely_abused_puppy_heaven_will_survive.html, and Stephanie Loder, "Heaven, the dog from N.J., gets worldwide sympathy," *Courier-Post*, Nov. 21, 2013, http://www.courierpostonline.com/article/20131121/NEWS02/311210033/.

56. Peter Kreeft, *Everything You Ever Wanted to Know About Heaven* (San Francisco: Ignatius Press, 1990), 45.

57. Joan Wester Anderson, *Where Angels Walk* (New York: Ballantine Books, 1992), 183–86.

58. Kathleen Norris, *Amazing Grace: A Vocabulary of Faith* (New York: Riverhead Books, 1998), 367.

59. Adapted from Erwin W. Lutzer, *One Minute After You Die* (Chicago: Moody, 1997), 75.

60. Stephen E. Saint, "The Unfinished Mission to the 'Aucas,'" *Christianity Today*, September 16, 1996, 26.

61. Alcorn, *Heaven*, 215.

62. Corrie ten Boom, with John and Elizabeth Sherrill, *The Hiding Place* (Grand Rapids, MI: Chosen Books, 1971, 1984, 2006), 43–44.

63. Tricia McCary Rhodes, *The Soul at Rest* (Minneapolis: Bethany House, 1996), 144.

64. Retold from Leanne Hadley, *Touching Heaven* (Grand Rapids, MI: Revell, 2013), 43–53.

65. Lutzer, *One Minute After You Die*, 100–101.

66. DeStefano, *A Travel Guide to Heaven*, 134.

67. Retold from Hadley, *Touching Heaven*, 23–31.

68. Kreeft, *Everything You Always Wanted to Know About Heaven*, 247–48.

69. John Calvin, *Institutes of the Christian Religion* (Philadelphia: Westminster Press, 1960), vol. 1, Book 3, Chapter 9, Section 5, 717.

70. DeStefano, *A Travel Guide to Heaven*, 170.

71. Retold from Spangler, *Dreams and Miracles*, 138–39.

72. Gordon Reid, ed., *The Wind from the Stars: Through the Year with George MacDonald* (San Francisco: HarperCollins, 1992), 335.

73. Crystal McVea and Alex Tresniowski, *Waking Up in Heaven* (Nashville, TN: Howard Books, 2013), 163–64, 175, 190.

74. Ibid., 180.

75. Ibid., 90.

76. Francis Frangipane, *Spiritual Discernment and the Mind of Christ* (Cedar Rapids, IA: Arrow, 2013), 45.

77. Reggie Anderson, *Appointments with Heaven* (Carol Stream, IL: Tyndale House, 2013), 48.

78. Ibid., 80–81.

79. Ibid., 82.

80. Ibid., 84.

81. Laura Schroff in McVea and Tresniowski, *Waking Up in Heaven*, viii–ix.

82. Desmond Tutu, Goodreads.com, accessed October 17, 2013; Desmond Tutu. BrainyQuote.com, http://www.brainyquote.com/quotes/quotes/d/desmondtut142349.html, accessed January 2, 2014.

83. Lutzer, *One Minute After You Die*, 55.

84. Ibid., 66–67.

85. Harris, *Glimpses of Heaven*, 29.

86. Ibid., 35–36.

87. Retold from Spangler, *Dreams and Miracles*, 176–77.

88. Drawn from Harris, *Glimpses of Heaven*, 55–57.

89. Alcorn, *Heaven*, xx.

90. A. W. Tozer, *Born After Midnight* (Camp Hill, PA: Christian Publications, 1959), 136.

91. Harris, *Glimpses of Heaven*, 116–17.

92. Canon Andrew White, blog post on October 3, 2013, https://www.facebook.com/CanonAndrewFRRME/posts/6133 54975395200.

93. Alcorn, *Heaven*, 28.

94. Drawn from Harris, *More Glimpses of Heaven*, 39–41.

95. Jonathan Edwards, *Letters and Personal Writings* (WJE Online, vol. 16), ed. George S. Claghorn, posted on http://edwards.yale.edu/archive?path=aHR0cDovL2Vkd2FyZHMueWFsZS5lZHUvY2dpLWJpbi9uZXdwaGlsby9nZXRvYmplY3QucGw/Yy4xNT03NDoxLndqZW8=.

96. Drawn from Alcorn, *Heaven*, 20–21.

97. Drawn from Harris, *More Glimpses of Heaven*, 68–70.

98. Harry Blamires, *On Christian Truth* (Ann Arbor, MI: Servant, 1983), 138.

99. J. F. Wright and L. Swormstedt, *The Ladies Repository*, vol. 32 (Methodist Episcopal Church, 1872), 129.

100. Lewis, *Mere Christianity*, 134.

101. Robert Browning, *Pippa Passes* (many editions).

102. Many sources. According to a British book, *The Joys of Christian Humour*, by Judson K. Cornelius, Spurgeon said it when admonishing a class of divinity students to use appropriate facial expressions when they preached.

103. Many sources, including Edward Eggleston, *Christ in Literature* (New York: J. B. Ford, 1875).

104. Howard Crosby, *The Healthy Christian: An Appeal to the Church* (American Tract Society, 1871), 53.

105. S. Ralph Harlow, *Guideposts* magazine, 1970, as quoted in Joan Wester Anderson, *Where Angels Walk* (New York: Ballantine Books, 1992), 227–31.

106. As quoted in Randy Alcorn, *We Shall See God: Charles Spurgeon's Classic Devotional Thoughts on Heaven* (Carol Stream, IL: Tyndale House, 2011), 124.

107. Ronald Reagan, "Remarks on East-West Relations at the Brandenburg Gate in West Berlin," July 12, 1987, http://www.reagan.utexas.edu/archives/speeches/1987/061287d.htm.

108. Alcorn, *Heaven*, 46.

109. Harris, *More Glimpses of Heaven*, 71–73.

110. Ibid., 171–72.

111. Ten Boom, *The Hiding Place*, 228–30.

112. Don Piper with Cecil Murphey, *90 Minutes in Heaven* (Grand Rapids, MI: Revell, 2004), 19–27.

113. Ibid., 29–31.

114. Ibid., 40–44.

115. Ibid., 45–46, 133–35.

116. Ian McCormack, *A Glimpse of Eternity* (n.p., 2013), 36.

117. Besteman, *My Journey to Heaven*, 56–57, 65.

118. John Ortberg, "Guide into the With-God Life," *Christianity Today*, July–August 2013, 64.

119. Medieval Sourcebook: St. Perpetua, *The Passion of Saints Perpetua and Felicity 203*, http://www.fordham.edu/halsall/source/perpetua.asp.

120. D. L. Moody quoted in *Moody* (New York: Macmillan, 1963), 316–18.

121. M. Craig Barnes, *An Extravagant Mercy* (Ann Arbor, MI: Servant, 2003), 65.

122. C. S. Lewis, *Letters to Malcolm: Chiefly on Prayer* (New York: Harcourt, 1992), 124.

123. The story is retold from Anderson, *Appointments with Heaven*, 141–43.

124. H. A. Baker, *Visions Beyond the Veil* (New Kensington, PA: Whitaker House, 1973, 2006), 77–78.

125. Joni Mitchell, "Woodstock," Siquomb Publishing Company, 1969.

126. Baker, *Visions Beyond the Veil*, 90–91.

127. From an address titled "Universalism and the Reality of Eternal Punishment: The Biblical Basis of the Doctrine of Eternal Punishment," delivered at the Desiring God 1990 Conference for Pastors, transcript posted on website of John Piper's Desiring God ministries, http://www.desiringgod.org/resource-library/conference-messages/universalism-and-the-reality-of-eternal

-punishment-the-biblical-basis-of-the-doctrine-of-eternal
-punishment, John Piper, ©2013 Desiring God Foundation,
desiringGod.org.

128. Besteman, *My Journey to Heaven*, 73.

129. Piper, *90 Minutes in Heaven*, 34.

130. A. W. Tozer, *I Call It Heresy* (Harrisburg, PA: Christian Publications, 1974), 139.

131. Helen Lemmel, "Turn Your Eyes upon Jesus," as found in
Praise! Our Songs and Hymns (Grand Rapids, MI: Singspira-
tion, 1979), 284. Lyrics in the public domain.

132. Anderson, *Appointments with Heaven*, 189.

133. Wayne Grudem, *Bible Doctrine: Essential Teachings of the Christian Faith* (abridged from *Systematic Theology: An Introduction to
Biblical Doctrine*) (Grand Rapids, MI: Zondervan, 1999), 465.

134. Alcorn, *Heaven*, 379.

135. Dallas Willard, *The Divine Conspiracy* (San Francisco: Harper-
One, 1998), 376.

136. Charles Spurgeon, "Fallen Asleep," Sermon 2659, http://
www.spurgeongems.org/vols46-48/chs2659.pdf.

137. Charles Kingsley, *True Words for Brave Men* (New York: Whit-
taker, 1886), 202–203.

138. Charles Spurgeon, Sermon #2659, "Fallen Asleep," January
28, 1900, as quoted in Alcorn, *We Shall See God*, 49.

139. C. S. Lewis, *The Weight of Glory* (SanFrancisco: HarperOne,
1949, 1976, 1980), 45–46.

140. Anderson, *Appointments with Heaven*, 190.

141. David Gregg, *The Heaven-Life or Stimulus for Two Worlds* (1895;
reprint, Charleston, SC: Nabu Press/BiblioLife, 2012), 62.

142. Amy Carmichael, *Kohila: The Shaping of an Indian Nurse* (India:
Society for Promoting Christian Knowledge, 1939), 156.

143. Ally Breedlove with Ken Abraham, *When Will the Heaven
Begin* (New York: New American Library, 2013), 30.

144. Ibid., 32.

145. Ben Breedlove, "This Is My Story (Part 2), YouTube, posted
December 19, 2011, http://www.youtube.com/watch?v=a4
LSEXsvRAI.

146. Kathleen Norris, *Amazing Grace: A Vocabulary of Faith* (New York: Riverhead Books, 1998), 368.

147. Kreeft, *Heaven*, 182.

148. George W. Sweeting, *Who Said That* (Chicago: Moody, 1995), 229. Taken from *Day by Day* with Billy Graham, compiled and edited by Joan Winmill Brown (Minneapolis: World Wide, n.d.), copyright Billy Graham Evangelistic Association.

149. Benedict J. Groeschel, *Arise from Darkness: When Life Doesn't Make Sense* (San Francisco: Ignatius, 1995), 125–26.

150. Richard Baxter, "Jewels in Our Heavenly Crown," from *The Saints' Everlasting Rest*, 1651.

151. Billy Graham, *The Heaven Answer Book* (Nashville, TN: Thomas Nelson, 2012), 171.

152. Peter Kreeft, "What Will Heaven Be Like?" *Christianity Today*, June 1, 2003, http://www.christianitytoday.com/ct/2003/juneweb-only/6-2-51.0.html?order=&start=4

153. Robert Lowry, "Shall We Gather at the River?" Words based on Revelation 22:1, public domain.

154. Mary C. Neal, MD, *To Heaven and Back* (Colorado Springs, CO: Waterbrook Press, 2011, 2012), 131–33.

155. Retold from ibid., 55–74.

156. Timothy W. Smith, "Byrd Is Partly Paralyzed as Jets Fall to Chiefs," *New York Times*, Nov. 30, 1992, http://www.nytimes.com/1992/11/30/sports/pro-football-byrd-is-partly-paralyzed-as-jets-fall-to-chiefs.html.

157. Mike Bickle with Deborah Hiebert, *The Seven Longings of the Human Heart* (Kansas City, MO: Forerunner Books, 2006), 70.

158. Scott Hoezee, "As in Adam…" *Calvin Theological Seminary Forum: Death and Dying* 17, no. 2 (Spring 2010): 6.

159. C.S. Lewis, *The World's Last Night, and Other Essays* (New York: Harcourt Brace Jovanovich, 1952), 112–13, as quoted in Randy Alcorn, *Money, Possessions and Eternity* (Carol Stream, IL: Tyndale House, 2003), 150.

160. See CBS News report, "Laura Bush Among Four Ladies in Red," Feb. 11, 2009, http://www.cbsnews.com/2100-500202_162-2233193.html

161. Frederick Buechner, *Beyond Words* (San Francisco: Harper-Collins, 2004), 130.

162. Martin Luther, *Table Talk*, "Of the Resurrection," DCCLVIX.

163. Tada, *Heaven: Your Real Home*, 84.

164. George MacDonald, *Donal Grant*, as quoted in *The Wind from the Stars*, ed. Gordon Reid (London: HarperCollinsReligious, 1992), 354.

165. Frederick Buechner, *Listening to Your Life* (San Francisco: HarperOne, 1992), 174.

166. Lyrics in the public domain.

167. Retold from Spangler, *Dreams*, 128–130.

168. Malarkey and Malarkey, *The Boy Who Came Back from Heaven*, 87.

169. Larry Libby and Wayne McLoughlin, *Someday Heaven* (Grand Rapids, Zondervan, 2001), quoted in *A Glimpse of Heaven* (Nashville, TN: Howard Books, 2007), 129–30.

Scriptures Noted